MONEY & SOUL

The psychology of money and the transformation of capitalism

Per Espen Stoknes

translated from the Norwegian
by Susan M. Davies

green books

First published in the UK in 2009
by Green Books Ltd,
Foxhole, Dartington,
Totnes, Devon TQ9 6EB

Cover design by e-Digital Design Ltd

This translation has been published with the financial support of NORLA.

ISBN 978 1 900322 46 1

Text printed on Five Seasons Stone-White 100% recycled paper
by MPG Books, Bodmin, Cornwall, UK

Contents

Part III: Towards an pluralist capitalism

Acknowledgements

Many people have given me inspiration and have made a contribution to this long-term project.

Thanks to Anne Britt Gran, Kjell Eikeset, Per Ingvar Haukeland, Guri Hjeltnes, Laila Stange, Kristin Hauge, Ragnhild Gredahl, Steinar Lem, Rita Westvik, Hedvig Montgomery, Per Gunnar Stoknes, Fredrik Kloumann, Ebba Opavik, Yngve Opavik, Mads Greaker, Kathrine Aspaas, Heidi Sørensen and Tine Store for their valuable feedback on earlier editions of the manuscript. A special thanks are due to Professor Jørgen Randers, Arne Jon Isachsen and Alexander Cappelen for discussions with their critical feedback.

I would also like to give particular thanks to Henrik Isebold for his many tips and painstaking linguistic reviewing.

All remaining errors and omissions are my own.

Thanks to Bjornconn cabins, Vindfjellhorn mountain and the forests at Meheia, which have accommodated me and all of these thoughts. I hope ideas and values continue to fly out from there, and possibly take root here and there in the souls of the two-legged creatures busy roving around.

Acknowledgements

Many people have given me inspiration and have made a contribution to this long-term writing project.

Thanks to Anne Brit Gran, Kjetil Eikeset, Per Ingvar Haukeland, Guri Hjeltnes, Laila Stange, Kristin Haugse, Ragnhild Grødahl, Steinar Lem, Rita Westvik, Hedvig Montgomery, Per Gunnar Stokness, Fredrik Klourman, Einar Opsvik, Yngve Opsvik, Mads Greaker, Kathrine Aspaas, Heidi Sørensen and Tore Høie for their valuable feedback on earlier editions of the manuscript.

Special thanks are due to Professors Jørgen Randers, Arne Jon Isachsen and Alexander Cappelen for discussions with their critical feedback.

I would also like to give particular thanks to Henrik Tschudi for his many tips and painstaking linguistic reviewing.

All remaining errors and omissions are my own.

Thanks to Bjønntjønn cabins, Vindbekkhorn mountain and the forests at Meheia, which have accommodated me and all of these thoughts. I hope ideas and values continue to fly out from there, and possibly take root here and there in the souls of the two-legged creatures busy roving around.

Foreword

Money & Soul emerges in the midst of the deepest recession since the 1930s. Any residual illusions about 'temporary downturns' have dissolved away, and there are many who now believe that concerns about a lengthy recession will soon turn into the reality of an out-and-out Depression.

No better time, therefore, to take a large step back and think very differently about the causes and the consequences of such a calamity. We haven't done that for decades, despite a large number of banking booms and slumps that have happened in the past twenty years in various parts of the world. These are always more damaging to the many people who suffer from them than to the bankers, regulators and politicians responsible for them.

As always, the responses of governments all around the world are focusing only on the symptoms, not on the underlying causes. A bit like builders trying to stop a house continually slipping downhill by repeated expensive repairs to the roof and upper floors, not realising that the foundations are profoundly unsound.

Indeed, here in the UK there is as yet no sense of relief that the government has been liberated from its servitude to the amoral imperatives of free-market economics. There is apparently little self-awareness that eleven years of running the economy in this way have left it more unbalanced now than it was in 1997, and even less resilient, in terms of its preparedness to cope with a world dominated by radical discontinuities. All that seems to matter is getting back to the same old consumption-driven, debt-burdened economism that got us into the current mess. As Per Espen Stoknes says, "Economism as an ideology has squeezed out everything else."

The need for new ideas has never been more pressing. *Money & Soul* provides those in generous proportions. The deliberately bruising juxtaposition of the title unfolds into a subtle, multi-layered examination of the two apparently separate domains, and then into a deeper account of the interpenetration of the two.

Money is the foundation of national and international financial systems. The way money is created and issued, by whom, and in what form (as in debt or debt-free, in one currency or another) largely determines how a financial system works. But money is not just a neutral means of exchange, a store of value or a unit of account. Its omnipresence in our lives inevitably opens up our imagination, for good or ill. As credit, it can be a source of untold creativity and liberation. But as debt (and interest), it becomes "the prison of the soul". Money can (and, today, usually does) "eat its way unrelentingly into the soul's area". But it doesn't have to.

This analysis builds on the work of a generation of environmental economists, academics whose vision has been all but ignored for decades, but who are now being sought out as the trailblazers of the kind of capitalism we will now need to invent. Per Espen Stoknes re-presents the conventional arguments about the limitations of economic growth, market failure and the inherent bias towards inequity and unsustainability that lies at the heart of today's capitalism. The analysis authoritatively demonstrates just how foolish we have been to stimulate economic growth by freeing up access to unprecedentedly high levels of credit; to license the continuing externalisation of cost for short-term economic gain, knowing full well how badly this would distort markets over the long run; to mis-price risk by assuming that asset values would continue to rise indefinitely into the future; and to allocate capital in such a way as to favour short-term profit maximisation rather than long-term value creation.

But *Money & Soul* goes a great deal further than this analysis. The final section invites us to think through different scenarios for an expanded capitalism, emphasising in particular the imperative of completely rethinking markets for both natural capital and social capital. It is unlikely that any reader will end up agreeing with each and every ingredient in this celebratory feast of ideas, but that is absolutely not its purpose.

What we all need to do, at a time of such intense dislocation and uncertainty, is to free ourselves of the iron-clad constraints with which we usually approach today's economic debates. Now is precisely the moment to start thinking very differently indeed – and Per Espen Stoknes certainly rises to that particular challenge.

Jonathon Porritt
Founder Director, Forum for the Future

"In broad terms, the economics field is, at root, human life in all its spheres."

Diane Coyle (2002), *Sex, Drugs and Economics*

"For the love of money is a root of all kinds of evil."

St Paul *(1 Tim 6:10)*

"It is easier to write about money than it is to acquire it. And those who gain it make great sport of those who only know how to write about it."

Voltaire (1764), *Philosophical Dictionary, Vol VI, Part 2*

Introduction

Senior officials in serious panic were screaming bloody murder and trying to look calm at the same time. "Eight hundred billion dollars stimulus package." "Banks go bust!" "Three trillion dollars lost on the stock exchanges." The sums gained before, the sums lost during and the sums of government spending after the crack of 2008 were staggering. Bigger than ever. There are far more people using much more money, involved in a greater complex of debts and credits, than ever before in human history. Just before the crack, property and other forms of capital had never been worth more in real terms.

One thing is the quantity of money. Real prices and the amount of money will sooner or later start growing again. But if we look past the violent short-term upheavals during the last three to four decades – and there have been several – we see something more remarkable. Despite the underlying long-term growth in capital and incomes, surveys show that levels of satisfaction and happiness in the population of the rich countries have *not* increased since around 1970. At the same time the condition of the natural environment and climate is severely deteriorating, according to a number of indicators. In total, the strain on natural ecosystems is simply too great.

The paradox is that money and financial markets have delivered the goods and triumphed everywhere, while the current design of the economic system is failing most people as well as other species of the natural world looking for long-term security and survival.

What are we doing about it – apart from frantically trying to get the financial system back on track?

The key question becomes: Is the mindset behind today's economic practices skewed or even flawed? This branches into other questions, such as: Do we need to expand our understanding of what money and wealth actually is? Perhaps develop new frameworks around international money, or even new types of money altogether?

These seemingly simple questions lead, however, to profound problems and excursions into obscure regions of both history and the human mind. This applies not just to the questions of what money is and how it is perceived, but also to the emotional, symbolic and psychological relationship between money and mankind. One central problem is the polarity between money and what we call our soul (or psyche). For most Westerners, these appear to be bitter enemies: money *or* soul, finance *or* feelings, markets *or* mercy, Caesar *or* God. Part I of this book tries to trace the origins of this polarity and the mixed feelings aroused by money. Can the two be brought together: money *and* soul?

Economic principles are often presented as if they were universal 'laws', globally applicable and superior to the particularities of place and idiosyncrasies of culture. Stock exchanges, Visa cards and IKEA are supposed to function the same way at all locations. Some people claim the world becomes flatter as the same financial rules are applied everywhere.[1] However, finance is hardly independent of culture; anchoring financial ideas in its hidden cultural roots is therefore necessary. Money is story and image just as much as it is a means of exchange and a store of value. By viewing money as culture and philosophy, it becomes evident that the money of today is a system of symbols that society itself has developed over several centuries. And further, the way money has been designed up until today has not yet found its perfect evolutionary end-state. It is fully possible to construct different monetary systems in future, if and when circumstances require it.

Part II of the book therefore delves deeply into the culture from which economic concepts have sprouted, and explores the links that money has with the emotional and subconscious mind. In Part III, I return to current economic theory and practice. This is where economic theory lies down 'on the couch' to psychoanalyse its own self-image and try to befriend its shadow. Based on the analysis of what money and psyche are (Part I), the way our culture makes us feel and think about money (Part II), and what the economy sees and does not see, I put forward a scenario that illustrates what an extended framework of money could look like.

The scenario, named 'poly-capitalism', is based on the idea of widening the scope of money and accounting – to include natural capital and social capital – in addition to accounting only for conventional capital. To make these other forms of capital visible to the economic view, *specific markets and specific types of currency* could be introduced *for each form of capital*, to give us 'natural' and 'social' units of currency in addition to the units of currency today. The scenario described in Chapter 12 is based on the ideas explored in the preceding chapters.

The central insight driving the scenario is that today's money measures values along only a single dimension – the one in use in traditional markets for putting a price tag on work, property and capital, as well as goods and services. Social dimensions such as care, voluntary work, the benefits of affiliation and cultural networks are not included in current accounting, or only in an indirect way. These assets do not fit in with current criteria. Neither do ecological realities such as air pollution, soil quality and biodiversity. They get a price tag only when they become 'resources' for sale on the human markets.

People have been working for a long time on producing clear, understandable figures – so-called social and environmental indicators – in order to be informed about the development of these other value dimensions. However, most social indicators generally gain little political attention as long as they do not directly concern most people or have any substantive economic effect (like the unemployment rate). By introducing separate and complementary currencies, however, social and natural values could be made more salient for economists and policy makers, and from micro all the way up to macro level.

The idea is that valuing and circulating these new currencies in separate markets can, in the long term, contribute to society's collective social quality of life *and* the quality of the natural world. Then it will no longer be just wealth and productive capital that will be capable of growth, but social and natural capital too. We will move from a system singularly focused on growth in financial terms to one directed towards growth in other forms of capital as well. Further, developments in these other forms of capital will probably make a greater contribution to the quality of human life in the future than could ever be achieved by further growth in conventional capital (in already wealthy countries).

Regardless of whether a scenario akin to 'poly-capitalism' becomes a reality or not, there are numerous methods by which soul and money could be brought closer together within today's frameworks and with a new economic philosophy. This is already happening in many places, and the concluding chapter weaves together some of those threads that are already bringing money and soul closer together as we move towards the future.

The current monetary system involves enormous costs that are hidden from economic view because they entice us to act on the basis of narrow profitability. But perhaps the greatest cost derives from the hold that money incurs by restricting our sense of what it is possible to do – the prison it builds for our imagination. The opportunity cost to what we are currently doing is therefore already staggering – we just don't recognise it.

In short, this book attempts to dance with a huge, agile two-horned topic: on one side grounding economic theories in the Western history of ideas and emotion; and on the other opening up new perspectives on money and how it can be put to use.

Part I

Like oil and water?

Chapter 1

Money everywhere

The world is shaped by globalisation and money. The economic system is by far the strongest driving force on the planet. Its basic philosophy has spread throughout human consciousness – and particularly during the last two or three decades – with an immense intensity. Its 'memes' seem to override even our genes. In our era, money is the one thing we all want. At other times and places, values such as pyramids, palaces, potlatches, horses, cattle, religion, dukedoms, knighthoods, armies or honour have taken precedence as ultimate values. Now the thing that causes us to struggle with each other is the hunt for money and capital; but it also unites us, since everyone has the same goal. It is tempting to borrow a phrase from Tolkien's *Lord of the Rings*: 'One ring to bind them.'[1]

Cultures have been constructed around ideas and stories of honour and shame, around family and lineage, land or livestock. The giving of gifts has been central to some cultures. But the thing that binds together the globalised world of today is neither ideas of truth nor gods nor language. Only the ideas of business and economics are actually universal. Our contemporary civilisation is held together by ideas such as property, trade, product, competition, market, price, interest and profit. Pervasive economic ideas have been internalised in all of us and now rule mankind's conscious and unconscious life on this Earth. "These ideas trickle down into each act of making, serving, choosing, and keeping that we perform," says the psychologist James Hillman. Day by day, these ideas conjoin to give business its power, establishing the Economy's world empire across all borders of geography and barriers of custom.[2]

All humans are today participants in economic rituals such as buying, selling, budgets, cost/benefit analyses, annual accounts and self-assessment declarations of taxes. And, almost regardless of the topic being discussed in society – energy, medicines, care of the elderly, transport, education, construction, refugees, the countryside, or agriculture and food – money and economic theories take the lead in debates. Development projects involving roads, parks, buildings, arable and livestock farming are all largely decided on the basis of economic calculations and arguments. Do we want suburbs? Housing schemes? Urban concentration? Do we want more nursery schools? Do we want to have an agricultural industry? How many farmers are really needed? What is the cost of a farmer to society – what is the per-annum net profit or loss? A total can be calculated and an economic average given. And the sum can be weighed up against alternatives such as importing food or using the money in some other way.

The figures are perceived as real, and as a central part of reality. This becomes possible thanks to the legitimacy and significance that economic theories are given by all parties. They are the central building blocks of our social everyday reality.

Here are a few examples of the way this shapes the public debate: how much does an refugee actually *cost* us? What is the net cost of accepting one extra immigrant? Let us calculate this for different categories of immigrant, so that the political discussions can use it as basic documentary evidence. The media compare food *prices*, seldom its quality. When the price of petrol or power rises, there is a political furore, since this affects the *poorest*. The daily newspapers ask 'Do you *earn* enough?' and offer 'help' in thinking that you can demand even more pay because others have a higher level of earnings. Are house prices going up or down? What is your house actually *worth*? Not that you must *sell* it now, but you have to remember, know and speculate about what it *could* be sold for. We think of our houses in the form of their *monetary value*.

People's health may be taken care of by health-care companies that have to be run 'profitably'. When the money follows the patient, the issue becomes how much the patient's diagnosis is worth. This mindset affects the way the hospitals operate on a day-to-day basis, and the treatment individuals are given.

Better care for the elderly? What would it cost for all care-home residents to have their own rooms? No questions asked of whether elderly people feel they have greater dignity, whether their skills are valued, whether they are capable of doing more, nurturing friendships or improving their relationships. Our financial mindsets make us calculate, talk about and consider the cost of single rooms or whether any extra person-years for care and nursing are affordable. Issues related to the soul and society, such as what it means to be old in modern society, hung up the new and youth, become subordinate. Often purely material improvements are made without any corresponding improvement to social networks and meeting places – these have no price tags and therefore no quantifiable value, and are thus quickly left out of decision processes in management meetings. When our economic mindset filters these other values out of sight, they disappear from corporate activities too – neither dignity nor capability are included in budgets to be quantified and monitored.

The economy's 'neutral' analysis shifts the attention irrevocably towards a calculative mode of mind. Gradually, relentlessly, our consciousness and our patterns of behaviour are formed on the basis of monetary templates.

"The Age of Chivalry is gone; that of sophisters, economists and calculators has succeeded," lamented British statesman Edmund Burke already in 1790. But is this really so lamentable – has money replaced our soul with an objective calculator?

Money – objective or subjective?

The fascinating thing about money is that it acts in such a concrete, factual, way, and is utterly quantifiable and seemingly objective. Each deal and transfer can be documented, counted and totalled. This is what the economic control systems relate to: facts. Emotional reactions have no place in conventional economics: money is dealt with rationally – or at least such is the attempt. And everyone assumes they act on the basis of their economic judgment.

But the shadow side of soul is easily brought forth in the encounters with money, such as in cases of greed, fraud or gambling addiction. According to traditional economic theory, that is best left to other professions. Conventional economists assume that when the individual human mind succumbs to subjective and irrational behaviour, this belongs to the domain of psychologists or social workers (or some other relevant professionals). Such deviations lie outside the core task of economics, which is to draw up general and objective analyses at the societal level.

However, the soul or psyche is not just individual and subjective. The *soul is participating wherever people enter into relationships with each other and feelings are evoked.* Markets and stock exchanges are prime exemplars of where such emotional relationships play themselves out. What I mean by the term 'soul' will be discussed further in Chapter 4, and in Part II I will examine the extent to which the soul can also be discovered even in accounting, in finance and credit, as well as in debt and interest. This book maintains that the soul and emotion are inescapably and necessarily interwoven into all economic life. The aim of the book is to 'venture boldly forth' into these hidden recesses of the economy.

Emotions and feelings have, in recent times, been the subject of renewed interest in economics. Recent research has – through experiments with people in economic laboratories – discovered a broader spectrum of motivation and human behaviour than traditional economics has taken into account. The old polarity between objective rational money on the one hand and subjective irrational feelings on the other seems increasingly less relevant to economic theory too. But normal economic practice lives on just as strongly, as if nothing had happened. We can talk about a widespread *belief system,* based on a set of convictions that used to be self-evident economic truths. *Economism* (Chapter 11) is what I would like to call this economic ideology, based on this type of inherited belief and how it continues to be lived out in politics, trade and industry. That is what I am primarily focusing on, more than the latest news from the research front where economics and psychology meet.[3]

Many people maintain, in a condemnatory tone, that we live in a society controlled by money. For my part, I am happy that we live in that type of society. The alternatives are usually worse. At the same time, I am convinced that we need a new understanding of money – and soon. In his book *A History of Money: From Ancient Times to the Present Day*, the British professor of economics Glyn Davies writes: "Despite man's growing mastery of science and technology, he has so far been unable to master money . . . And to the extent that he has succeeded, the irrevocable costs in terms of mass unemployment and lost output seem to outweigh the benefits. If money were merely a tangible technical device so that its supply could be closely defined and clearly delimited, then the problem of how to master and control it would easily be amenable to man's highly developed technical ingenuity."[4] But there is too much psychology in money to make it yield to mechanical controls, he asserts. And this psychological factor continually eludes the analysts and planners, so output is lost and inequity increased.

Unfortunately, it is not just economic output that we are losing out on. Many people feel they are also losing their *soul* in money. The spark of life, the emotional vitality, is drained out by the economic sphere into which so much effort is poured. There is a feeling that one has to flee from the power of money – to drop out or resign from it. Money seems to be robbing us of our social community, the natural world and a stable climate.

On the one hand, then, it seems that we can't determine how the subjective soul is at work in money issues. On the other, we can't find room for the soul within the stern, objective realm of money. It seems that the two just don't mix.

Money – loved and hated

A woman's daughter came home from secondary school one muddy spring afternoon and told her artist mother that she had decided to start studying business economics in the autumn. The mother immediately burst into tears. No, my dear, not you, not trade and industry!

Some people feel quite at home and comfortable in the economic world of markets and brokers, of shopping and shipping, of the quick buck and bountiful opportunities. Others can't free themselves from the perception of something rather distorted and suspicious in the movements of capital, profit and the fast money of business. They denounce it as the casino economy, or speculative turbo-capitalism.

Economics itself has a well-defined relationship with money. Money is seen as completely neutral. It is defined first and foremost as a generally accepted means of exchange. Having such means of exchange and payment makes trading in goods and services much more efficient than having to take along stacks of dried fish down south from Norway to Italy in order to bring a new Fiat back north. As economic reasoning puts it, money simply makes trading with one another much more efficient than bartering would be. In addition to being a means of exchange, money is both a store of value and a unit of account. According to the theory of money's neutrality, money has virtually no intrinsic value. Economists usually perceive money as only *a veil* covering the real economy which consists of actual assets, like houses and goods. Money is to real assets as a ruler to a plank of wood.[5]

However, psychologists object, human beings do not *experience* money just as a neutral means of exchange or as an arbitrary measuring stick. Otherwise why would we react so strongly, so emotionally, to money? Why do friendships change once money enters into the relationship? Why do people get so angry when someone does a deal to gain him- or herself – some extra of these 'means of exchange'? Why are inheritance settlements so agonising; post-divorce child maintenance payments so bitter? Why do rich people get an unfairly large share of society's attention? Why are we so interested in interest rates and the central bankers' convoluted utterances? And why are we so eager to interview share analysts, statisticians and brokers for their opinions on the pound against the euro? Why do we get so worked up if a manager gets a few extra millions in share-option profits from a company that has made a deficit? Why does a scandal erupt if a politician spends a little fortune on a dinner or a trip, whereas a manager in a private business can spend twice the amount on exactly the same thing without any fuss? Money is not, never has been and never will be neutral in the eyes of society's citizens.

We are probably approaching somewhere nearer the truth if we admit that money generates enormous emotion. In addition to being a means of exchange and a unit of account, money is also symbolic of a whole spectrum of expression relating to the soul: fear and vindictiveness, suspicion and envy, nationalism and the winner's instinct, longing and loyalty, euphoria and ecstasy. Money is so saturated with symbolic meaning and has such emotional power that it makes huge groups of people turn at the same time or run with the herd – and sometimes collectively cast themselves over the edge, like lemmings into the sea. Overlooking these powers of emotion in money by insisting that money be neutral is like choosing to be willingly blind.

The problem is that we have a fairly schizophrenic relationship with money: one moment we are rational, and the next irrational. Money can rip up and

"The universal regard for money is the one hopeful fact in our civilization, the one sound spot in our social conscience. Money is the most important thing in the world. It represents health, strength, honour, generosity and beauty as conspicuously as the want of it represents illness, weakness, disgrace, meanness and ugliness." – George Bernard Shaw

fragment our rational attitudes in a surge of emotions. One moment we are hanging on to it tightly, and the next we are spending it on some extravagant object because 'we deserve it'. Sometimes, money itself is the Problem, at other times it is the Solution to most things. While most people want and strive to acquire money, many people are disgusted by what money is doing to us, and large fortunes are regarded with an uneasy mixture of scepticism and envy. The reason for this is probably historical, for we have a long cultural tradition of inherited hatred and suspicion of money that we find difficult to free ourselves from. It is easier for us to understand 'soul *or* money' than it is 'soul *and* money'. For a long time, we have seen book titles such as *Your Money or Your Life*.[6] But the idea that soul and money should belong together rouses instinctive resistance, rather like the kick reflex point immediately below the knee: surely, we feel, that can't be the case.

If money is viewed as filthy lucre, this easily feeds the suspicion that something must be rotten in the state of the Economy itself. In particular, this applies to private businesses and major multinational corporations. *Big business* has been a bad word since at least the 1970s. At the same time, admiration and fascination for people and executives loaded with money are included in this mix.

Psychological research tells us that people's attitudes to money change as they grow older. Typically, richer and older people tend to have a very positive view of money, perhaps because money is a witness to their own deeds and accomplishments. Young, low-income groups are more likely to view money as an evil or negative force.[7] There is also a lot of secrecy surrounding money. One survey shows that 50 per cent of Americans do not want their parents or friends to know how much they earn. 80 per cent keep it hidden from their siblings. And the secrecy intensifies as income increases.[8]

Worse than that, perhaps, is that many idealistic people's distrust of money makes them view almost any business initiative with contempt. Economic motives *themselves* become suspicious. It is just another smokescreen, or greenwashing initiative, concealing the relentless hunt for higher profits. A fair number of environmentally or socially effective economic measures are obstructed because they clash with the political or public will. This could involve anything from the removal of old subsidies to privileged industries to the introduction of 'green' taxes or tradable quotas. On the one hand, suspicions among many idealists create resistance to taking part, collaborating with or even communicating with economic players. On the other hand, in the spheres of business and administration we find economic dogma about cost-efficiency, competition, self-interest and so on. Different attitudes to money, based on old cultural clashes, create conflict and confrontation, with all of their associated suspicion

[handwritten marginalia: *What ritual would have to do make happen .*]

ח money and soul played out at the level
:l.

y have to destroy interpersonal relation-
he effect money has depends entirely on
ηd the markets, and therefore how eco-
ctical action and regulations. It is there-
ɔney, regardless of what our professional
und we do not need to approach money
' and angry face. Rather, we could bring
e. Psychotherapy has discovered that, if
ιve to approach it with empathy and an
thically is a precondition for change to
approach money. Otherwise, this rogue,
ιn away, and we will end up shooting at

ırket as the Problem or the Solution, this
book intends to research the stormy relationship between money and soul. We shall delve into the background and try to understand why economic ideas and mindsets are so attractive and have such an impact on the lives of modern people, why twenty-first-century people devote most of their creativity and energies into just this field, and why we choose to assess our own efforts, and those of others, on the basis of exactly these ideas.

However, psychologists hardly take note of economic issues: the relationship of people to money has been a neglected area within psychology. You can open any textbook on the subject and find that money is not even mentioned in the index at the back. It seems almost as if psychology considers money irrelevant to human development.[9] But when it comes to the understanding of motivation and meaning, story and symbols, psychology has a contribution to make. This is where psychology meets economics, and where we can rediscover the soul of money.

I therefore invite money itself into this space, into the 'therapy room' that this book is trying to open up. Let us try to approach money – this strong personality with sociopathic tendencies – with an open mind. Let us see if it is possible to bring together money and psyche, finance and feelings; let us undertake a psychoanalysis of the economy's soul, possibly also defining anew what it means to be a 'financial analyst'. Maybe we will eventually find that, after going through a therapeutic reframing in the way it understands itself, money can also foster feelings of common humanity and consideration for the natural world.

Money is a cultural construct

As has already been mentioned, a large number of people perceive money as something objective, and external to us. It seems to be wholly 'out there': money presents itself as an utterly necessary part of the world, produced and regulated by the central bank. It belongs in wallets, cash registers, Internet banks and bank vaults. It is easy to count and account for, and mathematics willingly lends authority and logic to economic variables, so that they appear to be self-evident and concrete.

However, it is extremely doubtful whether money really is objective, in the sense that it exists independently of people's attitude to it. With a closer look, there is something weird about the way money exists. It is as if it is always dependent on a continuous infusion of human images, desires and yearnings in order to exist. It feeds on our attention to it. This is the main topic of Chapter 3, 'So, what is money?'

For now, we need only note that money has changed throughout cultural history. Old coins and notes with their images and concise wording tell the story of how the society of those times thought and felt about money. A fascinating thing is that coins, notes and even credit cards – from Caesar's time right up to our own, always *contain images*. It seems that the human psyche needs to add quality to the purely quantitative monetary system. Notes and coins are designed so that money becomes a type of mirror of the current self-image of a society. The ruling classes have always sought to insert their own ideals and their own images on to the money.

The oldest coins from classical times were frequently adorned with pictures of gods and their associated animals. The money was in touch with ritual and

A Roman denarius depicting
Juno Moneta, *c.*46 BC.

spiritual practice as well as the natural world.[10] The English word *money* comes originally from the Roman goddess Juno Moneta. Coins were minted in her temple. Precious metals gave value to the coins, but they were also blessed by the goddess. There was magic in money. It could bring good fortune and good health. Although most people today rely more on the Stock Exchange than Juno Moneta, we can still perceive remnants of this attitude in the custom of throwing coins into wells or rivers and making a wish. Money can connect us to something beyond.

Gradually, since classical times, the figures depicted were more often monarchs and emperors. The motifs chosen for note and coin designs were never accidental. There have always been social frameworks and laws concerning their issue and use. Money has played a central role in shaping cultural and national identity. With a national flag comes a national coin. The introduction of the euro since 2002, for which many countries hesitatingly had to give up their traditional currencies, illustrates how difficult this can be. For example, the UK continues to retain its British Pound, and not only on purely rational economic grounds. Money is one of the most important cultural expressions of a country.

One central point of this book is that if money is culture and story to such a great extent, we are also free to define our monetary system in new ways. It has not been determined, once and for all, what form the monetary system should take. Money and culture co-create one another. Previously, money changed when circumstances in and around a society required it to. If circumstances once again require this, money must once again change in order to reflect the new situation in which society finds itself.

The question is whether the time is ripe for new monetary reforms.

However, changing the money system is not something you do on a whim. Lots of things have been tried in the past – and have gone horrendously wrong.[11] There is nothing simple about changing such a central expression of a culture. We have a lot to learn here about the links between economic and national history. Money has a tight hold on our identity: just as money is dependent on people to keep it alive, so are people dependent on the stability and life-sustaining effects that money systems give in return. For this reason, for any changes to be effective they must be firmly founded in the culture's common understanding of and the deep stories surrounding money. In order not to be tempted to intervene too hastily, it is important to delve fairly deeply into such partially forgotten facets of money's significance, which will be the topic of Part II.

Captives of money

The fact is that money enters into all situations in life. With an expression taken from the imperialist tradition, German sociologist Jürgen Habermas says that the money system is *colonialising* the lifeworld.[12] Money is invading our relationship with food, home, the landscape of childhood. Money crops up everywhere, from issues of friendship, marriage, children and upbringing to skills, art, health, illness and death. The son asks his father why he cannot have a new bicycle; the friend would really like to pay for dinner; the bereaved speculate on who is to pay for the funeral and how the inheritance has to be split. Money is involved in most areas of life – sometimes with absolute and dazzling power, at other times imperceptibly woven into the fabric.

Think of your relationship with the natural world, says American philosopher Jacob Needleman, your relationship with ideas, with enjoyment, with your own identity and self-respect; think of the way you live and of all of the things surrounding you; think of all of the impulses to help others or serve a higher purpose. . . . Think about where you go, how you travel, who you spend time with and how, what you did yesterday or what you are going to do in one hour's time. Money is there. Wrapped around and mixed in with it all.[13]

The fact that money shapes our lives does not have to be a bad thing. Maybe we would not want to be without this invasion? People can do the most incredible – and necessary – tasks when money is involved, everything from dragging themselves to another day at the office to completing a long, burdensome education or moving to another city for better pay. Nothing has such lasting impact on behaviour as money. This basically means that when the monetary system changes, our patterns of behaviour will follow.

Also on a societal level, we follow the money figures – such as inflation, interest rates, wages and GNP – with close attention. In order to expand this horison, researchers have been working to develop social indicators for the development of society as well as environmental indicators for the state of the natural world.[14] The intention behind these sets of indicators is that they should be equivalent and complementary to the indicators that describe the state of the economy. A handful of economic indicators attract a lot of public and media interest. Many people carefully follow changes in bank interest rates, housing prices and wages as their wallets take a direct hit from them. These indicators are used when budgeting and planning, and have an effect on practical decision-making processes that affect all of us. Economic indicators thus get a lot of attention in the media and in politics.

The social and environmental indicators have not had any real impact – they are perceived as much less personally relevant. Even if any of these have been

Psychologist: Hi! I was just reading something in a book by economist Diane Coyle, in which she says that economics covers the entire scope of human life: "There can be economics in anything – marriage, sport, crime, drugs trafficking, education, movies and even, yes, sex."

Economist: Well, what about it?

Psychologist: Absolutely fascinating. Previously, I would have disregarded the whole thing. But now I think she is right: these days, money shapes all aspects of human life. Psychology will have to follow this direction, and let go of the subconscious, childhood, neurology, roles within the family and so on. It will have to look in more detail at the way money influences all of life's relationships. That is where it is all happening. Psychologists can't afford to ignore economics.

Economist: Well said. How else would we want it to be? When people say 'It is not about money, it is the principle', it is obviously about money.

Psychologist: Setting aside certain things will no longer be of any benefit – desiring to own things, harbouring bitterness about an inheritance settlement or a stock-market crash, fantasising about wealth, envying successful people, or fearing bankruptcy or changes in interest rates. We have persisted in talking through these things for far too long. As if couple-relationships and sex exist in a vacuum and not right there, all mixed up with a sofa from IKEA and a bed from John Lewis! We psychologists cannot possibly continue overlooking the effects of consumerism at Christmas, the mania for redecoration, pocket money, mobile phone bills, dodgy sales techniques, addiction to saving or to work, while at the same time stating that we understand the human mind in the twenty-first century.

Economist: No – psychology has always seemed a bit removed from the real world to me. Navel-gazing and delving down into a person's mind are much too individualistic for my liking. They distract attention away from issues of interaction and distribution. What we need, as good old Marshall said, are people who get involved in society with "warm hearts and cold heads".

---

formulated to have local relevance (such as the number of watersheds affected by acidification, or the number of nesting birds per municipality),[15] they do not directly affect people's wallets. They do not arouse the same immediate attention, emotion and day-to-day involvement as do the indicators for money. In our culture, money seems to have direct access to our private and public attention.

To gain a better understanding of how money and soul are linked, why money so easily captivates our attention, I am mainly going to use analytical tools that are cultural and symbolic (rather than typically economic or empirical). I turn to the world of the arts, to myths, language and the classical European tradition, to that tradition in which earlier economists, from Smith via Marshall to Keynes, were steeped – with Greek and Roman gods and classical pictorial art. This tradition has for two-and-a-half thousand years had a sustained influence on our Western philosophy, literature and emotional life.

Why uncover the mythical ideas in economics?

The way we humans think, our style of consciousness, determines the goals we set ourselves and how we behave to achieve them. Certain mindsets generate papyrus, pharaohs and pyramids, others produce feudal lords and Gothic cathedrals, yet others produce F-16 fighters and oil tankers. In modern times, we humans have had the technology and energy supplies that allow us to overcome most physical obstacles. We build tunnels under the sea and through huge mountains. We change whole landscapes in a short space of time and send rockets and probes far out into space. We have the world at our feet, and are trampling upon it to such an extent that other species are being eradicated thousands of times faster than the natural rate. The execution of this activity is driven mainly by economic ideas. This gives us, as humans, a responsibility for what we do to the world that could hardly be accorded to any other species.

150 years ago, the nineteenth-century American philosopher Ralph W. Emerson formulated it this way:

> Every country and every man instantly surround themselves with a material apparatus which exactly corresponds to their internal moral state, or their state of thought. Observe how every truth and every error, each a thought of some man's mind, clothes itself with societies, houses, cities, language, ceremonies, newspapers. See how each of these abstractions has embodied itself in an imposing apparatus in the community; and how timber, brick, lime and stone have flown into convenient shape, obedient to the master-idea reigning in the minds of many persons.[16]

The more technology and money, the more important it becomes to know oneself. In addition to being able to take a outward, factual view and gain economic perspective, we have to be able to take an inward look, so that we gain psychological insight into what we are seeing and busy doing. Today, we seem to have better outward knowledge than inward: we are very proficient at executing projects and technological development, but know little or nothing about what drives us to do so. The economic vocabulary rarely ventures beyond its favourite labels such as rationality, greed, fear and self-interest.

Knowing oneself means being aware of the ideas in which we believe and by which we are navigating. Even if economics is a relatively new science that has made particularly large strides during the last fifty years, its ideas are, and will continue to be, firmly rooted in a cultural history going back hundreds and thousands of years. The discipline has lots of new concepts, graphs, spreadsheets and advanced statistical tools, but its underlying ideas were not discovered yesterday or the day before. Most of them have long cultural and historical roots, although many modern thinkers like to believe that the new ideas are all one's own individual creation.

Similarly, we like to believe that it is I who have or hold the idea. But a central insight from psychology (and from philosophy of science), is that just as often the *idea has us*. The famous British economist John Maynard Keynes concluded his classic *General Theory of Employment, Interest and Money* in 1936 with the same insight. He formulated it eloquently as follows.

> The ideas of economists and political philosophers, both when they are right and when they are wrong, are more powerful than is commonly understood. Indeed the world is ruled by little else. Practical men, who believe themselves to be quite exempt from any intellectual influences, are usually the slaves of some defunct economist. Madmen in authority, who hear voices in the air, are distilling their frenzy from some academic scribbler of a few years back. I am sure that the power of vested interests is vastly exaggerated compared with the gradual encroachment of ideas. Not, indeed, immediately, but after a certain interval; for in the field of economic and political philosophy there are not many who are influenced by new theories after they are twenty-five or thirty years of age, so that the ideas which civil servants and politicians and even agitators apply to current events are not likely to be the newest. But, soon or late, it is ideas, not vested interests, which are dangerous for good or evil.[17]

Just how dangerous ideas can be was demonstrated only three years after Keynes wrote this, when ideas such as the Thousand Years' Empire, Third Reich and 'lebensraum' burst violently through with the War.

At the same time, Keynes' analysis is incomplete: he does not say anything about how these ideas gain their compelling power in the human psyche. From where do these ideas arise? What emotions drive them? What are the mythical patterns that inspire both practical men of the economy and 'madmen in authority'?

The Swiss psychiatrist Carl Gustav Jung pointed out that modern ideas also belong among archetypal patterns. *Archetypes* are innate predispositions for creating psychic images about the basic themes of human life, not unlike psychical instincts.[18] More on archetypes later. For now, suffice to note that once an idea comes into contact with an archetypal field, it will become emotionally charged. Sometimes such emotionally charged ideas get almost contagious, like 'memes', and spread quickly throughout society. Among recent examples are the 'Y2K-bug', the Internet boom and the 'war on terror' idea after 9/11.

By setting economic theory into its cultural context, into its European heritage right back to mythical times, I believe we can achieve a better understanding of the ideas that dominate our current economic lives. We can understand *why* we become so captivated by ideas such as 'the invisible hand', equilibrium, credit, growth, freedom of choice, self-interest or efficiency.

Ideas can be seen as autonomous, living entities in the ecology of the soul.[19] They come to us – often as a surprise – and then we say '*I* have an idea!' not knowing how we got it. There is a multitude of them, but each idea gives only one perspective on things. In that way, ideas have a nasty tendency to become tyrannical. Some do not tolerate any contradiction. They can attack other ideas, and therefore have both teeth and claws (in debates). They sometimes join together with lookalikes in determined bands called ideologies. They can persuade us and force us into action. They are perhaps the most valuable and crucial things, but also the most dangerous, in the human world. This makes it important to be aware of the contexts and the manner in which the ideas emerge.

Economic theory and understanding were not invented in our time; nor did they originate in the eighteenth and nineteenth centuries, although it might have been then that economics was founded as a discipline. Language and experience with and terms for trading with money had both been used for millennia. We have borrowed the most important descriptions and most influential impulses for the Western mind from the Ancient Greek and Judeo-Christian worlds. To gain a clearer insight into what the economy says about the soul and what the soul today says through the economy, we shall first and foremost see how the main economic terms are reflected in the fundamental *European*[20] myths.

This book's method

You will not find very many quantitative facts nor logical proofs in this book; the purpose is instead to reconnect the economic and the emotional sphere of the soul. The vision is, quite simply, to get money and soul to be friends. For that reason, I am tracking some central economic concepts back to their cultural roots, in order to ask what impact the concepts and their associated ideas have on the lives of modern people, in which the economy has become such a dominant element.

The method then becomes more speculative than empirical. But let us remember that the word 'speculative' has its roots in the Latin *specere*, which means to see, to behold, to reflect; in *speculum*, which means mirror, and in *specula*, which means a viewpoint. When following a speculative method, the criterion for the book differs a little from what would be the case in empirical research. It is not a question of true or false, of whether the hypotheses presented match up with some truth 'out there'. It is more the case that you, as the reader, should assess the material on the basis of whether it provides fresh perspectives on your own relationship to money as well as that of society. Put differently, it has more to do with the broadening of our understanding than with causal explanation of 'facts'.

The aim is to be able to *see* economics and the market in a rather different way from the one employed by textbooks in economics, yet to discuss the same topics and the same core concepts. I want to look at them, at the images they evoke, at how they present themselves, at the original meaning of the word, and then look again from yet another angle. By looking – but from a new perspective, we will discover fresh meanings in the worn-out concepts, I hope. In that way, the method has much in common with phenomenology. That is all about seeing and describing phenomena, carefully and in wonder, in order to extract the essence and see how the phenomenon of money and consciousness bring one another about.[21]

I will therefore not be using economic concepts and theories in the same way that textbooks do. Economics studies phenomena such as markets, growth or unemployment by the use of models, tables and supply-and-demand diagrams. Changes in variables are analysed by means of calculations, or by adjusting graphs, in order to explain historical changes to the markets. I will study the same concepts – such as welfare, wealth and credit – but try to see through them to *what they are saying about the human psyche*. To ask what the soul wants by telling such economic stories. Why have we, in modern times, chosen to believe in and use exactly these ideas to define our relationship with each other and society?

I do not intend to use very much from modern psychology – neither traditional psychoanalysis nor cognitive traditions. That would quickly lead to a form of reductionism: translating or reducing economic concepts to specialist psychology ones. These become *psychologisms,* as opposed to psychologising, which is what I intend to do.[22]

The American psychologist James Hillman has developed a post-Jungian psychology. This branch is called archetypal psychology, because it attempts to go beyond the therapeutic framework within which Jungian psychology often stands.[23] Archetypal psychology is a research tradition with a particular fascination for the *images* inherent in what we are doing. The concept of images is used in a broader understanding than the visual in photographs and paintings: it refers to the psychic images that reside in our actions, figures of speech, thoughts, music, dreams, history, narratives and models. In this sense, items such as statistical graphs, facts and layouts also express images. I would remove discussion of images from the realm of thought to the realm of psyche. There, it is not a matter of right or wrong in an empirical sense, but about becoming aware of the qualities, patterns and feelings these images evoke in us. Therefore, I try not to argue or convince using a form of logical necessity, but to juxtapose and re-story the flattened concepts in order to facilitate new depth and understanding.

The mythical and archetypal perspective makes it possible to organise myriad incidents from various areas of life into a network of 'family resemblances', as the philosopher Wittgenstein called it: images are connected by a series of overlapping similarities where no one feature is necessarily common to all. Still, they belong to the same family or patterning. Archetypes can be understood as the deepest patterns of psychic functioning. Concepts such as energy, health, father, God, Mother Earth, community, war, darkness, revenge, love, the hero and so on all have archetypal qualities. Images tend to cluster around them, as if they have some kind of family resemblance to each other.

All cultures express the more universal archetypal themes in their own specific ways. The same archetype can be expressed over a range of areas: The archetype of the hero, for example, appears first in *behaviour*: the drive to activity, outward exploration and enthusiastic response to challenges. It appears second in a typical way of creating *images*, as in the images of Hercules, Superman, Luke Skywalker, James Bond or Lara Croft. Third, as typical mindsets or *styles of consciousness* that emphasise strength, independence and decisive action. Fourth, in *emotions* such as a sense of urgency, fight-or-flight or the urge to win. Last but definitely not least, all archetypes are linked with a specific form of shadow or *pathology*, which with the hero, for example, might manifest as single-mindedness, being prone to conflict and turf wars.

But one thing is absolutely essential to the notion of archetypes, says James Hillman: their emotional possessive effect. They can bedazzle consciousness so that it becomes blind to its own stance. It does no good to argue rationally with someone who is possessed by an archetypal idea. That person just feels completely and unassailably correct, regardless of what others might say. The book *Limits to Growth,* published in 1972, attracted no end of unfounded criticism because it ran up against the archetypal idea of growth that was held sacred by many economists.

Since this approach uses the method of family resemblances, it enables the possibility of comparison between various economic levels that are often kept apart, such as private economics, corporate economics, micro- and macro-economics. These are different sub-disciplines, but they share lots of images and ideas. The archetypal approach of psychologising is more interested in the images present in the concepts or arguments than which discipline they belong to. Thus, it is an interdisciplinary method of approach. In the following chapters I'll be moving freely between economics and psychology, money and myths, finance and feelings; between fact and fiction, analyses and descriptions. The exploration of the economic ideas will also move between the academic and the literary, as well as between the personal level and the social level. I have consciously chosen a plurality of modes and levels as an aid to interweaving these domains, which are normally kept separate. I hope to show that there are other routes for the economy, organisations and society to take, routes other than the single vision that economism (see Chapter 11) is leading us towards.

First, I will have to address the widespread suspicion of money. Why is there such considerable ambivalence about money itself?

Chapter 2

The camel and the eye of a needle

"We modern religiously 'unmusical' people find it difficult to imagine, or even simply to believe, what a powerful role was played by religious elements in that age when the character of the modern civilized nations was being formed." So wrote Max Weber, the sociologist, in his classic *The Protestant Ethic and the Spirit of Capitalism*.[1] In it, he traced the impact of the Christian faith on our culture's attitudes to work, commerce and savings. Viewed in that way, all modern Western Europeans are still Christians, regardless of whether we consider ourselves believers in a religious sense. Our attitude to money is therefore, consciously or unconsciously, informed by the Christian view on money.

It is always difficult to obtain a clear view of one's own standpoint. That is why we need to look at some of the basic texts of our culture, the Gospels, in order to see what constitutes the Christian ideas and conceptions of money.

Let us start at the beginning. Jesus was born among the poor. There was no room for Mary and Joseph in inns or the whole town of Bethlehem. Joseph was far from wealthy, so they had to spend the night in a dirty stable, among the animals and shepherds. It is an interesting, fundamental fact that the first thing we come across in the story about our culture's superstar is poverty. Close to the dirt, shepherds' flocks, donkey and sheep droppings, hay, straw and an earth floor. That was where it all began. This is reminiscent of something original and genuine, sharply different from a noisy, festive inn. Gold, frankincense and myrrh entered the stable with the three wise men, but that was as if to underscore that these were riches belonging to altogether other world.

For the early Christians, being poor was one of the most important characteristics about Jesus. That laid the foundation for the faith's appeal among the poor of the Roman Empire. Many of Christianity's poor found a kind of consolation in this: it was an outstretched hand and an invitation to resign themselves to their lot – I have no money, but at least I have my soul intact, just like Jesus, who appears to have chosen poverty. Poverty thereby becomes raised to the ideal. The poor are good, and conversely a negative view of money and wealth arises. Francis of Assisi (c. 1181–1226), held complete poverty to be a fundamental norm for him and his brethren. The fact that the Church would later become super-rich did not alter the ideals. Monks had to abstain from two things: money and sex. The monastic oath bound them to a life of poverty and celibacy.

An anti-money attitude has thus been a woven in as a fundamental strand in our culture, and it can be traced back to the Gospel stories about Jesus and his attitude to money. These stories can be interpreted in many ways, but it is difficult to get away from the impression that most express an astonishingly harsh condemnation of money.

The story about the rich man who speculates on what needs to be done to win eternal life is central. Jesus recommends a decisive break: go and sell everything you own and give the proceeds to the poor (Matthew 19:21, Mark 10:17–22, Luke 18:18–23). The rich man went away grieving. Jesus was probably not the most patient and empathic personal coach that history has ever seen. And to really ram home the point, Jesus utters the sentence with which everyone in Western civilisation is familiar. It is exactly the same in the first three Gospels: "It is easier for a camel to go through the eye of a needle than it is for a rich man to enter the Kingdom of Heaven" (Matthew 19:24, Mark 10:25, Luke 18:25). What can you say to something like that? The Gospels state that the disciples were dismayed: "Who can then be saved?" Jesus looked at them and said "For men this is impossible, but everything is possible for God." Thus, it seems, only a miracle can save us from money.[2]

The parable about Lazarus and the rich man is in the same spirit. There was once a rich man who dressed in purple and the finest linen, and feasted in great magnificence every day. At his gate, covered in sores, lay a poor man named Lazarus. . . . "One day the poor man died, and was carried away by the angels to be with Abraham. The rich man also died. But when he opened his eyes he was in torment in Hades." (Luke 16:19–23). Now that's some economic downturn – not even the credit crash around 2,000 years later sent people to Hell because they had been celebrating in advance and lived life fast, with fun and frolics. The disparity between money and soul seems absolute.

In another story, the disciples and Jesus were beside the chest in the temple treasury into which the rich people put their gifts. "Then he noticed a poor widow putting in two tiny coins," writes Luke. "Truly, I tell you: this poor widow has put in more than any of those others. . . . She out of her poverty put in all of the living that she had." (Luke 21:1–3) Normal algebra does not apply here – two tiny coins are worth more than many tetra-drachma or whatever the rich were putting in. It is the poor person who has the ability to donate out of a rich soul. The rich person is hardened by money and ends up with an impoverished soul.

This story also raises the issue of whether money can carry with it any meanings or *qualities*. Modern economics does not accord such characteristics to

money. Money is solely quantitative. What is the relationship between the symbolic value of money and its quantity? Can sums of money, big or small, express
meanings or values beyond the exact total constituted by the sum? If so, the story
opens up a potential bridge between soul and money – that is, to see money as a
symbol: that money is 'good' if the narrative meaning in it is 'soulful'. By express-
ing precise quanta of value, sums of money become *images*: the two tiny coins
still live in our imagination.

- $ - € - £ - ¥ -

What about tax? Did Jesus pay tax? Did he also want to pay tax to the hated
Romans, or did he just want to pay the 'good' temple taxes? One moonless night,
some Pharisees decided it was time to set Jesus a test. They wanted to see
whether it was possible to catch him out with a clever double-bind that can only
be answered in two ways, and where both alternatives would trap him. The next
day they put the following question to him: "Master, we know that you are an
honest man, and teach in all honesty the way of life that God requires. . . . Tell us
now . . . are we or are we not permitted to pay taxes to the Roman Emperor?"

To understand the profundity of this question, you have to know that the coin
with which tax was to be paid to the Emperor was not the 'good' tetra-drachma,
but the Roman denarius. It was blasphemous for the Jews because it bore an
image of Caesar, with a quotation in which the Emperor declares himself to be a
god. But the Jews' commandment was as follows: "Take heed unto yourselves, lest
ye forget the covenant of the Lord your God, which He made with you, and make
you a graven image in the form of any thing which the Lord thy God hath forbidden thee" (Deuteronomy, 4:23). In addition to being deeply blasphemous, the tax
was being collected by a force of military occupation, so the Jews were financing
their own subjugation. The coin, in other words, was a persistent humiliation and
politically provocative. As the situation is portrayed in the Gospels, Jesus gives an
elegant answer: "Show me the money in which the tax is paid." They handed him
a denarius, and he asked: "Whose head is this, and whose name?" "Caesar's," they
replied. "Then pay Caesar what is due to Caesar, and pay God what is due to
God." (Matthew 22:16–21).

In that way, Jesus is able to demonstrate first that he himself has no coins, and
therefore neither does he own any blasphemous goods. But *they* clearly had the
despised coins in their pockets. I imagine him studying the coin that they have
passed him. He leans forward with his hands behind his back, or holds the coin
at an arm's length. He gives it back so that they can see the image on the coin for
themselves. If he had answered Yes to the question about whether it was correct
to pay the Roman tax, he would have confirmed that he supported the Romans.
That must mean that he had never wanted to lead a physical rebellion, which the

Jews were expecting from the true Messiah. If he had answered No, they could have betrayed him to the nearest Romans, and he would have been imprisoned as an agitator. When the Pharisees themselves have to say that the coin belongs to Caesar and has been made in his image, they cannot have him arrested.

Later, this answer has been used as support for separating the religious sphere from the economic, the Church from the stock exchange. The domains of Caesar against those of God – money against soul – are seen as eternally irreconcilable, as in the story of the money-changers in the temple.

Easter is approaching, and Jesus is received with jubilation on his way into Jerusalem. According to Matthew (21:12) he does not hesitate, but goes straight up to the holiest of holy places – the temple. "He drove out all of those who were selling and buying in the temple precincts. He upset the tables of the money changers and the seats of the dealers in pigeons, and said to them: 'The Scripture says: My house shall be called a house of prayer. But you are making it into a robber's cave.'" This episode is described in all of the Gospels. To really make the drama sizzle, and to emphasise the point even more clearly, John says that "he made himself a scourge out of rope" which he used to chase away the merchants and money-changers. John places this story at the start of his Gospel, and we find there the word 'market-place', instead of 'robbers' den' as it was in the others. It might seem that the Evangelists and early Christian writers found it hard to see any difference. If we are to take this original scene from Western conceptual history as a guide, the soul ought not to be tempted to go out among the robbers in the marketplace, but forcefully chase away money with a scourge. In the house of the soul there is no room for the money-changers.

And yet, we have not related the story of Judas, the treasurer and economist among the disciples. As everyone knows, he sold the Son of Man Himself for a miserable thirty pieces of silver.

How could money be given a more negative angle and value? Is it strange then that we still remain ambivalent, when we are bearers of that sort of heritage? These Bible stories are not just a historical curiosity; they still wield active emotional force in Western society. For example it is still taboo for many people to talk about their own income, debts and assets: money has to be covered up and hidden. With money comes shadow, sin and darkness. And still we can hear the echo of the ancient Christian cleansing of money-changers from the temple precincts when today the finger is pointed at the profit-seekers, bankers, deal-makers, short-sellers, speculators and turbo-capitalists.

But all that scolding for centuries hasn't helped much, for whatever is suppressed sooner or later comes back again. Moneymakers and markets have not gone away after being chased out by Jesus. Instead, it now seems that the entire temple has been leveraged out by the money people. They have rebranded the temple, retrofitted it as a tourist destination and are selling entrance tour packages and tickets as an element of the thriving experience economy: "Discount today! Come and see where Jesus chased out the money-changers!"

Misers and usury

St Paul is utterly unequivocal in his epistle to his good friend Timothy: "If we have food and covering, we may rest content. Those who want to be rich fall into temptations and snares and many foolish harmful desires which plunge men into ruin and perdition. For love of money is a root of all kinds of evil." (1. Timothy 6:8–10). No minor statement that short, last one.

The opposition to money was a central tenet of churchmen during the following centuries. In the Middle Ages, there were many stories about money-lenders or rich merchants who were taken by the Devil before they got a chance for their money to make them happy. Other stories tell of how money was transformed into withered leaves inside a locked money chest. One, from around 1240, tells of a money-lender who was to be married. When he stepped into the body of the church and walked up towards the altar a statue fell down from the archway, and he was squeezed dead against the floor. On closer inspection, it became clear that the statue – by God's grace – depicted a miser, holding tightly on to his purse as he is being taken by Satan. How appropriate!

Such stories, more clearly than any statute book, depict the attitudes and ideals with which money was linked during this epoch.[3] In the fourteenth century, a learned monk wrote: "The person who has sufficient to cover his own requirements and still unceasingly works to build up riches, in order to have enough to live without working or to seize a higher social position or so that his sons shall be rich and important men – all such men are driven by the mortal sins of lust, greed and pride."[4] In the Middle Ages, the Church made it clear that sufficient material goods were important for a society. But economic motives as such were suspicious. Earning more money than required for your own needs was provocative and intolerable. An appetite like that bore witness to strong desires. Merchants and markets needs discipline and control, not freedom to caper about with unbridled passions and desires. Riches are made for people, not people for riches, warns St. Anthony.[5] Any man who uses the needs of others to sell at a high price and make himself rich *must* be evil. Otherwise he could not be poor yesterday and rich today.[6]

For that reason, people who lend money to be paid back with interest were lost to eternal damnation. In particular, this applied to those who charged exorbitant interest, in other words more than five per cent. No good Christian could be involved in such hideous practice, the deadly sin of usury. Law courts were just as strict in relation to usury as they were with adultery and forgery.[7] In Florence in the fourteenth century, it was illegal for Christians to be involved in lending money. That is why they imported Jews to cover the need for capital. The Jews were prohibited to lend at interest only to other Jews. They could, however, lend money and charge interest to non-Jews ("Thou shalt not lend upon usury to thy brother," Deuteronomy 23:19,20). Christians became economically dependent on services such as this, while they also despised and frequently mistreated or killed the hated money-lenders.

In 1639, there was a lawsuit against a Robert Keayne in Boston, who was accused of having made sixpence profit on the shilling, an outrageous gain. Terrible! The court is debating whether to excommunicate him, but dismisses him with a fine of 200 pounds. Keayne admits his sin, weeps tears of regret, and pays his fine. In his sermon, the minister of Boston cannot resist this golden opportunity to profit from the story of this wayward sinner. He rails against the immoral principles that are corrupting trade. Among the worst of these are 1) that a man might sell as dear as he can, and buy as cheap as he can, 2) If a man loses by casualty of sea, etc., some of his commodities, he may raise the price of the rest, and 3) that he may sell as he bought, though he paid too dear . . .

"All false, false, false!" cries the minister. To seek riches for riches' sake is and will always be avarice, one of the seven deadly sins.[8]

It seems clear that economic principles have come a long way from pre-industrial times to today. The view of money and its relationship with the soul has undergone some radical changes. However, we can still find four fundamental attitudes to markets and business operations, from the Middle Ages to today.[9]

First, we have the *ascetic* aloofness, in which markets and money are seen as morally wrong and damned, as hopelessly corrupt. People lose their souls there, so they must escape to the straight and narrow path and not get mixed up with vicious people and moneylenders. The corrupting influence of money can only be overcome by having the smallest possible amount. Money and markets ought to be avoided, as they entangle and trap the soul.

Next, we find *indifference*. This attitude takes money and markets for granted, as things that are unavoidable. However, they are peripheral and irrelevant to the important things in life. They are needed only to cover basic needs. This attitude will be expressed in arguments such as: There have always been markets, as we have to have something to live off, but money is not something to live for. Consider prices, debts and the need for money soberly. Acknowledge them and be done with them, then move on. Money and economics are not dangerous, but tiresome. Money ought to be an unremarkable means serving higher ends. It can cover basic needs, but never the need for meaning.

Third, there is the requirement for *reform,* which starts out from the premise that money and markets are fundamentally unfair and create a lot of suffering. Money and riches are means of inequity and suppression. This, therefore, calls out for compensation, change, mitigation, revolution or salvation. On this basis, ethically aware people must get involved and agitate for change in the economic system. Money can be put to good use, but first it has to be wrestled out of the hands of the over-wealthy.

The fourth type involves a fundamental *acceptance:* Money and markets are manifestations of genuine human needs. Regardless of how unfair or incomplete these manifestations are, they ought to be welcomed as expressions of humanity. Society's economic life is the matrix of desires, needs and yearnings from which human development emerges. Neither markets nor money nor wealth are foreign or hostile to the realm of the soul.

It might appear that during the course of the last century there has been a movement from the first two types in the direction of the last two. I would suggest that this change has been gaining strength since around 1980. Surveys about values have supported the idea of this kind of development.[10]

Money's victory – the return of the repressed

So we have a long history in which the relentless chase for money has belonged to the sinful power of darkness. But after two thousand years of fulminations, denunciations and repression of money, we see a powerful reversal. Strong forces in Christian culture tried to tame the soul-related reality of money with discipline, restraints and threats – but things that are suppressed do not simply disappear from the soul. The father of psychoanalysis, Sigmund Freud, described the subconscious as a simmering pot of repressed passions and desires. There, the repressed feelings await an opportunity to slip out past the ego's defence mechanisms. Now, with money, we have probably been seeing what Freud would call *the return of the repressed.*

The cultural reversal is by now complete. Many people have seen this and remarked upon it.[11] It is quite a commonplace observation that economics is now our *de facto* belief system, having developed into a full *religion* which can illuminate "every aspect of human nature".[12] The economic sphere fills the needs that religion previously filled: it provides a general understanding of how the world's drama is playing out, it provides guidance at difficult crossroads, it provides us with tasks, and it prescribes the correct course of action. Economic ideology defines purpose (growth), means (competitiveness) and meaning (prosperity) for people. Money has taken over anything there may have been of shared language and value systems. Today, it is the economy that is given most attention and devotion in world society. It is where we form our identity, hone our strengths and express ourselves. Sin and salvation have gained new worldly interpretations as deficits and profits. This unconscious religion promotes the message that material growth and prosperity are the most important values as long as we live, and that after that there is nothing.

Business and economic activity – inspired by the ideas of Western capitalism – has become the fundamental driving force in human societies throughout the world. And it promotes, in the manner of any monotheism and ideologies before it, a fundamentalist belief in its own basic tenets. Market-driven capitalism has triumphed over everything and everyone in its path, claims James Hillman.[13]

Exactly when and how this reversal happened – from the earlier religious hostility to money and business, to our current full embrace of markets and finance – is a historical topic that is treated in depth elsewhere.[14] The thing that is important here is to be aware of the deep cultural and emotional impact of the sustained historical conflict between money and markets on the one hand, and soul and compassion on the other. Emperors, trade, riches, taxes and inequity belonged to the first part, while God, integrity, generosity and humility comprised the second.

The antagonism between money and soul lives on today. It pops up, for instance, in discussions about the introduction of economic principles such as management by objectives in academic circles at universities, or in the unit-pricing of patients and diagnoses in the health-care services. The disparity creates many conflicts, and it is high time to do something about it. Why? Because it has serious consequences for both sides.

The split between God and Caesar denies the soul entry into economics, and expels money from the life of soul. The effect of this is that economic decisions are taken without the participation of the soul, while the life of the soul takes place far from the influential decisions that direct the flows of money. This is the mostly unconscious background to the deep oppositions that divide artistic life from economic life, culture from market, the humanities from economics and science from business.

Instead of the desperate choice between having either a spiritual religion that is explicitly hostile to money or a economic religion that implicitly worships money, an alternative may be to study how money can serve the soul. This implies observing how soul and money are actually entwined in and mutually dependent on each other. Is it possible to discover the soul at work in money, and to see the use of money as one of the soul's many modes of expression? In that case, a new vision is required. This implies a re-visioning of economics as well as a reclaiming of a worldly sense of soul. Only then can we see how the two former antagonists can begin to dance together in a more intimate and interactive manner than the two conflicting traditions can conceive.

Chapter 3

So, what is money?

I have asked many people what money is. A common response is that money is just a means to achieve other things, not a goal in itself. The answer frequently stops there. This argument leads attention away from money, almost apologising for the nature of money by pointing away from it. Only a means to other ends! That answer does not help us understand how money affects us by focusing our attention and leads to a calculating mode of mind. Nor does it say anything about how it incessantly changes the relationships between people. And nothing about how it feeds on our fantasies and wishes and even feeds back into them. It omits to mention the stories that money flows can tell about the past and the future. It also conceals the difficulty economic historians have had in defining money, and the ways of understanding it has changed in different cultures and throughout history. The closer you look at the phenomenon of money, the more it reveals of its complexity.

So, yes, money is a means to other ends. But that is not the end of the story. It is where the story of the magic of money begins.

Economic textbooks give short and succinct definitions on the functions of money. They state that money can be anything at all as long as it functions as: 1) a means of exchange, 2) a store of value, and 3) a unit of account for value and debt. Having specified this, the textbooks and many economists too then con- sider themselves to have finished with topic of money and direct their attention to prices and markets. But have they really answered the question about what money is? Several sociologists have commented that economists appear strangely disinterested in the topic.[1] Classical economics maintains that money is 'neutral' and limits itself to discussion of pricing, interest, scarcity and distri- bution of resources. It is not concerned about money as such.[2]

The question about the nature or essence of money is probably as much a philosophical and phenomenological matter as a specialist economic one.[3] What characterises money's mode of 'being'? How does money approach us, and what types of relationship does it invite us into? How do we know that something can be said to be money? How does the phenomenon of money present itself? Let's

Here are some of the many ways in which money can be defined. Take your pick.

Money is . . .
- the universal instrument of commerce (Adam Smith)
- the oil which renders the motion of the wheels of trade more smooth and easy (David Hume)
- a veil over the real economy (Arthur Pigou)
- human happiness in the abstract (Arthur Schopenhauer)
- labour. Labour is the first price, the original purchase money (Adam Smith)
- coagulated man-sweat (Åsmund Olavsson Vinje)
- energy / life energy (Joe Dominguez)
- gold (The Gold Standard)
- time, and time is money (Benjamin Franklin)
- the sinews of war (the factor holding armies together, Tacitus and Cicero)
- like manure, of very little use except it be spread. (Francis Bacon)
- like water, when it flows freely it purifies, but when it stagnates it becomes toxic (Lynne Twist)
- like sex – only too much is enough (John Updike)
- like beer, golf and sex – even when it is bad it's good (Jimmy Williams)
- like excrement (Sigmund Freud, Sandor Ferenczi)
- vagina-envy (Robert Sardello)
- what makes the world go round (English saying)
- memory, a meaningful link between persons and communities (Keith Hart)
- futile, unless cultivated with imagination (Robert Sardello)
- coined liberty (Fjodor Dostoevsky)
- power (Thomas Hobbes)
- a requirement of society (George Simmel)
- our madness, our vast collective madness (D.H. Lawrence)
- a value made by law (Nicholas Barbon)
- the poor man's credit card (Marshal McLuhan)
- an agreement within a community to use something as a means of payment (Bernard Lietaer)
- power to turn fantasies into fact, to make wishes come true (unknown)
- institutionalised mistrust (Michael Hussey)
- a new form of slavery . . . it is impersonal . . . there is no human relationship between master and slave (Leo Tolstoy)
- incarnate desire, frozen desire (James Buchan)
- human relationships (William Bloom)
- a measure of social interaction; no more, no less (Keith Hart)
- the Holy Grail, the thing we are all in search of and want to have (Jacob Needleman)
- like electricity: everyone uses it, but no one understands it (Paul Hwoschinsky)
- a symbol of the emotional relationship between an individual and . . . the group (William Desmonde)
- in the end CONFIDENCE, which lives only in human minds and hearts (Bernard Lietaer)

go back in time to the really old days – that is, before the 1980s, when money was typically still in the form of paper notes.

I well remember the feeling of holding a 10 Krone note in my hand at the start of the 1970s. It was yellow, and issued by the Bank of Norway with the serious face of the Prime Minister, Christian Michelsen, on it. Ten serious Norwegian Kroner, with a beard. That was an impressive sum of money for a little child. I once also held an incomprehensible hundred thousand lire note in my hand. I hesitated at the thought of that sum. Today, my own sons have those same notes in their toy box.

There is not much you can do these days with a 10 Krone note like that, apart from putting it in with the coin collection. They are like old postage stamps; they tell the story of bygone days, with the detached traces of forgotten links between people. When money ends up in a museum or in a coin collection, it is no longer alive, no longer really itself. It is a remnant of life once lived, like insects on pins behind the glass in an insect collection. Look here, that's what money looked like when it was alive, when it was flying about and getting goods and people going! Now it is all dried up and stiff. The wandering Greek god of trade, Hermes (on the back of the old Norwegian 10 Krone note, and given a thorough introduction in Chapter 6) has moved on and left these notes inactive in the dust. Do those notes dream of the good old days when they were passed from hand to hand, dancing all day long?

The 10 Krone has since morphed into a coin. Now the 100 Krone note is on almost the same type of paper, the same size and issued by the same authority, and another face looks at me wonderingly. What would she say? How can it be that money which had Christian Michelsen's face from 1972 and Fridtjof Nansen's face from 1982 is unusable now, while papers with the face of opera singer Kirsten Flagstad, from 2002, is able to circulate freely? How can it be that money which seems to be alive and attractive works within one period but not in another? One of the criteria for the function of money is that it should be capable of preserving value. But clearly it seems that this is no longer true for my old 10 Krone note. It is like a snakeskin that has been sloughed off. The snake has moved on and has grown a new skin. Banknotes have a finite time on the Earth, just like us. But money lives on.

What is it then that keeps money alive, giving it its vital, seductive monetary features? What is the difference between money in a museum and money in circulation? The fact that something is legal tender implies that someone has said that precisely this money may circulate now. There is somehow an invisible social contract around it. On American notes there is a saying: 'In God We Trust'. Do they want us to believe that it is God standing behind the dollar?

Like the genie in the lamp?

Money, in the form of coins, banknotes or credit cards, is of a different kind of reality than a cup, a bicycle or a car, for example. A cup is a cup as long as it holds water, but if the bottom falls out of it, it is no longer essentially a cup. A car is a car, even if it is no longer able to move from place to place. But a car that has been torn in two is no longer a car; it is then a wreck. A 100 Krone note, on the other hand, is a 100 Krone note even if it is torn in two or has been washed and wrinkled. You can hand it in and be given a new one, or add it to the balance of your account. And it is the same money. Money seems to live a life that is independent of its physical (on paper) or virtual (on screen) expression – an extremely real life that can be measured and accounted for. Money has no necessary physical counterpart. Still, money remains a concrete, necessary part of our shared world even when it has become invisible and digital. If you think that money is not real, try surviving in a foreign town for three or four days with no money.

Money seems to have a *migratory* or *borderline reality*, says the British journalist and monetary philosopher, James Buchan. Like a ghost or a Flying Dutchman, it seems neither to belong to the living – or to the dead.[4] Whether money takes the form of shells, beads, gold, copper coins, paper or digital signals on a computer monitor or a magnetic strip is of no real consequence; its essence is something invisible yet still effective that surrounds its concrete expression.

So it is in the room *between* us and its visible expression that the phenomenon of money can come alive. *Only in relation to other people's interest in it does money actually become money.* It is here that the magical fascination for it arises. Money is nourished by mutual human interests. It is people's constantly renewing input of wishes, wants and fantasies that gives money its actual existence. Without such new wishes and desires pouring into it, there would be nothing money-like about its expression. Then it would just be plain figures, paper, metal or bits and bytes.

Money can then be understood as one of these human inventions that makes an psychic intuition tangible, just as a clock makes the intuition of time tangible or as a sheet of paper containing characters makes the intuition of a thought tangible. And, just as with other inventions, it becomes more than a passive slave of the inventor – it begins to have a return effect on us. The relationship works both ways – the invention changes the inventor. The clock has changed us, who we are, how we behave and live our way through each day. The characters on the paper make it possible to be in discussion with ourselves and to bring about an ideal abstract world in which concepts and ideas appear to live lives of their own.[5] Inventions such as coal steam engines and industrial weaving looms changed the British landscape, how people thought about the world and where people lived throughout the nineteenth century. They spread all over and affected people everywhere. Such inventions have a strong, undeniable society-forming power.[6]

If the clock gives us the time, written language provides us with abstract concepts and industrial machinery provides us with goods, what does money provide us with? Let's expand a little on the definitions of economics: money is a unit of account that stores value over time and functions as a means of exchange. But why do we want exchange in the first place? Well, because we would like something other than what we have. Wishes and trading stem from an absence, a yearning for something else. The intention to buy and sell with money springs from a psychic image depicting our wants. Money in the hand awakens imaginative possibilities: to do this, go there, have that. And that means, perhaps surprisingly, that money belongs primarily to the world of fantasy and imagination.

This is key: we are hot on the trail of the mystery of money here: Money appeals to, communicates with and tells much about human desires, fantasies and yearnings. Notions about something that does not yet exist can become reality with the help of money – it becomes a sort of dreamcatcher. It arouses dreams *and* lures us to arrange them in real life. On this basis, money primarily lives in a psychic reality which leads people to associate with others who have also let themselves be lured by money, thanks to *their* images and yearnings.

Let us therefore define money as *that which possibilises the imagination.*[7] Money is an invention that allows our psychic images to materialise. It is like Aladdin's genie in the lamp from the Arabian Nights: We rub the lamp, and money asks us what wish it should fulfil for us today. Money allows the images of desire to put down roots so that they can start sprouting in our common life. Money gives the images substance and sets them off in the direction of new changes in society and the world. Your commitment to money is, viewed in this way, also a commitment to the world.

The images within money

If, one day, you get a letter telling you that you have won the lottery, or you stand with a sizeable sheaf of banknotes after a successful investment, or you see you have received a tax rebate that was a lot bigger than you thought, *that* arouses the images: images about going there, buying that, doing this. But what kind of images come to you? If we look closely at these we might discover that the images tell the story of those gods that dominate my imagination, or the myths through which I live my life: do I put the entire sum into my savings, like an old skinflint (Chronos), blow it all on one tremendous party (like Dionysus), invest in productive industry (like Prometheus), or give it all away in a grand gesture (like Zeus)? Will there be a shopping trip for beauty and cosmetics items (like Aphrodite), or will I actually go off on a two-week hunting and wilderness trip (like Artemis)? Maybe gamble or speculate in daytrading on the stock exchange (like Hermes)? Money brings to life different ideas and patterns of behaviour in different people.[8]

In that way, money becomes an opening to the many different archetypal backgrounds that dominate human life through all of our possible and impossible wishes. There is therefore no reason for people to agree on where the best investment is to be made, what sort of things to consume, or which horse to bet on. Disagreements about money are something we will have to live with, because money seems to be a genuinely polytheistic phenomenon (more on this in Part III).

The problem today is that, on the basis of conventional economic theory, we have tried to tame this beast with one mode of mind alone: quantitative rationality. But economic theories simply cannot control money to make it behave in line with this. Long columns of figures, worksheets and cost/benefit analyses are not able to cope – regardless of how precise they may be – with getting the mongrel to sit, to lie down or do the tricks we might want in practice. Money raises its hackles and growls back, before it runs out of the yard in the opposite direction from the one intended. Money is also difficult to control and impossible to predict at macro level. Even in the short term, inflation and interest rates are difficult to predict – into next year, for example.[9]

Money is like sex, death, work, love, hate, war, power or religious yearnings in that it is an *autonomous* power that has a life independent both of the individual and of a universal rationality. We would like reason to prevail, but money is stronger, and surrounds us. Even central banks lose control when money storms break loose in the credit markets. We end up in the leash of money and have to follow it, even if we would prefer to have had control and made the money behave in the way *we* think is sensible. Sometimes, the tail wags the dog.

This is not unlike our relationship with language. We certainly do not have full control over the language we speak. Not only does it sometimes happen that what we say isn't really what we mean, but sometimes what other people pick up differs substantially from what we are actually saying. More profoundly, it is also as if the language *is speaking us*, rather than us speaking it. On the whole we can say only what the language allows us to say. Very few – mostly poets, philosophers and madmen – venture beyond the borders of the commonplace. We are handed over to the language and the power structures that lie within it. This is also the case with money: it flows out, washes over our lives, creates uproar here, rich people there, poor elsewhere – apparently arbitrarily. If the language speaks us, we could perhaps say that money is *moneying* us. By that I mean that money is a*ctively* forming our relationship with the world, and therefore also effectively forming who we are.[10]

For a few thousand years the monetary system, like a mongrel, has sometimes been thrashed and told off on the one hand, but secretly fed with the other. Today, it seems as if money has completely escaped from the harness. Many people live in fear of the devastation money causes. No one is regulating the financial flows any more. Every day, an average of US$3,000 billion whizzes around the planet in short-term trading in different currencies. That is more than ten times the entire daily share trading on all of the world's stock exchanges. In total, daily trade in actual goods and services form only one per cent of this.[11] The figure is inexact because the flow of money is difficult to measure in all of the forms it takes (derivatives, insurances, reassurances, etc).

Nevertheless, we ought to know that huge floods of money are racing around and over us – money pouring in over us, over ports, cities and borders in the hunt for opportunities. Often, the 'same' money can travel right round the world several times during the course of the same day. Governments and central banks are virtually powerless if this deluge just decides to submerge the currency of a country. In practice, it could halve all values in a country during the course of a few weeks.[12]

Many people believe that this is financial anarchy. They are looking for international institutions that are able to control it. Let's look a little more closely at that idea of anarchy. The word *anarchy* comes from the Greek and means 'without *archai*'. The word *archai* has several roots: We find it in *arkhaios*, which means old, and in *archos*, which means master or chief. It also appears in *archetupon*, as the archetypal dominant patterns. Money understood as 'an-archy' is *without* all of this: Money has lost contact with where it came from. Nobody is in charge any longer, and it no longer is contained and held by one larger pattern or one story. This is money that has a life of its own and has lost contact with any caring human community. It devastates unpredictably, more or less in the same way as the Åsgårdsreia (the wild midwinter hunt of gods and goddesses) in ancient Norse mythology. Rational theories can try to explain the money flows *post hoc,* but so far they have not managed to tame them.[13]

Money 'talks' – but what language?

If we cannot domesticate money, perhaps we can play with it? The American artist J.S.G. Boggs has specialised in improvisations of images of money.[14] After a restaurant visit, he sometimes offers to pay by signing an artistic variation of a note of money. He asks whether it is all right to pay with it, and not infrequently also gets change in return. A work of art might be called '10 fun' or 'tan dollars', for example. No one could mistake them for real money, but the public authorities do not altogether see the humour in 'the fun'. Because what does it mean if people accept the pictures as genuine money? Boggs has been taken to court several times for forgery (but has been acquitted). The US Secret Service has carried out raids and has been monitoring him.[15] Why?

Probably because the monetary system requires money to be perceived as something hard, real, serious and solid. It is not appropriate for people to start questioning what money means, how it works and what it is really worth. The point is that money is *a psychic construct whose value depends on the confidence most people have in it.* That is how airy-fairy it all is. If the consumers' confidence in money and its future value drops towards zero, if they start cutting up their credit cards everywhere and stop taking out loans, then the entire monetary system will go into a flat spin and implode. To be money, money requires people to have confidence in its future value.[16] If we collectively start losing the *belief* that it can fulfil our wishes next year, it will be finished.

Boggs's images illustrate that money is something that we ourselves design and create. If only money could be linked to something lasting and objective (such as gold, silver, oil, grain or diamonds), perhaps we could all rest in the knowledge that money is 'real'. Instead we enter into collective repression of the

nature of money. The threat from Boggs consists of people possibly being able to see money as an idea made up by our collective imagination and not at all as something objective and solid. It could appear so shocking that the world just could not cope with thinking about it.[17]

The magic exercised by money is dependent on the power of metaphor and image. In the same way as art, money represents something beyond itself. A poem can ask us to believe that it represents a nightingale or a tiger of wrath. A note asks us to believe that the figure written upon it represents a sack of potatoes, a few hours' work or a little silver. Neither money nor poems would be possible without the ability of the human mind to grasp that something can act as a replacement for something else. The ability of money to be a means of exchange is based on its ability to translate one kind of thing into another, and one kind of work into another.

Money talks because money is a metaphor, a transfer and a bridge, as the media philosopher Marshall McLuhan points out. He continues: "Money is a language for translating the work of the farmer into the work of the barber, doctor, engineer or plumber. As a vast social metaphor . . . [money] speeds up change and tightens the bonds of interdependence in any community."[18]

Both art and money are dependent on our capacity to create and handle metaphors. If 'my love is a rose petal' provides meaning, we can also find meaning in 'a £1 coin is a loaf in the shop'.[19] Money becomes a metaphor that (also) belongs to the world of poetry, play and the imagination.

A few preliminary conclusions

As has been mentioned, economic theory states that the *function* of money is as 1) a means of exchange, 2) a store of value and 3) a unit of account. But what money actually *is* can be difficult to understand when it is seen 'objectively' and thus detached from the human psyche. The inexhaustible source of the *vitality* of money derives from human wishes and desires, combined with a confidence that money will retain its power in future.

So, from a psychological standpoint, we can expand on the understanding of money with three more functions that should be integrated into economic theory.

4) Money is *attention*. Money affects our consciousness, and easily shifts it into a mode of calculation. We are in an intense reciprocal influence with money, almost like a living dialogue; it makes visible certain values and obscures others, depending on what other people think of the same values: It leads us to pay attention to certain sides of reality that can be easily calculated with money and to overlook others.[20]

5) Money *defines relationships between people;* it shapes and maintains certain social networks; money is shaped by and shapes social norms and institutions. People with similar interests become effective in markets and mutually drawn to one another. People with lots of economic contacts become more closely linked to one another. Those who are not participants in the money exchanges are left outside these networks.[21] Thus, money is a social relation.

Finally, 6) Money *possibilises the imagination* and lets it materialise. We have seen that for money to come to life it springs forth from desire as images – it is primarily a psychic and social reality. Money is imaginative and owes its existence to the realm of metaphor and its permanence only to human confidence in the future. To the extent that it seems to live an independent and objective life of its own on notes or in computers, it is because it has coagulated or solidified, in the way that letters on paper are solidified thoughts. In this sense, following the monetary philosopher James Buchan, we can say that money is *frozen desire.*[22]

The soul is dependent on money for giving expression to its images and wishes. And vice versa: money belongs to the lifeworld and is dependent on the metaphors and fantasies of the soul in order to come to life. Otherwise it is just a lot of meaningless pieces of paper or bits on a hard disc. Here we get a glimpse of the inner secret dynamics when we see money and soul together: they are like an old married couple in a mutual love-hate relationship. Precisely because the soul, deep down, knows that it is dependent on money, it has to shout and slam things, and tell money how terrible and immoral it is. Money, on the other hand, brings home the bacon and is fed up of all the moralising. Still money knows that life all alone by itself would be very empty. Divorce? Soul leave money behind? Money without soul? Unthinkable.

That's enough about money for now. Before we can go on, we need to know a bit more about the soul, the psychological fields in which money moves. How to speak better of the soul is the next step.

Chapter 4

Why money and *soul*?

Are there any reasons for making an attempt to resuscitate the concept of soul? For some people, the word is 'soft' or 'feminine'. Others link it to theology, the Church and purgatory. For several centuries, it was like this:

> As soon as the coin in the coffer rings, the soul from out of Purgatory springs! [1]

Fantastic business idea: payment now, delivery in the hereafter! As a marketing strategy from the Middle Ages, this is not far behind campaigns for modern brands. Not at all strange, then, that the Church ran at a profit.

So, for many people 'soul' is still closely associated with the Church, priesthood and religion. To some the word smacks of dust and hymns. Many scientists and atheists will not even utter the word. For others, the soul is a type of mystical hazy concept, an ethereal cloud that is attached to the body, but which can go on existing when we die, through a tunnel and out into the light or out of the window and up a bright stairway, as has been described during near-death experiences. All of this seems very far away from today's monetary world, as it appears in account statements, wage negotiations, shopping malls and international trade. Economics is primarily a *worldly* philosophy, says economics historian Robert Heilbroner.[2] For many people, the worldly is also in a contrasting position to the ideal or spiritual. Money *or* soul.

In the psychological field, too, the word 'soul' is not particularly creditworthy. The father of psychoanalysis, Sigmund Freud, wrote numerous volumes in German about *die Seele,* but when he was translated to English, the word emerged as *the mind.* The soul fell overboard and drowned on its way across the English Channel. It was important for English-speaking psychologists to establish a distance between Psychology and its big brother Theology ever since the former's birth in around 1880. I too studied psychology at university for years without coming upon the words 'soul' or 'psyche'. A hundred years after pioneers such as Fechner and Freud, the profession still prefers words like cognition, mental schemas, behaviour, scripts, consciousness, the subconscious, intelligence, perception, family systems, relationships, self, self-image or simply 'the brain'. Anything other than 'soul', which is perceived as imprecise, outdated and unscientific.

Nevertheless, as long as we involve ourselves with psychology, we will never get away from the soul. It is inherent in the very name of the discipline. *Psyche logos* means speech or study of the soul. The English word for the Greek *psyche* is and will remain 'soul'. We may be able to talk about 'psyche'; for me they are virtually synonyms. Still, soul has some meanings that are not identical with psyche: in everyday speech we can still describe a chair or lamp as having soul. We hear music that has soul, and that does not just apply to *Soul* music. Or we tell stories about someone who might have won the whole world but has lost his soul. Or we feel something in young people that bears witness to an 'old soul'. Why, if psychologists don't like the word, are the construction industry and real estate agents happy to build and sell houses that have soul?

'Logos' can also be translated as *coherent or reasoned speech,* the word. To the extent that an estate agent succeeds in talking in a justified way about the soul of a house, it is also engaged in psychology. The things being done at psychology departments we might more rightfully call statistics, cognitive science, neuro-biology, interaction training, coaching, linguistic analysis, behaviour analysis, testing or something similar. If we are not speaking of the psyche or soul, then we are not engaging with psychology in a real sense either. Large parts of psychology have become like the economy – soulless – because the discipline has no interest in things relating to the soul (any longer), as the moral philosopher Adam Smith and the soul-doctor Sigmund Freud were.

Therefore: money and *soul.*

Psychology means a coherent discourse about the soul – how we can think about it, talk about it, come into contact with it, care about it and serve it. But if we are to be able to discover soul in the world of money and the economy, we have to know what to look for.

An unambiguous definition of 'soul' is still not possible, since the soul can never step outside itself to an objective position where definitions can be deter-mined. When the soul (by means of its verbal consciousness) speaks about the soul, it bites its own tail. Absolute definitions are rare – particularly outside logic and science – and not always even desirable. The philosopher Ludwig Wittgen-stein taught us that this is linked to the way language operates.[3]

Instead of definitions, therefore, I will put down a few fence poles and some signposts to point the way and mark how we can talk about the soul in a coherent way. The term 'soul' may be of crucial help in understanding emotional reactions and the experience of meaning. If people experience economic life as emotionally cold and meaningless, things of the soul become all the more important.

The soul is the *form* of everything

I would first like to borrow from Aristotle's work on the soul, *Peri Psyches*. In this 2,500-year-old text he describes the soul as the unique form of every thing and every creature. The notion of soul used by Aristotle is only distantly related to the usual modern conception. He holds that the soul is the *form* of each and any thing. Thus, it is not a distinct substance separate from the material body that it is in. Rather, the soul is the form through which the thing is present in the world. Thus the notion of a body without a soul is simply unintelligible.

Perhaps the thing we are unaccustomed to with this description is that the soul is positioned safe and sound in the sensuous, tangible, perceivable world, and not in the hereafter or in an abstract, transcendent world. You can sense and see the soul. The soul is in the eyes, says the Danish essayist Carsten Jensen;[4] or, as the French philosopher Emmanuel Levinas formulates it, in the face of the Other.[5] Both locate the soul in the sensuous field.

A person's soul then becomes directly accessible to us in the way he or she spontaneously appears to us. It is not only human faces that speak to us through their form, but also animals, products, trees and buildings. They tell the story of who they are and how they co-create the perceptual field around them. We easily take their existence for granted. The very word 'existence' comes from the Latin *ex* – out and *sistere* – take a stand. Thus, things and people are able to *stand out in front of us*. Then we forget the very mystery of Being, as Heidegger says. We think of being as a noun and not as a verb, something *active*.[6] We easily forget that the silent world of things and objects produces the world afresh every day by displaying their forms to each other and to us.[7]

The Austrian philosopher Martin Buber says that we can adopt an I-it or an I-you relationship to everything we meet.[8] In my use of language here, I would clarify that an I-it relationship means an attitude that fails to notice the soul in the other person or thing, while an I-you relationship means that I am meeting this other co-creation as a soul, a unique form in the world, in a reciprocal relationship in which I am also called to account for this Other. If I say (as the former US President Ronald Reagan is supposed to have said) "If you have seen one redwood, you have seen them all," then I am not interested in nor do I respect the unique characteristics of the Other's form that this tree is showing me. Like Aristotle, on the other hand, we can say that we are able to catch sight of and gain contact with the soul of the Other. We note the unique character of the form of this co-creation when it comes to meet us.

Another consequence of this definition is that we do not need to go *behind* anyone or anything to encounter its soul. We can stick to the surface, to the sensuous impression. Thus, the soul of a tree is not inside the stem. The soul of a dog is not inside its nose. Neither is the soul of a personal computer hidden among millions of transistors in the microprocessor. Correspondingly, we do not find the soul inside the brain, even if the brain's neurons undoubtedly have a crucial role in how we manifest ourselves. The soul is not an 'epiphenomenon', a by-product of neurons' interactions with one another through the synapses. We can confidently let the neuro-researchers work on studying the brain without having to await their findings in order to understand the soul. Brain and soul are concepts on different levels altogether.

Here, I'll speak of the soul as something *sensuous*. You can feel it, see it, suffer it, imagine it, try to understand it if not explain it. In this perspective, the soul of something is accessible to anyone who stops his or her busyness and starts observing the unique character of the form of someone or something. How does this form appear or speak to me? It is a matter of an aesthetic sensitivity relating to the unique form of something appearing in the here and now. Soul thus does not refer to otherworldly dimensions or neurobiological mechanisms.

The world comes with shapes, colours and textures. As expressive forms, things speak; they show the shape they are in. They announce themselves: 'Look, here we are.' The soul is here, now, in the immediately given form – as it appears to you.

- £ -

If we are to find the soul in the world of money, we therefore have to ask whether the things we come face to face with – people, products, places – invite an I-it or an I-you relationship in which the soul is allowed to be noticed. For a product on the market, this means that its soul lies in *how it presents itself to me,* and how it feels when being used. Does this mug feel comfortable in the hand? Does this bun express a touch of care and thoughtfulness? Does the roar of the engine make my head thump? The building that company is based in – is it inviting? Do their employees treat me like an insensate object or with respectful attention? Is the design, lighting and air of the office space favourable? Is the letter written in an welcoming or alienating, standardised and bureaucratic way? Is there care for the language used?

Many communications experts are interested in the body language of the person passing on a message. 'Up to 80 per cent of communication is non-verbal,' they say. Whatever the number used, 40, 70 or 80 per cent – it is maybe better understood as a metaphor for the often-underestimated importance of aesthetic form. What they are implying – phrased somewhat differently – is that the soul is inherently and fully present in the way we appear to one another. The soul is not hiding somewhere under the skin but emerges fully in our self-display. We display who we are through the images we present to the world. And this commonly speaks louder than the words we utter.

The soul is *in*

The other signpost to the realm of the soul points in a specific direction. It states that the way to the soul goes in: in as in inwards, interiorise, intimate, intensify, insight, intuition and inspiration.

We could say that we find the soul whenever 'external' events acquire an 'internal' meaning.[9] Through interiorising events into one's life these events are deepened into experiences. We may talk about someone having a rich soul. That does not necessarily mean that he or she has been at many events, travelled a lot, seen many cities, had exciting lovers, been to the right conferences, or has the most stylish house. Simply taking part in events, or suffering them strongly or collecting lots of them, does not produce what we might call a wise or old soul.[10] The events must be incorporated into the web of life in order that the experiences are things that relate to me, and that I can learn from. They have to be interiorised and interwoven into the story of who I am. There must be both emotion and an understanding of what is happening. The emotional events must be intertwined with ideas for creating deep and long-lasting experience. Otherwise it is just consuming one thing after the other. 'Been there, done that' – almost as variable as a music video, with several new pictures per second. Or like the newsreader on the daily news review TV programme: 'And now over to' something completely diffcrent.

The soul is not something superficial, even if it perceptibly present on the surface of things. The depths of the soul are witnessed in the complexities of its image and the way it invites us into engagement with itself.

The soul incorporates incidents and weaves them into the story of who we are. The soul is what forms identity from intense experiences. It is not difficult to sense in people who have an honest relationship with themselves and others. Nor is it hard to gauge when you meet people who constantly flit from one new experience to another because they would not cope with, succeed in or want to make the necessary internal changeover that is necessary to absorb these experiences into the soul.

This does not just apply to people. Consider cities with 1,000 years of history like Rome or Barcelona, and compare them with Philadelphia or Las Vegas. Or a 400-year-old oak tree in relation to a new shoot; old and new soul. The older one has absorbed hundreds of years of experiences and appears to have a different kind of intensity and gravitas.

People can develop a rich soul in a monk's cell, a prison, a suburb or a smallholding. Nelson Mandela is an example from South Africa. The bachelor and poet Olav H. Hauge might be an example of this from Norway, He lived almost his entire life on his fruit farm by the fjord, producing short poems of stunning

beauty. Moving from the outside in is *interiorisation* – we move from impersonal facts and incidents to a personal understanding and involvement.

However, some more precision is required here. The fact that the soul is *in*
does not mean that it is literally under the skin. The perception of being *inside*
does not refer to coordinates in a three-dimensional space. 'Internal' is a
metaphor for the soul's invisible and yet inherent power to participate in whatever it encounters. On the other hand, 'external' is a metaphor for a more un-
involved, detached or superficial stance.

If we take 'internal' literally, we are caught up in the old question of the location of the soul: is it in the pineal gland, as the French philosopher Rene
Descartes believed in the seventeenth century? Or in the heart, the stomach,
behind the eyes, or perhaps in the synapses inside the cerebral cortex? Do we
find it as information within the core of the cell, in the helixes of the genetic
codes?

'Internal' and 'external' are therefore not locations in physical space, but
metaphors for the way we relate to things and phenomena. Do we absorb them
with intimate understanding and allow them to affect us? Or do we keep them
at a distance, reject them and say that they do not concern me?

- € -

If we take this into the world of money and economics, we see that it raises a
number of practical questions. Are economic theories and methods used in
order to disengage from the people suffering or profiting from the markets?
Does the firm involve employees in the decision-making processes that apply to
them? Does it have an intimate relationship with its customers? Is there room for
friendship and intimacy at work? Or is all communication of the external kind:
about the weather, water temperature at the beach or last year's holiday trip? Are
the organisation's vision and values just words and formulations, with an external understanding? Or is there a deeper will actually to live them out? Is the
vision just a platitude, or something that employees really internalise? Are other
stakeholders invited to be involved in the discussions before important decisions
are made? Or do we exclusively keep to customers and owners while other relationships are externalised in an attempt to externalise costs and maximise
profitability?

We thus can have internal or external relationships with ideas, people or values.
It is easy to surround yourself with fashionable terms such as 'intellectual capital', 'synergies' or 'teamwork' without having taken in the content. This book
attempts to intensify our relationship with money and the economic ideas that
guide us. That also involves a conscious relationship with the metaphors and
language we use.

The soul is *down*

The money supply, the total amount of money available, generally increases, like the number of cars, roads and skyscrapers. Most economic graphs, with volume or quantity on the vertical axis and time on the horizontal axis, point upward towards heaven, like a rising morning sun; towards a greater, brighter future where it is 'warmer' and where there is more of everything.

However, the third signpost on our walkabout reminds us that the soul is also about death and the underworld. It points towards the Earth, towards the dust to which we'll return and the Earth's hidden depths. Death, breakups, bankruptcies, endings and descents are all things that the business world does not much like. But it is still all part of it. We cannot have soul without death or loss lurking somewhere in shadow. We cannot enrich the soul without being able to let go. Being human is also to be fragile, vulnerable, exposed to disease and mortality. Living bodies are, at the same time, dying bodies, regardless of how good they look or how strong and healthy they appear to be.

There is rarely talk about death within organisational life. At most, pensions are discussed. Death, however, can remind us of the most important thing: what sort of life is worth living? What do we want out of life? But, as with 'in' and 'internal', we must not be too literal when we talk about death. Death is not just a point far ahead in an as-yet-undetermined date, a point in linear time at which the brain stops making its waves, the lungs stop breathing and the heart has given its last heartbeat. Death is also the many small deaths that occur along the way. Everything we give up on the journey. The roles we shed. Anything we do 'for the last time'. Some people around us pass away. Houses we lived in disappear. Colleagues vanish out of our lives. Duties cease. Important relationships fall apart. Teams are broken up and projects end. Capital depreciates. Investments are written off.

Death can be seen as a process that is parallel to life, and is going on all the time. The ancient Greeks were conscious of this with their whole gallery of gods, where Hades rules over the underworld in parallel with his brother Zeus, who reigns over Mount Olympus and the daylight world. There is always something going on in the shadowy world of the soul, in parallel with what we are doing at work, during the daytime. We can get closer to this consciousness of death (which Freud called *thanatos*) by asking the question: Just think if I am doing what I am doing for the last time now? The last time I make breakfast for the children. The last time I go in to this kitchen. The last time I see my beloved when she gets on to the plane and goes away on a course.

Many people are struggling with images of death or loss that force their way in to their consciousness. Some feel guilty about having them. Some tell themselves they should not think in that way. But it is important to have an opening into the death processes, as these are processes that are always going on in the soul. In soul work losing (and gaining) take on another significance: losing isn't just all negative. The presence of loss and death gives more depth to the here-and-now, and contributes to making events more intensive. It is the soul's close relationship with death that makes intimacy strongest of all. The pull from below, the face of death, forces us to form an opinion of what has lasting value and what does not.

In my role as consultant, when I am interviewing managers in conjunction with a strategic project, I often use a remembrance question. I ask: "What do you want to be remembered for? When your job here is over – what would you want to remain?" They get the chance to think out their memoirs in advance. This brings us nearer again to the soul-related question: What am I here *for*? Biological death is inevitable, it will one day arrive. But encountering death in the here-and-now, as in the thought of 'what if I die now?', can be like an injection of consciousness. Suddenly the current moment opens up to deeper issues: *Why do I do what I do? What purpose do I really serve?*

- $ -

In industrial and organisational life, the emphasis is on visions, the optimism of progress, high ambition and rapid growth. Successes, triumphs, peaks, bull markets and all-time highs. Busts and depressions always come as surprises! But the soul draws us down from the peaks, down towards the ground and the Earth, towards wet and dark areas. Losses, setbacks, errors and vulnerability are no threat to the soul. It grows just as much from errors and defeats as it does on success and peaks. Periods of conflict and despair can be food for the soul, even if our ego perhaps feels only loss and retreat. Soul-work also goes on when hope is crushed.

How does management view employees' failures and setbacks? Does it overlook them? Fire the employees? What is its attitude to losses and deficits? Is the reflex reaction in downturns to immediately start cutting costs and head counts? Or to try to massage the figures, pretending deficits just aren't there? There are many modes of denial to hold these smaller deaths at bay.

In modern times, few people believe in Hell as a final destination after death. But maybe we encounter a smaller Hell in the situations that the loss of money triggers. Suddenly we experience a descent to the underworld while still alive. Seen from the perspective of soul work, the opportunity is to accept this as paths to the deepening of the soul.

There is an enormous shadow to money. Few things can awaken as much anxiety, despair, violence and criminality as does an intense, acute lack of money.

Money is linked to intense emotional forces in the psyche. Political psychologist William Bloom asks us to imagine all of the despair and yearning in which humanity lives as a result of a lack of money as a collective black-and-blood-coloured cloud of fear and panic.[11] This is a place of monsters, grotesques, debt-prison inmates, drug addicts, outcasts and the dying. When we ourselves experience a sudden lack of money, unexpected increases in the interest rate, the mouldering away of our savings or extra bills coming in, it can trigger contact with this black cloud – the black hole of money worries. We may be thrown on to the street. Bankruptcy threatens. We fall down, and the fall gives way to panic. But perhaps that is necessary if we are to develop further.

This is an emotional field that is not primarily about the quantity of money. For some people the sums may be very large; for others they are smaller. The field is a more collective area of the soul which has always been there, and which the lack of money can effectively open the trapdoor to. The Greek myths tell us that money also belongs to the underworld. We have to take some coins with us into the grave so that we can pay the ferryman Charon to take us over the river Styx on our way to the realm of the dead. And once we reach the realm of Hades, we are able to see his enormous riches. Both Hades and his Roman counterpart Pluto were known to be wealthy. If soul and money belong together, it is also because they meet in the underworld. The journey downward can be just as valuable as the journey upward.

The soul is *between*

At the first signpost, we found the soul to be the unique form of everything, as each being *displays itself.* The soul is therefore not just the form but also the capacity to enter into *a relationship*, thereby creating an encounter. The fourth signpost indicates that soul is neither over there nor in here, but in the actual relationship. The soul emerges in the between.

This is possibly most clearly demonstrated in music. The soul is not the piano's hammers and strings, not is it inside the ear and the auditory nerve pathways. The music lives *between* pianist Leif Ove Andsnes' sensitive touch on the grand piano and my relaxed body in the concert hall. 'Yes! I'm surrendering to the music. It's coming alive!' The wonderful music fills the air between the musician and me, my fellow listeners and my self.

Or with a rather less pleasant example: What if I am sitting deep in sensitive conversation with you and then someone else, in a bad temper, abruptly comes into the room. The entire atmosphere, the entire space around us and between us, changes. The intimate conversation stops; it is impossible to continue when this dark cloud comes between us. The soul is not just inside me or inside you, it is in the encounter between us, in the air, in the room in which the encounter takes place.[12]

The idea is similar to systems thinking: the relationship between two is more important than each unit in isolation.[13] So, we find the soul in the intermediate field that arises when two or more unique forms meet and interaction takes place. The soul emerges in the difference between you and me. A differential arises in which something new can take place. To work with soul is to observe, dwell on and express what is happening within this relationship. The soul is no 'thing' or separate substance. It is more like a reflection in the mirror or the moon reflected on water or a rustling in the leaves. Discovering the soul is to become attuned to the relational spaces.

It is as if our human consciousness rests in an autonomous field that extends between us and the part of the world that surrounds us. This is the inter-subjective world of life that phenomenology calls 'Lebenswelt' or 'life-world'. The life-world is the world of our immediately lived experience, *as* we live it, prior to all our thoughts about it. The life-world is the world that we count on without necessarily paying it much attention: the world of the clouds overhead and those trees over there, of getting onto your bike and greeting your colleagues at work. Easily overlooked, this primordial world is always already there when we begin to reflect on what is around us. It is not private, but a collective dimension – a common field of our lives and the other lives we encounter.[14]

That means, expressed in clearer terms, that the soul *is* our relationship to other things and other people. We exist in the power of our relationships. In Western society there is a strong perception of people as independent and self-sufficient individuals. The ideal figure is someone who gets through life by his or her own efforts. We also find this in the hero who rides off alone into the sunset or who climbs to the mountain's peak by his or her own power alone. Such perceptions are not necessarily wrong, but they often lead away from the interdependency of soul. Even in films, independence is short-lived. The hero also exists in relation to a beautiful rancher's daughter, to the land or to someone at home. Human identity is based, like the soul, through differences and relationships, not by being alone and separate. We become who we are only in relation to an Other.

- £ -

What significance does this have for money and for organisations within the monetary world?

Economic theory regards individuals and companies as self-determined, atomic and rational players. Each player is presumed to take his or her own, independent decisions. It becomes difficult to maintain this conception if the economic actors – individuals and companies – are primarily relational. We can now start viewing the company's soul as a network of relationships to customers, suppliers, owners, the environment, the local community and the public authorities. Things that are in the company's *own* interest therefore become more extensive and complex than previously thought. Self-interest must be expanded to encompass the network of relationships to a series of interested parties. A perception that the company has only internal responsibility for employees and owners – if necessary, at the expense of the other relationships – becomes profoundly problematic in this perspective. In the long run, the company forms part of an ecosystem in which it is unable to survive except by its relationships. Participating in interaction and co-development with a close, rich network of players is more important than outcompeting them, maintains Professor of Strategy James F. Moore.[15] Success is then conditional on how the entire network develops, not on an isolated profit for the individual company. If the company *is* its relationships, it loses its soul by neglecting these.

Money, too, can exist only in a relationship. That implies a new perspective on money. Suddenly it may dawn on us that money defines social relationships between people every time they are transferred. When we make a payment to someone else who accepts the money, the deal is an expression of trust in the relationship and in the money itself. As purchaser, I rely upon the vendor, and the transfer of money confirms and strengthens this confidence. The transfer of money viewed in this way becomes a record, a remembrance of a social relationship. I was there, I met this person and I bought a picture from him. Or I was on that website, studying this or that product and placed an order from this Internet vendor.

In this way, money expresses a specific type of contemplation of or response to what it was like to meet the other person at that time and location. Money and markets radically expand our social outreach. With money's help, we can enter into constructive and effective relationships with a network of people we do not know, and whom we otherwise would not have met. Helped by the magic of money, the relationship becomes possible: 'Here you have it,' says one person. 'Yes, thank you very much,' responds the other, putting the money or the bankcard on the counter. 'Many thanks,' replies the first person. Money changes hands, sums are debited, goods are moved, services are carried out and new experiences open up. New relationships materialise in joint action. So, if the soul is *between,* money's capacity to create relationships can thus serve the soul.

Soul and corporate values

Starting in the 1990s, we saw the emergence of an ethical wave in economic life. Talking about values and ethics was 'in'. This was hailed as a way to integrate money and soul, economics and ethics. Philosophers were invited to meet business executives, and everybody agreed that values were important. New trends and management tools such as Value-Based Management and Corporate Social Responsibility (CSR) emerged. Companies with respect for themselves crafted new visions and values documents. Courses in ethics were initiated at business schools, and some companies started training their employees in the core values that the corporation had chosen.

Are these not genuine attempts already at integrating soul and money? Is it not the case that soul deals with values while money deals with profitability, and that bringing these together will solve our problem? There is undoubtedly much to be gained from awareness of the significance of ethical values. But there are also obvious and unsolved problems with this approach. The great challenge has been to avoid making values – which are by their very nature inherent – into a means to an end: profitability. A joint stock company is established by its owners *in order to* create a return on the capital invested. Management and employees may well discuss and adhere to values, but never truly at the expense of profitability. As an example, the Norwegian corporation Orkla resolved this potential dilemma by making profitability its undisputed primary value, ahead of openness, respect, loyalty and so on. That way, a number of values have been made instrumental means to another end: they have been put there to serve a distinct purpose, namely the interests of the shareholders: 'One ring to bind them.' Admitting profitability as the primary value is, at least, a clarification.

Another problem is that values are formulated in an abstract, 'soulless' language. Elaborate images and stories that give form to emotions is what nourishes the soul. After the inspiration from workshops and dialogues, the values are left lying there like the dead, as expired formulations on Powerpoint slides: Loyalty! Honesty! Teamwork! The values became abstract and generic instead of being processed into becoming concrete and specific. They are sometimes set up as disembodied, universal ideals. From the perspective of the soul, it is one's *relationship* to values that is important rather than the values in themselves. At such corporate sessions the values were declared in front of a huge audience. If group work was involved, there would usually be a predefined 'correct' result. I know some honourable exceptions to this, in which an attempt was first made to make the relationship to the values more intimate by applying them to select ethical dilemmas at work. That created more participation and an internalisation of each individual's relationship with the values.

The ethical wave resulted in values that were only 'up', not 'down'. By that, I mean that the values pointed towards abstract higher ideals, towards light and harmony, and that everything would be really good. No attention to shadow or death, and hence, less soul. The implicit model for this way of applying values seem to be from Moses's Ten Commandments. Making a list of good values always resonates with that type of cultural template.

The corporate ethical wave has since receded. Hardly anybody can 'afford' values in downturns. Once again, profitability (in its narrower sense) rules.[16]

This book recommends a more sensuous and relational, internal and downward approach to values. Another path is possible: we can revoke the rich cultural imagery of values from mythologies, like in the Greek–Roman tradition in which the values were given names and personified. These myths are, above all else, a language in which to speak of values. Each of the gods – Zeus, Hermes, Apollo, Hestia, Hera, Demeter, Dionysus – expresses a certain set of values. At the same time, they also all have their own shadows built into their stories. Values also come with a flip side, which is important to know if pitfalls such as hubris are to be avoided.

- $ -

The past two chapters have laid out some ideas on money and soul respectively. Now this way of thinking can be put to work on some central economic ideas and concepts in order to see how money and soul, in spite of all their bickering, are interconnected.

Part II

Searching for soul
in economic ideas

Chapter 5

New welfare

Does money make the soul happy?

The economic system has been set up with the purpose of achieving continuous growth. The assumption is that greater wealth is always better for the inhabitants of a country. However, do higher incomes increase social well-being and happiness? Direct measurements of happiness have not had much credibility to date. But new psychological research reveals processes that undermine the happiness effect from increased income. Value dimensions other than those measured using current money appear to mean more and more for well-being. Will these gain increased significance in future politics?

The word 'welfare' originates from the phrase of *faring well* throughout life. Faring is also rooted in *faru* from Old English and Norse, which means to travel. Correspondingly, we have *velferd* in Norwegian and *Wohlfart* in German. According to the dictionaries, 'welfare' means well-being, happiness, health, prosperity and secure living conditions for individuals and society. Bear in mind also what we wish people when we leave them: Farewell!

The concept of welfare thus brings with it images of a *safe, good journey* towards the evening of life for each and every person living in the country. The role of the State should be to guarantee help when citizens are subject to failing health, social need or loss of income, as in unemployment or old age, and at the same time to secure the right to education. The State assumes the role of a kind of gigantic insurance company which utilises its huge money chest to ensure no one loses his or her dignity. In this image the State takes on a mythical garment which is reminiscent of Christianity's God the Father, or the Greek god Zeus: a great, bearded, benevolent father who promises order and security for everyone.

In American politics the word 'welfare' still implies too-big government and is frequently perceived as an authoritarian threat to individual freedom, responsibility and autonomy. In this book the word 'welfare' would cover both *wealth* and *well-being,* the first relating to prosperity and the second to the experience of happiness – see the igure below.

The idea that welfare was something that should apply not just to rich people but to most people is – historically speaking – quite new.[1] The word 'Wohlfartsstaat' was probably first used in the early twentieth century, about Bismarck's social insurance arrangements. The idea was thought through economically, and systematically expressed in an official report in the UK dated 1942. In a 1949 book, the Archbishop of York contrasts the welfare state with the 'power state', that is the states of Stalin and Hitler. The idea was put into practice by the Labour Party in the UK after the war and was then copied and modified by other countries, particularly in Europe.

But the problem is no less relevant today than it was when it was formulated during the extreme poverty and need in post-war Western Europe: How much is *enough*? What do you really need to fare well throughout life? To be satisfied; have peace of mind? More specifically: exactly what do you need as an annual income in order to be free of financial worries? £25,000? £50,000? £80,000? If we add everything together for a whole work life and calculate the current value of the future cash flows, it would quickly become a considerable sum for the type of life many people have got used to and want to live. Maybe 1 million? Or 2 million? From an economic point of view, what is the current price of peace of mind or well-being throughout the rest of life? Or is this a meaningful question at all?

No doubt we have all become richer since the start of the twentieth century. But the question is whether total welfare has increased. That is (material) wealth, (mental) well-being and (physical) health. See the Figure below to see how the terms are being used here.[2]

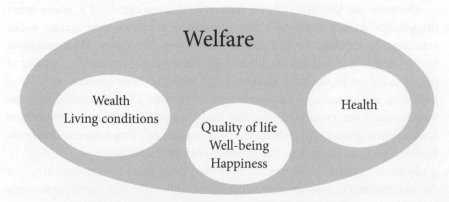

A few welfare terms viewed in relation to one another. Welfare is the whole area. The key issue is the way the three small circles relate to one another.

So, does money buy happiness?

The short answer is yes. Richer people are, on average, happier than poor people. And rich countries, on average, clearly have more happy inhabitants than most poor countries. But the connection is not simple, nor linear. And money does not steadily buy more happiness – although, for example, an advertisement for Lexus cars says that it depends on your ability to buy the right product. Investigations into human happiness appear to confirm the assumption that, as soon as you have enough for clothing, home and food, each extra amount of money that you acquire has less significance.

Whoever said money can't buy happiness isn't spending it right.
(advertisement for Lexus Auto)

Questions such as 'Are you happy?' have long been regarded as not being serious issues for research. It has been thought that people respond to surveys of this type with opinions and not with facts. According to this view, talk is cheap: superficial responses on surveys don't deserve serious consideration. It is also doubtful whether such surveys could say anything about economic utility. Better to study what people are actually doing and willing to pay for than opinions on subjective internal states that change from one day to the next.[3]

However, the last twenty years have seen the emergence of a whole interdisciplinary science concerned with measuring happiness and similar social conditions in an objective and scientifically approved manner. More and more survey methods have been established for defining and quantifying quality of life. In addition to the term *quality of life*, terms such as *objective well-being*, *happiness* and sometimes *satisfaction* are often used as synonyms.[4] There are now standard survey methods for this, and even professorships in happiness at leading international universities. The field has gained its own international professional periodicals, such as the *Journal of Happiness Studies*.[5]

In these research toolboxes we find everything from simple questions like 'Would you largely describe yourself as very happy, quite happy, not particularly happy or not at all happy?'[6] to very complicated survey methods containing several dozen sub-elements.[7] Neuropsychologists have also measured brain activity and have found these patterns to match up quite well with feelings of happiness reported verbally.[8] Health researchers have detected higher levels of the harmful hormone cortisol in people who say they are unhappy.[9] In addition to a person's personal score, researchers have asked other people to state how happy they perceive the person being surveyed to be, how often he or she smiles, and so on. The feeling of happiness naturally goes up and down during the course of a day, and from one day to the next (and, yes, good weather does produce a higher level of happiness!). Nevertheless, some people, assessed by a combination of several methods, reliably show a higher level of happiness over longer periods than others.

The interesting thing is that almost regardless of how happiness is measured, it seems as if people respond consistently (reliably) and also provide answers that can actually be meaningfully used in economics and politics when discussing quality of life (valid responses).[10] After thousands of studies, researchers agree about it being possible to study happiness in a scientific and quantitative way. This means that an important aspect of the soul, its overall level of affective states, has become publicly accessible through a language that our society understands – empirical numbers.

So, what do the data tell us about the relationship between money (wealth) and the soul's feelings?

They say the following: money creates more happiness up to the level that rich countries reached around the 1970s. Increases in income above this level do not create any more happiness or any more satisfaction. The relationship between increased income and the proportion of very happy people in the US over fifty years of economic growth (see the Figure below) shows this plateauing very clearly. Fifty

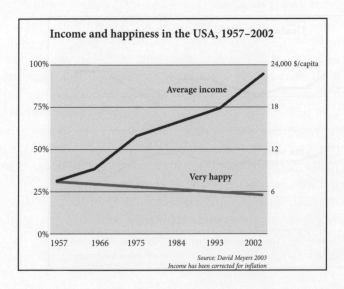

Income and happiness in the USA, 1957–2002

Source: David Meyers 2003
Income has been corrected for inflation

years of economic growth have not produced a greater number of happy pe
And neither has the proportion who say that they are unhappy diminished.
findings do not just apply to average figures for the entire population throu
period. If the same people are followed over a period of time as they becom
affluent, it seems that they do not become any happier when their inco
reases. Surveys in almost all other affluent countries show a corresponding t

We are faced with a major paradox: affluent countries give their inhabitants
increasingly high incomes, but no more happiness or satisfaction.[13] At the same
time, the income level remains low in poor countries, where extra income and
wealth would have a greater effect on happiness and satisfaction. The rich part
of the world also has a greater incidence of depression, alcoholism and criminality than it did thirty to fifty years ago.[14] Even in Norway – the country that has
been acclaimed by the UN as being at the top of the world's human development
index [15] – the figures show that the proportion of people who are materially very
satisfied decreased during the period 1985 to 1999 and, further, there was no
increase in happiness in the general population in the last twenty years, as seen
in the Figure below.[16]

Even though this is not an altogether new discovery [17] – and something that
common sense has long has suspected – the long-term implications of these data
series amounts to a social, economic and political tectonic shift. We have just not
noticed the effects of it yet, because we are sticking to old ways of thinking about
the relationship between money and utility. But *if* we take it in, we will see that the
foundation on which current economic policies has been built (an inheritance from
the industrial age between 1800 and 1970, in which governments had designed

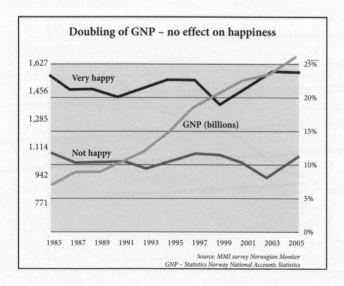

Doubling of GNP – no effect on happiness

Source: MMI survey Norwegian Monitor
GNP – Statistics Norway National Accounts Statistics

Richard Easterlin defines as the ~~money~~ ~~illusion~~ the belief that more money will make us happier. The new science proposes conversely that, as our general welfare model, we should replace material wealth with happiness and human development as the final goods. Then, completely different political instruments will be required from those which are directed towards increasingly high incomes.

Because of the money illusion, we allocate an excessive amount of time to monetary goals, and short-change nonpecuniary ends such as family life and health. The time has come to move away from pushing the happiness pills to pushing the happiness policies.

Why do we not become happier as we become (ever) more affluent?

Many responses can be supplied as to why money does not increase feelings of happiness. The poet Arne Garborg has formulated a response in his poem 'Om pengar' ['About money']:

About Money

It is said that for money you can have everything,
but you cannot.
You can buy food,
But not appetite;
Medicine, but not health;
Knowledge but not wisdom;
Glitter, but not beauty;
Fun, but not joy;
Acquaintances, but not friends;
Servants, but not faithfulness;
Leisure, but not peace.
You can have the husk of everything for money,
But not the kernel.

The political economist Robert E. Lane gives a number of reasons for this, based on scientific investigations.[19] There are some well-documented psychological processes that gnaw away and demolish any happiness benefit that increased incomes could have provided. The first of these is connected to the individual's relationship with him- or herself (habituation), and the second is connected to the relationship between people (comparison). A third is connected to people's tendency to have increasing levels of ambition, and the effects of advertising on the production of desires. It is to the first two of these in particular that I will devote space to here.

Slaves of habit – habituating to wealth

It seems there are almost no limits to what we can habituate ourselves to, as long as the situation persists. Just the fact that people live and are happy in such cold, dark and wet regions as Norway is often something difficult for southern people such as inhabitants of the Mediterranean to understand. People get used to using fiercely hot spicy foods, barbecued grasshoppers, jellied dogs' feet, and even Norwegian 'lutefish'. We cope with life in hurricane zones, scorched desert areas and tropical rainforests. Some live happily in monasteries, apartment blocks or large villas. After a few months of new living conditions, most people have got used to most things. Not much later, we start regarding what was new as *normal*.

As a psychologist, I have worked with women who, after gradually becoming habituated to a destructive couple-relationship, feel it is normal to be shouted at and beaten 'once in a while'. Populations and soldiers can gradually get used to using violence and gradually come to believe that no other existence is possible. They habituate and become resigned. Here, we encounter something fundamental to the human way of facing up to the world. Our experiences are gradually incorporated into our identity and then start defining what we experience as 'natural'.[20]

In particular, we find this in our relationship to money and our standard of living. As soon as we have more money and more possessions in our hands, we regard this as normal. And we take this with us into the future. We believe that a new house – when it is finished – will provide us with a higher sense of happiness for ever, whereas the effect actually lasts for three to twelve months. Estimates of how much extra income people get used to during the course of a year appear to converge at around 40 per cent.[21] If, for example, you are very satisfied with the increase in your income one year, almost half of that contentment will disappear through the course of the following year. The Norwegian singer Anne Grete Preus captures the point very well when she sings "Happiness has a hole in its pocket".

Contentment with an increase in salary certainly produces a clear, quantifiable effect on the feeling of happiness at the time it occurs. However, that contentment is linked more to the *actual increase* than to the higher, stable *level*. Happiness keeps slipping out and requires to be replenished. By what? Well, with another increase, of course. This dynamic has a special name: addiction. The same applies to alcoholics, drug addicts and oil-dependent nations when they become addicted to an increasingly strong dose to achieve the same feeling of satisfaction.

Whereas contentment from a job well done or spending time with family and friends provides the same contribution of happiness each time, steadily stronger injections are required for increases in income in order to increase happiness correspondingly. This might be part of the explanation for why many poor countries have far higher levels of happiness than income level alone might indicate. The input factors within 'gross national happiness', GNH, are clearly quite different from gross national product, GNP.

Habituation and increasing expectations put many on a *hedonic treadmill*.[22] That is a wheel in which a person has to run faster and faster to stay in the same place. It is reminiscent of Alice in Wonderland, when she meets the Red Queen:

"The Queen cried 'Faster! Faster! They ran . . . with the wind whistling in Alice's ears . . . they went so fast that at last they seemed to skim through the air, hardly touching the ground with their feet, till suddenly, just as Alice was getting quite exhausted, they stopped, and she found herself sitting on the ground, breathless and giddy. The Queen propped her up against a tree, and said kindly, 'You may rest a little now.'

'Why! I do believe we've been under this tree the whole time! Everything is just as it was!'

'Of course it is,' said the Queen, 'What would you have it?' 'Well, in our country,' said Alice, still panting a little, 'you'd generally get to somewhere else – if you ran very fast for a long time, as we've been doing.'

'A slow sort of country!' said the Queen. 'Now, *here*, you see, it takes all the running *you* can do, to keep in the same place. If you want to get somewhere else, you must run at least twice as fast as that!' . . ."[23]

In the physical world, running faster might help, but in the emotional world, in which habituation pertains, you have to run faster and faster to maintain the same level of satisfaction.

The welfare economist Tibor Scitovsky differentiated between passive and active happiness in his book *The Joyless Economy*. The passive type is the comfort that things we buy can give us, like a new sofa or a more slick kitchen. These are comforts that fade with time. The active type of happiness he calls pleasures. These come from a person's own involvement in creating an experience such as meeting friends or walking in a beautiful forest. The passive type is all about comfort; the other with active pleasures that avoid habituation. Certain types of consumption, Scitovsky says, are 'joyless', other 'joyful', and the difference between them depends on factors like challenge, mastery and active participation.[24]

If we are not aware of how quickly we get used to the comfort of new things, it is easy to over-invest in possessions. Then, there is little time left over for anything other than keeping up income to pay for them. Studies seem to confirm that most people underestimate the strength of the effects of this habituation.[25] The new flooring, the TV, the holiday cottage, the kitchen and the boat do not provide any long-term increase in satisfaction. One unintended result of this is that life gradually moves in the direction of paid work and earnings, and away from other areas.[26]

When that happens, money can eat its way unrelentingly into the soul's area, finally leading to an inner battle against the invasion by money. Like the last Samurai or the last of the Mohicans, the soul is making a desperate effort to be heard, and the person who is dependent on money can be attacked by feelings of emptiness or burnout. A potential integration of soul and money slips away. We are caught up in the historical split between soul and money, thereby confirming St Paul's words about love of money being the root of all evil.

Kill my neighbour's cow

God the Father was out one day walking on the Earth and happened to meet a poor Russian peasant. This particular day, the peasant was feeling very low and upset because his neighbour, another poor peasant, had managed to acquire a cow. God saw that the peasant was feeling low. "What can I do for you?" He asked.

The answer came quickly: "Kill my neighbour's cow!"

That might not exactly be the answer that God had in mind. The story does not say how things went for the cow, but it would not have been much of a story if it did not resonate with us: we can get used to most things, provided the people we compare ourselves with are not particularly better off than us. Comparison of social status sneaks, like a poison, into our own quality of life and well-being. Research confirms what the Russian peasant was experiencing: if you compare yourself to others and find that you are falling behind, there are quantifiable reductions in levels of happiness and satisfaction.[27] It might have helped if God had killed the cow. But for how long?

Many people compare themselves with other people (who are important to them) when they evaluate their own happiness and satisfaction. Within happiness research, this is called your reference group. Those whom you compare yourself with become crucial to your own satisfaction with life. A rule of thumb for increasing your own happiness is to compare yourself downwards – in other words, with someone who is clearly worse off than you are yourself. If you want to reduce your level of happiness, you should correspondingly compare yourself with someone further up the tree, someone praised by the media or acquaintances.

Other-directed people, who largely gain confirmation of their own value via other people, often let their feelings of satisfaction and happiness be determined by their position in some type of ranking system. The dark side to this is that it helps if these other people head for a fall. The American essayist Gore Vidal pointedly formulated this in his epigram "It is not enough to succeed. Others must fail," and "Whenever a friend succeeds, a little something in me dies."[28]

There are lots of things that confer status, and money is probably the most important in our era. But money that is invisible, hidden in a bank account, confers little status in relation to other people. Money must preferably be spent on consumption that other people are able to see, in order to provide the status effect. One early, famous economist who researched into these less rational methods of using money was Thorstein Veblen, an American of Norwegian descent. He dissected with sarcastic precision 'the leisure class' – the way the affluent could declare themselves better than the masses via 'conspicuous consumption'. This is a type of consumption that is based on the philosophy of expensive being better than cheap, regardless. This idea lives on just as well today as it did when *The Theory of the Leisure Class* was published in 1899:

> We all feel, sincerely and without misgiving, that we are the more lifted up in spirit for having, even in the privacy of our own household, eaten our daily meal by the help of handwrought silver utensils, from hand-painted china (often of dubious artistic value), laid on high-priced table linen. Any retrogression from the standard of living which we are accustomed to regard as worthy in this respect is felt to be a grievous violation of our human dignity.[29]

An economic rational individual would not pay £10,000 for cutlery studded with diamonds, if a good knife costing £5 would do the same job. But the well-heeled can do that — if the idea is to show the world that they are so rich that they can raise themselves above the merely functional. Veblen was not just intending to criticise the nouveau riche or aristocrats who base their well-being on outdoing others in possessions and consumption. He was asking deeper questions, about what function such obvious economic psychopathology might have. Conspicuous consumption (widespread throughout modern society, as is the castigation of moralists who intend to stand on the side of the soul against unscrupulous money) could not be explained within the conventional model of Economic Man.

Veblen was not convinced that rational self-interest was the bond holding society together in the way that Adam Smith maintained, nor that consumption and leisure were to be preferred over work. But he saw that both poor and rich people no longer competed with muscles, weapons, sport or skill, but rather via money and consumption. Workers, citizens and the rich all sought to demonstrate their superiority in wealth in comparison to others.

Veblen continues: "In order to stand well in the eyes of the community it is necessary to come up to a certain, somewhat indefinite conventional standard of wealth; just as in the earlier predatory stage it is necessary for the barbarian man to come up to his tribe's standard of physical endurance, cunning and skill at arms." He sees parallels between the sword and shield of earlier ages, and the walking sticks, silver pens, briefcases and elegant document folders of his day. Viewed in this way, modern players on the markets are still barbarians – they just roam other hunting grounds.

Veblen here leads us onto the track of more deeply motivated behaviour than the economic theory of the nineteenth century, about behaviour controlled by rationality and self-interest. What is it that really binds market-based societies together? Adam Smith believed it was the invisible hand of the market that would gradually lift the nation up from poverty. Marx saw no solution in collaboration between the classes, and believed that the poor would eventually cut the throats of the rich by revolution. However, Veblen saw that the competition for status behind conspicuous consumption was exactly what was holding society together! How? Well, the lower classes are not, and do not want to be, at swords' point with the upper. Workers do not want to get rid of management. Rather, they simply want to become rich themselves!

Veblen's analysis is that this is the glue that holds society together. Anarchists and revolutionaries did not succeed with their 'Eat the rich!' message in the twentieth century. Instead, the market has succeeded with an outlook of 'Me too!' All are joined together by the intangible but steely bonds of common attitudes.

In theory, comparison with others might, as Veblen points out, be straightforward enough as a glue for holding society together. But its ghost comes back to haunt us, however, when everyone, at the same time, clambers towards the constantly moving targets of conspicuous consumption. When that happens, happiness and satisfaction both decrease.

The mutual struggle for greater wealth or income *than other people* is completely destructive to society as a whole. If my income (or my consumption) increases relative to yours, yours simultaneously *falls* by just as much relative to mine. The process does not produce any general increase in happiness or well-being, regardless of how much of our lives is spent increasing our income and consumption.[30] That is what is known as a zero-sum game: the amount of status for distribution does not grow as long as everyone is being measured on the same dimension: money. And because everyone has to work more, the result may be that well-being actually goes *down*.

New happiness research has tried to quantify how much I lose in well-being in relation to your pay rise (or vice versa), and the findings point in the direction of 30 per cent. If everyone else earns an extra £1,000, my happiness falls by one third as much as it would rise if I alone earned an extra £1,000.[31] As the economist Richard Layard puts it in his book about happiness: there is "clear evidence that a rise in other people's income hurts your happiness."

In addition, we rapidly become accustomed to receiving pay rises. And, as mentioned before, around 40 per cent of contentment with your own increase disappears every year.[32] Such figures illustrate how these processes chew away large chunks of the happiness that higher incomes and wealth could otherwise have brought with them. Habituation sets money up against the soul by gradual dependency, and social comparison can set souls up in a self-defeating struggle with each other. We start out from it being either your money or my money, not our money or the nation's or the Earth's money.

However, as has already been mentioned, the soul is not limited to what is inside the individual. Guided by the ideas from the previous chapter, we know that the soul is always in relationships. What the soul wants is circulation and community. So does money – it exists only in exchanges. Money creates and expands relationships between people in markets.

But when those relationships are dominated by comparison and competition, money and income get framed by *conflict*. To many people this feels like coming to a crossroads with only two choices: Either a life of more-money-than-you in which we race around on the treadmill, or a life in which we opt out of money altogether – try to cultivate carrots, look after the cat, cook waffles – and hand the rest of society over to the climbers, Veblen's barbarians. Once again, either money or soul.

A new model for welfare and happiness

In summary: in many ways, life is much better than it was fifty years ago. We have riches as never before, more leisure time, more equality, better health and less physically demanding workplaces. Only a few would want to return to earlier times. Nevertheless, we are not any more satisfied or happy. Mechanisms such as habituation and comparison take away a lot of the improvement in well-being that money could have brought.

That would probably have surprised John M. Keynes, who in 1931 put forward the following hundred-year forecast:

> Let us, for the sake of argument, suppose that a hundred years hence we are all of us, on the average, eight times better off in the economic sense than we are today

... I draw the conclusion that, assuming no important wars and no important increase in population, the *economic problem* may be solved. ... The struggle for subsistence always has been hitherto the primary, most pressing problem of the human race. ... This means that the economic problem is not – if we look into the *future – the permanent problem of the human race* ...

Must we not expect a general 'nervous breakdown'? Thus for the first time since his creation man will be faced with his real, his permanent problem: how to use his freedom from pressing economic cares, how to occupy the leisure, which science and compound interest will have won for him? How to live wisely and agreeably and well?

When the accumulation of wealth is no longer of high social importance, there will be great changes in the code of morals. The love of money as a possession – as distinguished from the love of money as a means to the enjoyments and realities of life – will be recognised for what it is, a somewhat disgusting morbidity, one of those semi-criminal, semi-pathological propensities which one hands over with a shudder to the specialists in mental disease ...[33]

Keynes' scenario is thought-provoking. But he does not break away from that mode of economic thought in which money is nothing but a means for other ends. In this frame of mind effective markets and well-regulated flows of money are only a means for the wealth of nations. In his conclusion to his 700-page classic textbook on economics, the Nobel Prize winner Paul Samuelson writes in the same vein: "We end here with the eternal question about how we should use these material advances to improve our private and social lives.[34] The economics profession regards its job as done once material wealth has been created in an effective manner (and reasonably well distributed). From there on it must be up to the politicians and the individual to use and invest wealth so that we obtain human development and better communities. Let us call this the old welfare model based on money as something instrumental. Only once material wealth is in place can soul-based needs be provided for. First money, then soul. They are still split.

The tradition of microeconomics is even more specific. It states that we primarily work – offer our capacity to work on the wage market – *in order to* earn money. Once we have the money, we can use it for well-chosen consumption which provides increased benefit and therefore increased happiness. Work too is *instrumental*. In economic theory work is in itself an input factor, a personal cost, a non-satisfaction, which can be used for procuring money that is again used for welfare and quality of life. The inherent value of work itself, the satisfactions and human relationships developed there, simply do not count.

But then the figures from new psychological-economic research indicate that almost no matter how much our incomes and material consumption grow, happiness and satisfaction do not increase at all. In wealthy countries the old model of welfare as 1-2-3 does not apply any longer:

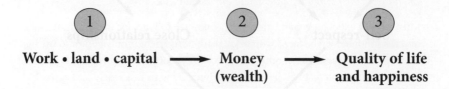

It is wrong to think of work as the sacrifice made by workers to acquire commodities and leisure, when work has intrinsic value for many workers.[35] Adam Smith's original idea was that economics is the science of how markets could make nations wealthy. The question now becomes whether the market might have another purpose than to create increased wealth that can be used for improved welfare. Robert Lane suggests two new goals for the market: human development and the greatest amount of happiness possible. There is no need, he says, to take a detour around greater wealth – particularly when that detour leads us astray, to a dead end.

The economic idea of work being a disutility – a 'bad' – implies that in a market society people will work only for the money. This does not match up with what employees actually say. Instead, they report that they work for a multitude of reasons, not least for the opportunity to exercise their proficiencies and to achieve respect.[36] Happiness research tells us that the greatest source of well-being and satisfaction often lies in the actual work *process*, not in the consumption paid for by work. Meaningful work has inherent values which are not evident in economic assessments. Work well done and the respect attained from it has greater impact on happiness than more pay would (once a certain standard of living has been achieved). That is conditional on the work providing opportunities for development and a certain degree of financial security.

The second major source of development and happiness is relationships with other people. Family relationships, friendships and communities consistently come further up the list as sources of satisfaction and happiness than does increased income.[37] Sigmund Freud's old definition of what makes up a meaningful life was work and love ('Arbeit und Liebe'). These two pop up again like a jack-in-the-box out of the tables of happiness research. The Figure opposite describes the model for what the new welfare then becomes.

These two figures illustrate the transition from an understanding of welfare as wealth, to a more comprehensive understanding of welfare as quality of life and happiness.

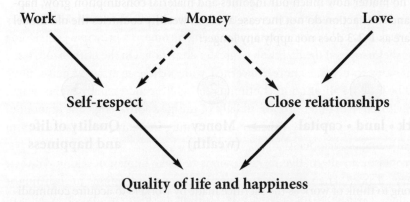

My proposal for a new welfare model, based on what contributes to an increased level of happiness. (The dotted arrows indicate weak connections.)

Is the time ripe for Gross National Happiness – GNH?

Politicians and the conventional economic system have been preoccupied with growth in economic activity (measured as growth in the Gross National Product, the GNP). The science of happiness is making a shift to becoming more occupied with growth in objective measures of quality of life and happiness. Perhaps in 2030, society will be more interested in the development of GNH as an indicator of welfare than it is in GNP? [38]

Happiness research has begun to put down roots in more and more theorists and political-economic environments. The strategy unit at the Prime Minister's office in the UK prepared a report some years ago based on this new way of thinking.[39] Central UK politicians talk about launching GWB – General Well-Being.[40] What would be the consequences of this, and where could change happen? Three areas stand out: work, taxation and new models for public governance.

Let us start with the inherent value of work. The idea is to give work priority over consumption. It is most often in the sphere of work, not consumption, that the greatest potential for human development and well-being lies.[41] Workplaces with room for learning and creativity increase 1) our cognitive complexity, 2) our sense of mastery and self-attribution, and 3) our self-esteem. These are three key points in human development.[42] At the same time these three counteract stress, learned helplessness and external loci of control – three familiar contributions to reduced well-being and happiness.[43] In the labour market, people learn characteristics that it is not possible to develop as a consumer. An active welfare policy would therefore put things in place for more learning and creativity in all jobs, thereby including more people in the 'creative class'.[44]

This forms a special challenge for trade unions in wealthy countries. It is easy to get stuck in the old role of having increasing income as a principal goal. Doing that pushes people in the direction of greater addiction. On the other hand, if the unions were to become more concerned with welfare in its new guise, there would be little justification in continuing to fight for increasingly higher wages *in comparison with* other groups. In light of this new knowledge, the amount of social comparison increases, thereby contributing in a directly negative way to the well-being of members!

It could be an alternative for the unions to make human development their primary purpose. Then the demands would be for more options for learning at work and greater scope for creativity. In addition, performance-based systems of payment should be discouraged. These increase stress and the effects of comparison, and usually reduce self-respect and intrinsic motivation.[45] They are also rather dubious from a corporate economics perspective.[46]

Based on this argument, the traditional political left can tone down its demand for economic parity between different groups. Firstly, increased income (beyond a certain level) does not improve the quality of life significantly. Second, subjective well-being is already more equally apportioned than income.[47]

Another important consequence of the new welfare model would be necessary changes to the taxation system. This is quite at odds with the traditional political right. We have seen that consumption has little effect on subjective well-being. On the other hand, being out of work greatly reduces well-being. That would indicate a general shift from the taxation of work (in particular via employer contributions) to a big increase in taxation of energy-intensive consumption. The welfare effect of this would coincide with consideration for the environment and would support strongly the idea of 'green taxes'. To a large extent, the wage tax system is ripe for revision, and this time under a heading of human development and well-being. The good news is that the same solution can contribute both to better jobs and to less energy-hungry consumption.

We have seen that increases in wages can create addiction and have hidden costs via increased social comparison. When someone enjoys a jump in income, it contaminates the surroundings. Neighbours and colleagues want to kill his or her cow. To solve this, we could borrow a tried-and-tested model from insurance companies, with customers being rewarded if their car rarely has a crash. They get bonus points and progressively higher discounts on their premiums. Maybe we should try out a tax system that gives bonuses to people with stable incomes? Every year, if your income level stays the same (corrected for inflation), your bonus would increase. The tax would go down and you would still have more money but without your income increasing. The longer you stay at the same level, the lower your tax would be. If your taxable income goes up a level, you would lose your bonus. This would counteract the dependency on pay rises and would be like charging a tax for frequent car crashes or pollution incidents. In the language of economics, incentives would be created which reduce the frequency of wage rises and their corresponding social externalities.

A third and more fundamental consequence of the new welfare model is the necessity for changes to economic welfare theory, public policy and national accounting. The central point is how we measure and account for welfare. GNP was developed originally in the 1930s for analysing changes in unemployment, but has since been hijacked to become a dubious target for national welfare, so that nations and regions can be compared and can compete with one another. Politicians in power take the credit for any increase in wealth (GNP up) during their period of office, while the opposition blame those in power for irresponsible policies (for that, there is nothing better than a weak growth in GNP). The instrument of analysis has become a goal in itself, with growth in GNP being like the Holy Grail – a goal that should bring the nation together. This is a sad story of a concept that has gone astray, says economist Richard Layard of the London School of Economics, who hurries to add that most economists see many weaknesses with GNP as a measure of welfare.[48]

The way for economics and politics to continue must be to revise theories and indicators on the basis of new findings in areas overlapping with psychology, sociology and ecology.[49] In this first pass, measurements of quality of life (like 'GNH') could be given equal political weighting to GNP. Studies could be made of the effect of new policies and public investments on happiness and well-being, to the same extent that purely economic effects have been studied. Theories and findings in happiness research are now on their way to becoming so well developed that they can be used for shaping policy.[50] And we have seen that the factors of production of GNH (human development, financial security, family, friends) differ significantly from those for GNP (land, labour, capital and technological change).

There has been a great outpouring of suggested development indexes and social indicators.[51] However, they have not yet found their final form, nor have they attracted enough attention to bring them into general use. But a long-term perspective is needed here. Traditional bookkeeping that led up to the GNP has a 400-500-year head start – once double-entry bookkeeping, in the late Renaissance period, had defined the economic language that made the modern capitalism possible. We will just have to hope that GNH – or ISEW (Index of Sustainable Economic Welfare), GPI (Genuine Progress Indicator) or some equivalent indicator – does not need many decades to become taken up as a policy tool.

Some conclusions about welfare

We have seen that the idea of welfare came originally from a benevolent intention for security for everyone, after the social catastrophies of early industrial capitalism, Hitler's fascism and Stalin's communism. We have seen how the economic idea of wealth – the result of market-driven growth – in its early stages contributed to welfare. And we have seen that gradually, as prosperity has grown even further, welfare is becoming more and more dependent on quality of life in the form of happiness and subjective well-being.

Welfare can then be viewed as a combination of material wealth, health and happiness, but steadily increasing wealth provides increasingly less of an impact on collective welfare. In rich countries, welfare is more sensitive to changes in happiness and well-being than to changes in wealth.

Unfortunately, a lot of politics and economics is based on the assumption that increased wealth brings a corresponding increase in happiness. This has been named the *economistic fallacy*.[52] This condition has not been true of Western countries since the period 1950–1970. If economics is a science about increasing human welfare, then growing wealth will become less and less relevant. It seems we are getting lots more of what we really don't want. Contributing to the well-being of the soul requires a deeper understanding of the relationship between money and the human psyche than is provided by the ideas applied by the economism of today.

It may be time to leave the traditional political left–right axis behind when it comes to the respective roles of the state and markets in the distribution and growth of wealth. A new axis will arise between the people who still put economic growth first and those who place human development and the development of happiness first. It is no longer the case that wealth automatically conveys more happiness and more human development. The second position implies new roles both for governments and for markets. In Chapter 12 we shall also look at social and ecological value dimensions in relation to human development. That is where the new welfare lies: in developing a broader economics of the soul.

But, can markets really be thought to contribute at all to human, social and ecological development? Are modern markets not characterised by exploitation, deception, instability, greed and manipulation? Lots of people feel that markets are the enemy of both nature and humanity, rabidly promoting growth, stress and increasing inequity. Maybe it is time to delve down into the mythical layers of our ideas about the markets.

Chapter 6

Markets

Who owns the invisible hand?

In economics, the markets are 'king'. Outside economics, markets are often associated with the rights of the strongest, with profit and manipulation. This chapter investigates the cultural and mythical basis underlying markets, in an attempt to rediscover the relevance of the markets to the soul. Can the market be viewed differently? Can radical innovation enable markets to serve several value dimensions – such as social networks, happiness and the natural world – in addition to the target of financial results? What characterises the 'soul of the market', then and now?

A market in the year 2007: I drive in to the shopping centre's car park. As luck would have it, I have the right coins for the ticket machine. I know I just have forty minutes before I have to drive on and do the pick-up at the nursery school. I feel a kind of fogginess in my brain, a slight knot in my stomach muscles. I have to focus on what I need to buy – cannot hang about now.

I make a little plan of how to get to five different shops in less than forty minutes. There is a queue at the chemist's, but luckily I can pick up the medicine without a prescription, I don't need to wait in line. The pharmacist puts the small, lightweight boxes into the dark green plastic bag. She is kind, smiles at me. Tells me how much it costs and pops in an extra sheet of paper without asking me if I want it; maybe it is some kind of pharmacy information. I didn't catch the sum she mentioned, but I am sure it is right. She turns the card reader terminal round towards herself. Keys in the amount and turns it back to me. 'Enter PIN + OK' it says on the display. I just want to get finished.

I manage to fetch the repaired specs, buy a birthday present in the children's shop and finally trundle the trolley through the always equally well-filled food shelves at the supermarket closest to the car park. The same ritual: smiling lady, but it would be difficult to call that smile sincere. I manage to pop a number of goods into the shiny new plastic bag before she is finished beeping all of the goods past the red beams of the barcode reader. She also says an amount of money, while the pay terminal automatically displays the sum. The card slides through the machine again. Four digits keyed in. 'Accepted', it says on the display. That was good – we have avoided the modern version of the stocks, where everyone in the queue behind me wonders what kind of a person I can be if I do not have sufficient cash in my account.

I put the rest of the goods into the bag. Hurry now. My eyes sweep over the open area beyond the cash desks. People everywhere, in twos and threes, but many of them alone. The exit leads straight to the car, but there are some young men in smart clothes who ask me if I want a quotation for a security system for the house. An anniversary offer. I stick on an inane smile, shake my head a little and make my way past as quickly as I can with carrier bags cutting into my fingers and handles that are threatening to rip.

- £ -

A market in the year 1305, in the south of France: Travelling merchants arrive early in the morning with their armed guards. Merry colourful striped tents are put up. Not long afterwards the merchants get started on haggling and trading among themselves and the local population. Exotic-smelling goods are on sale at the fair today: silk fabrics, spices and perfumes, leather and furs. Some have been brought from easterly Mediterranean areas, some from Scandinavia; other goods have just been carried there from a few miles away. The local nobles and their ladies walk about among the ordinary people between lively stalls and tents, keen for a little bit of a change from their monotonous, elegant lives. They ask questions to try to extract the greatest amount of news possible in between information about the wondrous goods that have come out of Arabia. They learn new words from foreign lands: divan, syrup, artichoke, spinach. The quantity of goods is small, even though the fair is a major local event. In a whole year, the quantity of goods that pass through the largest border crossings are no more than could be carried easily on one of today's goods trains.[1]

- £ -

It seems that markets have existed for as long as recorded history. The stone tablets from Tell el-Amarna in Egypt tell of lively trade between the Pharaohs and the Syrian kings three-and-a-half thousand years ago:

Market anno 1405 BC, Egypt: an open, sunburnt plain between two low ridges. War chariots with sharp knives mounted on the wheels race across hot sand, drawn by snorting pure-bred Arab horses with flaring nostrils. The sweat foams around the harness. Gold and war chariots are exchanged for slaves and horses. A few people negotiate; hundreds of soldiers, slaves and servants are standing, looking on.

Barter is probably as old as humanity itself, and the instinct for self-interest even older than that. But markets, whether they be exchanges between tribes where objects are dropped on the ground or the travelling fairs of the Middle Ages, are not the same as the market system.[2] The old markets were magnets for local freeloaders, the nobility, drunkards and the pillars of society. Clowns, profane singers and musicians had this as their stage, perhaps also as an unofficial critical arena. Everyone in the vicinity was drawn to these annual social highpoints, busy festival days that were in stark contrast to everyday life.

Other towns and villages also had monthly or weekly local markets. Today, market flows still ensure that society does not fall apart. A modern market economy involves the majority of society continuously being interwoven into the market processes that sustain the entire society. If the unbelievably intricate flows of goods were to fail, every city would come to a standstill from one day to the next. It can be useful to differentiate between markets and the market. The former are specific to places or products. The latter is more general and global; the market which encompasses all markets.[3]

This transition from *marketplaces* to a *market system* is no more than 200–300 years old. It is only with the emergence of market-based societies that we can start to talk about a *distinct discipline* of economics, as a science of market systems. It was the idea of a market system where individual actions contributed to larger, systematic effects that made Adam Smith famous. He described the way in which all material needs can be effectively met by means of one specialist producer or another, wherever they are. All bidders conform to the price the market can give for what they are making. The market thereby resolves – with no centralised direction from above or from outside – economic challenges by deciding *what* should be produced, *how* and *for whom*.[4] The market sets up "wagon ways through the air"[5] – another high-flying Smith metaphor – and sends goods across any distance in order to satisfy even our weirdest desires, as long as we have the money to pay for them.

The widespread trade and division of labour which goes with our participation in the markets could not happen, Adam Smith observed, unless we were predisposed for it. Markets seem to be in line with something in human nature. He states: "Division of labour . . . is the necessary . . . consequence of a certain propensity in human nature . . . the propensity to truck, barter and exchange one thing for another . . . By the disposition to truck and barter, their talents are brought into a common stock, where every man may purchase part of the produce of other men's talents!"[6] In a famous sentence he points out that the baker, brewer and butcher gain greater benefits from their own goods if they can exchange them with one another than if they were to consume all of their own bread, all of their own beer and all of their own meat. The idea of mutual benefits of trade is one of the fundamental insights of economics.

Smith looked into the bustling throngs of the then budding industrial society – with paupers and princes, pin factories and spinning jennies, home-grown produce from the nobility's estates in competition with imported grain – which characterised the times he lived in. And he managed to discover and describe a certain order and system in all that chaos. While Kepler and Newton uncovered the hidden order of the paths taken by the planets, Adam Smith uncovered a hidden order within the market society. He saw a pattern that made everyone, when bargaining on the basis of their own self-interest, to be led as if by *an invisible hand* to promote the best interests of the nation as a whole. Every individual's self-interested actions are transformed by the market, in an almost magical way, to contribute to greater wealth. Those who chase the thrills of making a profit for themselves, in competition with others, become the best contributors to society's common wealth. Through market exchanges, new value is made that was non-existent before the exchange. The more you specialise, trade and earn, the better it is for the wealth of the nation.

The workings of this invisible hand, which brings forth an efficient, partly self-regulating market system out of a thronging chaotic everyday world of offers, credit cards, goods flows and accounts, is one of the founding insights of economics. Most economists believe that public authorities ought to tinker as little as possible with the market's internal activities. Upholding and keeping stable frameworks like property rights, law and order, yes – but government should keep its fingers out of the market's pie and let the invisible hand organise the internal dynamics as much as possible. Politicians who imagine that they are in a better position to regulate the market than the invisible hand are the subject of hundreds of pages of caustic, bitter criticism from the hand of Adam Smith. And since the publication of *Wealth of Nations* in 1776, the criticism has been repeated and expanded for more than two hundred years.

- £ -

All of this will be very familiar to anyone who knows basic economics. But, as far as I know, no one has ever asked the question of *whose* invisible hand is Smith speaking?[7] And which emotions, what fundamental characteristics in human nature have conspired in the unstoppable rise of the economic market system despite all resistance from feudal systems, monarchical hierarchies, religious institutions, traditions and national borders? Where does this incessant need to truck, barter, and exchange come from? What perpetual sentiment, which god is it that drives us to become so fascinated in shopping and trade? What attracts people to shopping malls – who is the pied piper who ensures people always make their way there? Who inspires hordes of people to participate in virtual markets like eBay and amazon.com, and who gets so many people involved in following stock market developments every day?

The image of an invisible hand has continued to receive attention since Smith's sparse use of it in his two major works and right up to the present day. What gives the metaphor such a power of attraction that it is still, 200 years later, being used as a political argument for how we ought to organise our society? I believe we can gain a deeper understanding of what motivates all of this, of the human urge to barter and trade, by looking into a few of the cultural roots of our conceptions of the market. In Western culture, these roots go right back to the old Greek myths from the pre-Socratic period. In particular, they circle around the mythical being whom the Greeks called *Hermes* and the Romans *Mercury*.

Myths are not superstitious stories about what supernatural beings once did. Myths are stories about what always *is*. The mythical beings are great metaphors that keep evoking the imagination. Precisely because they were formulated in another era, as nuanced depictions of deeply human behaviour, myths are able to give us a new understanding of how such ancient mythic plots are played out even in modern times.

Adam Smith was, like every eighteenth-century professor, well versed in rhetoric and classical mythology. With the reference to the invisible hand, Smith firmly set economics within a classical school of thought about the inexorable human desire to travel, trade and break boundaries. The mythical level has not disappeared from economics simply because it proclaimed itself a science. Hermes is still active in the markets, even if he is not explicitly mentioned in the modern economic textbooks. He might even be more dynamic at work now than ever before.

Only a few people currently working in the stock exchanges today know much about him. But at the Oslo Stock Exchange he is actually standing cast in bronze outside its main entrance. The people who erected him there in 1911 knew one or two things about the theoretical and emotional foundations of the Stock Exchange.[8] But for most stockbrokers today the statue is nothing other than a decoration, or perhaps a insignificant logo. At the same time, the brokers, both in Oslo and elsewhere, live for and are passionately devoted to free, flexible trade. They are also frequent critics of any kind of political restrictions. They share the foundation of their beliefs with some highly educated and knowledgeable fellow adherents all over the world, and they have all sorts of 'solid' economic arguments against undue regulations.

I myself am an adherent of trade and markets, and I admit that I am an apostle of Hermes. This is why I am writing this book – it is dedicated to him. At the same time, I would like to maintain a certain distance, a certain playfulness and scepticism in relation to how he seduces us to think about the world. Yes, I am a lover of Hermes and the market, a loyal toiler in supermarkets and kiosks, in virtual booksellers and at auctions, and therefore a persistent consumer. But I am not a market fundamentalist. I often feel confused, disgusted and exhausted in the temples of Hermes: stock exchanges and shopping centres. He often offers more than I can cope with.

If we want to bring the soul back into the economy, rediscover the soul of the market, a detour to the mythical source of the market is a necessity. Let us get acquainted with him, the god of the market.

Hermes the trickster

Greek mythology describes Hermes as the god of boundaries and of travellers who cross them. He is also the god of storytellers, shepherds and inventors. His domains cover trade and markets, of orators in general and sales pitches in particular. All thieves' slyness, grey and white lies, fast and smooth talking belongs to him. He is the gods' favorite messenger, from the Olympian spheres to the Earth and then further to the underworld. Finally, he leads the souls of all people through the gateway of death, across the River Styx and on to Hades, the realm of death. He is the guide for souls who have got lost or who have come to a standstill.

The actual root of the name comes from *herm* – which means stone post or boundary marker.[9] A lucky find – ("Look what I found!" as Askeladden, the 'Ash Lad', the wandering hero of many Norwegian folktales, says) – is called a *hermaion* in Greek. A translator of foreign languages is called a *hermeneus*. From Hermes we have *hermeneutics,* the science of interpretation. The planet Mercury and the metal mercury have been named after him. From his Roman name we have the words merchant and merchandise. Even the very word 'market' comes from the Latin *mercari* – to buy – and thus to point to him. I mention these examples just to illustrate how the figure of Hermes-Mercury has had a lasting impact on Western language and thought for several thousand years. If markets ever had a father, the genealogy all points towards Mercury/Hermes.

The original myth about Hermes tells that he was the son of Zeus and Maia, a particularly vital nymph. She was the oldest and most beautiful of the Pleiades, but she was also extremely shy. She had long, luxuriant hair, and Zeus found her irresistible. They ended up being tightly entwined in a deep shady cave at Mount Kyllini while Zeus' wife Hera was sleeping on Mount Olympus. Ten full-moons later, the Homeric hymn to Hermes relates, a son forced himself out of her body, "a robber, a cowherd, a bringer of dreams, a deserter, a thief at the gates, someone who would carry out the most incredible feats among the immortal gods".[10]

After the birth, his mother wrapped him up and put him down in a cradle deep inside their cosy cave. But he grew incredibly fast, and as soon as his mother had turned over to rest, he slipped past her and out to hunt for adventure. Right outside the cave he met a large tortoise. "Ha! What luck! Look what I found!" Hermes cried. "If you die, then you shall make sweetest song," he said to the tortoise. He had already perceived that the tortoise was a resource, a raw material, which almost called out for modification and innovation.

He took a sharp stone, turned the tortoise over on its back, cut off its limbs and scraped out all of the soft insides. With skilful dexterity, he drilled holes in the shell and attached strings into pieces of horn on both sides. Then he sampled and tuned the notes, and was ready to play on the first stringed instrument in history – the lyre. It sounded surprisingly beautiful. Hermes now had something to barter with, an innovation, a product ready for the market! It was just that there was no one to barter with – yet.

He placed the lyre inside the mouth of the cave and set off down the road. He started to feel hungry, and after a little while he discovered fifty fine cows. They were the property of the brilliant sun god, Apollo. At that time, cattle were the predominant form of capital.

Hermes wondered which tricks he could pull off to get fifty cows without the owner realising what had become of them. He came up with the idea of driving the cattle backwards, while he himself put on large sandals made of twigs to make the tracks impossible to follow, not unlike shrewd financial acrobats in the shadowy realms of the monetary markets. He drove the cattle in this way away from the meadow, over sandy soil and on to the hard rock. Here he threw the sandals into a river and herded the cattle over the mountain and, under cover of night, into a large, empty barn. Outside, he lit a bonfire, slaughtered two of the cows and divided them into twelve equal-sized pieces, one for the each of the gods on Mount Olympus. Arrogantly enough, he included himself as one of the twelve, and although he was starving, he sacrificed the other parts on the fire.

Dawn approached, and it was time to return. He shut up the barn, crossed back over the mountain and slipped into the mouth of the cave. There he fetched his lyre and tried to sneak up into the cradle unnoticed. But his mother Maia was not so easily fooled: "You robber, you have been out during the night and committed a crime against the forces of order. You rascal, you wear shamelessness as a garment!"

"But mother, why do you try to frighten me as if I am a delicate child?" answered Hermes. The rest of his answer gives away a lot about his nature, his vision and his set of values:

Mother, (. . .)
We're not going to stick around here,

as you want, the only two

among all the immortal gods

without any gifts

without even prayers!

It's much better

to spend every day

talking with the gods

rich, bountiful, loaded with

cornfields, than to just

sit around home here

in this creepy cave.

As for honours,

I'm going to get in on the same ones

that are sacred to Apollo.

And if my father won't stand for it,

I'll still try,

I'm capable certainly,

to be thief number one.![11]

While these two were talking in the cave, the mighty Apollo awoke. He discovered at once that his capital, his marvellous herd, has shrunk in size. He carefully studied the tracks and was confused at first, then amazed and frightened, to see tracks that he, Foibos Apollo, reason and acuity personified, could not interpret. The cattle tracks pointed into the pasture and none out of it. And around the cattle tracks were also footprints such as had never been seen before. What WAS this?

Some long-winged birds had caught sight what had happened, and they gave Apollo a sign to indicate that the culprit was to be found in a cave on Mount Kyllini. The birds had discovered the two hides. He raced towards the mountain and found the hides that had been left beside the fire. He pieced together a clear picture of the crime. He then strode into Maia's cave, out of breath.

- £ -

When Hermes saw Apollo's stern face, he shrank down into the bedclothes and squinted at Apollo. "You little wretch there in the cradle, explain quickly now, directly, about my cattle – otherwise we two will soon come to blows. And I will throw you down into the dusty hell of Tartarus, the most fearful darkness, and neither you nor your mother or your father will be able to set you free again." Hermes drew some clothes aside to free up his mouth: "Clear-sighted Apollo, son of Leto, what terrible words are these? What are you talking about – cattle?"

I didn't see anything,
I didn't learn anything,
I didn't hear anything,
From anybody else.
I don't have any information to give,
and the reward for information
wouldn't go to me
if I did.
(...)
I was just born yesterday!
My feet are still pretty soft.
The ground underneath
is pretty hard.
If you want,
I'll swear a great oath
On the head of my father:
I declare that I am myself
not guilty,
nor did I see any other thief
of your cattle,
whatever cattle are, anyway –
I've only heard about them.

Apollo had to smile: "You rascal and beguiler! You talk so smoothly that I am convinced you must already have broken in to many well-built houses at night and robbed more than one poor man, so that he probably hardly has one stool to sit on after you were finished." They continued to squabble, each as stubborn as the other, about every little detail of the story. Finally, Apollo said: "You walk in front of me so I can keep an eye on you, because I'm taking you to Zeus, on Mount Olympus, who will pass judgement on you." On the way out of the cave, Hermes picked up his lyre and then made off on his small quick legs.

On snow-white, gleaming Mount Olympus the immortals were gathered together in the hour immediately after dawn. Apollo pushed Hermes in front of him, until they both stood before Zeus: "Who is this you are bringing here,

Foibos Apollo, a child who looks like a messenger?"

Apollo answered his father: "He is a thief, a rascal, whom I found after a long journey in the mountains of Kyllini. I have never found anyone so impudent among gods or people. He stole my cattle, drove them backwards and with strange tracks." Apollo went into all the details, and laid all of the facts clearly and distinctly before Zeus and the immortals at Olympus. With irrefutable logic and clear conclusions, he pointed out how the culprit had tried to lie and smooth-talk his way out of it. "Well, what do you have to say to that?" Zeus asked Hermes. Hermes winked at Zeus, whom he realised had recognised him as his son, and began in low tones: "Dear Zeus, my father . . ." A gasp went round the gathering. "I want to talk truthfully to you, because I am an honourable innocent soul, and quite incapable of lying. This brilliant Apollo came rushing in when I was in the cave early today, and commanded me to confess, under threat of throwing me into Tartarus. He is big, strong and full of the power of manhood, whereas I am a little baby, born yesterday and, as he also knows, I am no rootless bandit nor experienced cattle thief. Just look, I am still not dry behind the ears," said Hermes, and with his thumb in his mouth he bent one ear forward to that the entire gathering had to laugh at him and at Apollo's stern face.

"Believe me," Hermes continued when the laughter had died down, "that I did not drive his cattle to the cave to become rich, whatever cattle may be, for that is a word that I have only heard today. Neither have I crossed the threshold out of our cave. Believe me, because I love you and fear him, the stern one. You yourself, all-knowing Zeus, know that I am innocent child, and I can swear a great oath on that. And one day I will probably punish him, strong as he may be, for his inconsiderate treatment of a newly born slumbering child in his cradle. But now *you* must help me, the younger one."

Zeus burst out in peals of laughter at this scheming, well-spoken son who so smoothly denied all guilt. Instead of giving a judgement, he commanded them to go outside and to agree on a solution together.

Outside, Apollo wanted to tie Hermes' hands together. But the ties loosened and slid off his hands by themselves. While Apollo stared open-mouthed, Hermes picked up his lyre and began to play. To accompany the beautiful notes, he sang some flattering verses about Apollo's stable character, his shining countenance and sparkling eyes, about the exceptional perspective and brilliance he brings to the world. The sweet music broke down Apollo's defences. A yearning for this wonderful instrument filled his heart and softened his anger. For the first time, his voice was friendly: "You, Maia's inventive son, has this instrument been with you since your birth, or were you given it by a god or by a human? And who taught you such a heavenly song?"

"I would like to be friends with you in both thought and word," answered

Hermes. "You speak in a considered and orderly manner. So I will give you this as a gift and ask that I should be given the cattle in exchange."

Apollo took hold of the lyre and tested the strings carefully. They sounded overwhelmingly beautiful at his touch. "Of course, you can have the herd," said Apollo while he listened, quite carried away, to the sounds of the lyre. So they went together and herded the cattle back to the pasture. This laid the mythical foundation for all *bull markets* thereafter. Hermes, the herdsman of behaviour in the market's herds of cattle and sheep, was ready for his eternal task. The first deal ever was closed: innovation for capital. And the world's markets have been growing ever since.

Zeus was also satisfied and ceremoniously declared that the two were friends. But Apollo was afraid of Hermes' ingenuity and greed: "What holds you back from stealing or bartering back the lyre, or perhaps my far-shooting silver bow, because it is clear that you have a task involving

Giambologna's statue of Mercury/Hermes, c. 1564, with Mercury's wand (Caduceus) in one hand and the marking of a point with the other.

bartering and shady trades with people and gods throughout the productive Earth."[12] These two therefore formed the first negotiated contract between buyer and seller. It contained a clear division of roles, in which Hermes promised not to steal anything that Apollo owned, nor to go near his house. In return, Apollo honoured Hermes with the golden wand of riches and wealth. Since that time it has been known as Mercury's wand or Caduceus. With it, Hermes can use the magic of the markets to produce wealth and health. Prediction and prophecies remain Apollo's domain. Hermes himself remains utterly unpredictable.

The Homeric hymn to Hermes ends with some well-chosen warnings about relying too much on him or his willingness to distribute wealth fairly:

And even though

he helps a lucky few,

he cheats an endless number

of the race of mortal men
in the darkness of night.
So then,
Son of Zeus and Maia,
farewell!
But I will think of you in my other poems.[13]

The spirit of crossing-over

What are we to think about this story, this trickster? What does this have to do with modern economics and markets?

A story like this is not just a random collection of entertaining elements. The myth has survived for hundreds of years of oral storytelling tradition in which the poets of every generation looked after the core details, while they embellished what suited their own tradition and culture. That was the philosophy and psychology of the period: painstaking observations of behaviour in people and the natural world in well-crafted narrative. In the story about the god of storytelling and communication himself it is fair to assume that they were taking particular care.

Primarily, the Hermes story is all about crossing over and transgressing all types of boundaries. No cave could hold him in. No property is respected. No hand could bind his quick hand. Neither could anyone silence him. As for emphasising this, most illustrations show Hermes with wings on his legs and with a hat of invisibility. With the hat on, no one notices that he has crossed any boundaries at all or come into a room.

As mentioned previously, the name Hermes derives from *herm*, which meant a stone post or boundary marker. Lots of herms were erected at crossroads and at boundaries throughout Hellas (Ancient Greece). Most of them depict a bearded masculine face on top of a pillar, like a phallus, with the genitalia at the base. A fertile, potent man.

We therefore find Hermes in the

A 'herm' was a stone pillar, a boundary marker with Hermes' head on top. It was associated with fertility, luck, roads and boundaries.

fertile crossing over of borders from the known to the unknown, connecting one field to another. He is similarly present in all moments where people meet and engage with one another in conversation, conflict or negotiation. Hermes' characteristics are shown by words such as transfer, transition, transgression, transmission and translation. But also in transaction, transport and transit. We find them in barter, gossip, mediation and eloquence. He is present in all communication from one party to the other. He is like language itself, transferring meaning. Or like the invisible wind blowing a message from one place to another, while remaining invisible himself.

Adam Smith, disciple of Hermes

When Hermes was wearing his invisibility hat, no one was able to notice his presence when influencing the outcome of conversations and events with his 'invisible hand'. Hermes is presented as a god because he is an *autonomous force* in the psyche. He's larger than the I, the human ego. This does not mean that Hermes (or any other Greek gods) are behind or outside us, directing our human activities from above, so to speak. Rather, we can understand him as an inherent force within human actions. Hermes is the inner force in the transaction, giving the archetypal pattern to the transactions going on in all markets every day. Each deal is made in his image, so to speak. The psychological reason behind the success of Smith's famous metaphor is that it draws its evocative power from this mythical figure in the human psyche. It resonates with something inside us.

At the start of the story Hermes simply follows his self-interest, as he clearly states when speaking to his mother, Maia. He wants out, forwards and up. Yet, by the manner in which he accomplishes this via negotiation and bartering, he contributes to the best of all on Mount Olympus. Apollo obtains his beloved lyre, Zeus gains a messenger and all of the gods gain a permanent mediator and storyteller. At the same time all markets and thieves are given their own god. This is how he illustrates – and inspires – Smith's idea that when someone pursues his own self-interest in a market system, he also promotes development in society. This is often a better contribution than when someone with idealistic intentions tries to change society in a specific direction, says Smith.[14]

In addition to the invisible hand, Smith talks of trade's wagon-ways through the air.[15] Here he develops the image further of Hermes with wings on his legs, the god of all travellers, *en route* from here to there with goods. When Smith also talks of a universal propensity of human nature to "truck, barter and exchange",[16] he is possibly referring to the Hermes in all of us.

It is not without reason that established authorities like Apollo try to limit the

power of the markets and merchants. In 2001, Ken Lay, the financial trickster
and CEO of Enron, was arrested and trialled for his accounting wizardry. In
2003, the Russian president had the oligarch and head of Yukos, Mikhail
Khodorkovsky, arrested. From a mythical-historical perspective, these are just
two of many more recent examples of the conflict between market and hierarchical authority. In the fifteenth century, China had ships, innovations and voyages of trade and discovery that far exceeded the situation in Europe. But the
conflict between the hierarchical Zeus-Apollo alliance on one side and impro-
vising Hermes on the other was not resolved in the same way in China as in the
Greek myth. Instead of being allowed to sail across open seas to explore new
routes, the ships, after the voyages of discovery of Zeng He, were put under
arrest until they started to rot. The merchants were taken in custody. The Ming
dynasty sensed – quite correctly – disruption and change, and ruled out any further expansion beyond established core areas. The authorities chose stability
ahead of breaking down boundaries and expanding networks.[17] Six hundred
years later, however, Deng Xiaoping chose to set loose the unsettling powers of
the markets.

Where markets start growing, old structures and top-heavy hierarchies may
topple. Apollo quite quickly perceives that if Hermes releases his frontier-
breaching bartering and markets, change will be coming. So he tries to tie
Hermes' hands down. But the restive quality of trade and entrepreneurship, with
all of its crossing of traditional boundaries and new networks, will not be tied
down. Every market of a certain size is linked, in one way or another, with other
markets, and further to a border-free network of constantly new and more far-
reaching markets.[18] While local rulers seek to control their subjects, the god of
trade always tries to breach frontiers.

The market route from innovation to capital

The story about the slow tortoise that Hermes finds and turns into a lyre illustrates that it is quickness and inventiveness that is valued most highly in Hermes'
world. Raw materials and other resources form the basis, but it is through innovation that they really gain value as commercial goods on a market. Inside Maia's
cave, the lyre has limited value. The important thing is to rouse someone's – i.e.
the purchaser's – desire for your product. Hermes' quick gaze sees the possibility of making gains from the processed shell of the poor tortoise. He has the
entrepreneur's desire to break down boundaries, to turn conventional things 'on
their head', which is exactly what he does with the tortoise.

It is technological innovations, more often than the capital itself, which promote wealth: 'creative destruction', as the Austrian economist Joseph Schumpeter called it.[19] And Hermes is inconsiderate enough not to dwell on the resource in itself. The slow tortoise is not able to make itself heard until it has been divided up and scraped out, like the last sea turtles on today's market. They end up in stews more quickly than they manage to reproduce. In Hermes' world this is not important because, as the hymn tells us, even while he is testing out the sound of the lyre he is preoccupied with other matters. He longs for more, for cattle and capital, and is wondering how he is going to satisfy his desire for profitable beef. This god has a fearsome appetite.

I have placed the words 'cattle' and 'capital' together in the previous paragraph. It is no coincidence that cattle were exactly what Hermes was out after. The origin of the word capital, capitalism's most central concept, is the word *caput,* which means head, and, more specifically, head of cattle.[20] It comes from the time when wealth were valued according to how large a herd you had, how many head of cattle you had in your herd. Looking out over the herd and counting the heads of your cattle was the original taking account of your capital. It is still not good manners to ask a Sami (previously known as the Lapps) how many reindeer he owns, in the same way as you would not ask a capitalist, over a cappuccino, what his personal net worth is.

We find a close historic relationship between money and herds of animals: sheep, goats and cattle have all functioned as money in trading transactions. 'Pecuniary' represents things that are connected with money; the word comes from the Latin root *pecu,* which means, in turn, cattle. 'Chattel' likewise comes from cattle and the Latin *capitale.* The English word *fee* comes from *faihu,* Gothic for cattle, which is also the root of the Norwegian word *fe* (cattle). The Greek coin *obelos* refers to the sacrificial meat from an ox that has been blessed, and the Roman coin *as* corresponded to a piece of roast beef.[21] Periods of rising share prices on the stock markets, when capital seems to be multiplying all by itself, are still called *bull markets.*

Capital, as one of the three original factors of production in modern economics, is thus culturally and linguistically deeply rooted in our prehistory as nomads, animal herders and farmers. The animals, in particular the cattle, were the original factors of production. That is where Hermes goes: towards the capital of the wealthy and established Apollo. The entrepreneur needs the investor, even if he has to steal or furtively borrow start-up capital to get going. Later on, as this hymn to the market god points out, capital breeds capital just as bulls and cows produce calves in the rich mountain pastures. Hermes, the pathfinder and guide that he is, continues to conduct entrepreneurs to success and increasing access to capital. Through the capacity of the market to create value from trade, as if from thin air, the magic wand brings increasing wealth.

After having taught us about resources, innovation and capital, the story of Hermes also provides a key lesson on a forgotten topic, but one that is crucial to a revival of the economy in a more holistic direction. It revolves around something we do not find in economic textbooks, from Adam Smith right up to today: Hermes slaughters some of the cows as a *sacrifice*. He divides this part of the capital into twelve equal-sized pieces and sacrifices them to the main gods on Mount Olympus. In contrast to what we learn from Adam Smith, he does not take care of his own self-interest by devouring the entire meal himself or saving it for later. No, he abstains from eleven out of the twelve parts and gives these to each of the other gods (Zeus, Hera, Hestia, Demeter, Athena, Aphrodite, Artemis, Apollo, Ares, Hephaistos and Dionysus).

Several scholars of classical myths have seen this as a symbolic expression of the tolerance we find in the Greek polytheism – the existence of many gods at the same time, in contrast to monotheistic religions.[22] The number twelve can be seen as an expression for wholeness, just as the year has twelve months and the daytime has twelve hours. The go-between Hermes multiplies the concept of capital by granting a sacrifice to each of the gods. This puts capital into a general framework, a diverse social and ecological context, presumably a necessary feature of the market's own long-term survival. The idea of utilising a plurality of capitals to evaluate different dimensions of value, not just in classical times but also in modern markets, is a main topic of Part III of this book.

Hermes, the spirit of crossing over, is uniquely designed for such tasks. No one can move in between and facilitate exchange in the way he can. He himself is pluralistic. He does not allow himself to be locked into conflicts or dualisms such as good versus evil, upper versus lower, light versus dark. Some globe-trotting financial innovators, like a George Soros, appear to be in touch with this form of consciousness. Playfully and freely, and sometimes with cheats and excesses, Hermes works to break out of the standard confines into new avenues. Sometimes this opens up new and surprising relations and alliances. Perhaps that sacrifice to the other gods was precisely what ensured him a friendly welcome to Mount Olympus when Apollo pushed him there to be judged as a cattle thief.

After the theft of the cattle, Hermes is confronted by his mother, Maia. She is afraid that he has trodden on Apollo's toes and fears the worst. For Hermes, however, her isolated life as a cave dweller is already the worst thing he could imagine. He wants out. He wants to be mobile and to do business with the big guys. He himself wants to have sacrifices and to "spend every day in conversation with the gods, rich, munificent and honoured". The direction is shifting from being rooted in one location to opening up greater worlds. He wants networks and sociability. The vision is clear: Hermes is dreaming about becoming the most successful capitalist ever: "I am guaranteed to be in a position to become the foremost of all thieves!"[23] But, in Hermes' world, theft is neither inconsiderate, brutal or violent. The brutal robbery belongs to another mythical pattern – belonging more to Hercules with his club than Hermes with his mercurial wand. Hermes both takes and gives with cunning and style. He is a kind of amoral Robin Hood figure, who just as happily takes from the poor and gives to the rich as the opposite. He goes after what he wants, but is just as ready to make new deals and compromises. This smoothness means that he gradually manages to become friends even with the very upright Apollo. The main plot of the myth deals with how Hermes artfully manoeuvres his way out of an isolated position, driven by a self-obsessed, infantile desire for riches and power. He finally succeeds through eloquence and negotiation to create movement towards mutual benefit and respect.

The general direction of the Hermes story is from an isolated existence in caves and pastures to society and participation. This journey has its own inherent value and satisfaction for those undertaking it. Hermes is someone who loves to make agreements, oiling the wheels, talking and bearing messages between people and between people and gods for its own sake. There is a basic need in the soul that constitutes something essentially more than the propensity that Adam Smith mentions to 'barter and exchange' for the sake of gaining material wealth alone. The story of Hermes points towards the inherent soul-based function of market trading. Conversation and exchange conducted out of mutual interest promotes both more wealth and the deepening of relations between people. When one party has something the other wants, a good negotiating process can create mutual respect and social capital in addition to an increase in prosperity. Hermes seems to be more interested in the social conversation than in the cattle as such.

This goes right to the core of how markets function: each transaction is a voluntary exchange that the parties can accept or reject according to the valid rules for this market.[24] The story about Hermes leads up to the crucial turning point at which he and Apollo become mutual partners.

The French philosopher of the Enlightenment, Montesquieu, formulated it like this in 1748: "Trade arises everywhere where human enterprise is peaceful. And everywhere where there is trade, human enterprise is peaceful."[25] That last part is obviously up for discussion. But warfare limits trade, and war between the nations of Europe has become unthinkable since the EU's internal market was established. Hermes is not belligerent or violent, does not issue threats or ultimatums. He clearly prefers nimble networking and seduction to brute force.

Good businesspeople recognise the importance of maintaining their social networks. Hermes builds a relationship with Apollo in the same way as a good businessperson knows to create new connections with the right people.[26] A central point of the myth concurs with new research: markets can create forms of sociability and networks based on voluntary mutuality that other social arrangements cannot.[27] From Hermes' point of view, the true goal of the markets may be a steady promotion of negotiation and innovation, ingenuity and new relationships. Perhaps conscious use of these characteristics could contribute to strengthening a renaissance of markets for regenerating social and natural capital (see Part III). Perhaps, with the Industrial Age now behind us, we can take further steps on the way to realising the full potential of the markets?

The joys of the markets

In the myth we meet an eloquent Hermes. More than 3,000 years later, we can still enjoy the surprising twists and humour of this figure. He is the protector of trade and the markets, but Zeus also appoints him as messenger of the gods, the Master of communication. Markets can be understood as information networks, and a smooth flow of information is critical to the functioning of the markets.

The classical economic model of efficient markets assumes a perfect flow of information. In other words, all of the participants are assumed to have immediate and correct access to all relevant information about prices and quality.[28] But such an ideal model does not take into account the effect of asymmetries in power and information. The stories about Hermes are more in line with modern information economics, as it shows that the flow of information is far from perfect. Hermes is also the god of white, grey and regular black lies, and he wins friends and opportunities rather than following rational calculations. Frequently the authorities (represented by Apollo and Zeus in the myth) have to make corrections and regulate for failure in the flow of information. Today, we can see this in the joint stock companies' reporting obligation to the administrators of stock exchanges, or in requirements for scientific documentary proof and public approval of drugs. Without any form of control, extreme disciples of Hermes can happily pass on what they want to gullible investors and consumers.

The market as a source of joy, meaning and human development has not been given a central place in economics. The market and finance are serious matters: hard facts and black suits. An acquaintance of mine worked for a while in the City of London. The dress code there is fairly strict. It was conceivable only on Casual Fridays that people would take off their ties. One Wednesday, my friend came in wearing brown(!) shoes, which immediately attracted the comment "So, going casual today, are we?" Deviation from the norm, in language or clothing, is no trifling matter.

Economics has never managed to rid itself from the epithet of "the dismal science", as the Scottish historian Thomas Carlyle labelled it in the middle of the nineteenth century.[29] When the annual results are to be presented to analysts, or when the head of the central bank gives a speech, the economic uniform emerges. The latest estimates for quarterly profits, consumer confidence or the retail price inflation index (RPI) are not things to be flippant about. The heavy-weight players enter market the arena armed with their mobile phones, laptops and thin document folders, today as well as in Thorstein Veblen's day. It is a question of survival, loss or triumph. Only the most adaptable will succeed. Business is serious.

However, are these the essential qualities of the market? Or are they just an expression of an attitude based on succinctness, rationality, seriousness and hardball competition? More Apollo than Hermes? When I read about Hermes, I get the impression of trade and market being more 'funny business', involving play, puns and fantasy, rather than 'serious business'.[30] On Mount Olympus, Hermes is in a bit of a squeeze and has every reason to be serious. He is under threat of being sentenced and cast into Tartarus, the punishment part of the underworld. Nevertheless he manages to retain his sense of humour, be a seducer and to build relationships. With no trace of performance anxiety, he moves away from the serious charges against him into play mode and gets the other gods, finally even Apollo, involved in the playfulness.

Have we forgotten the art of play in business? How can this have anything to do with play, a stressed knowledge worker might object, with a 150 page heavy technical tender document for an industrial supply valued at £34 million in front of him and a short deadline? We are not playing at shops! But Hermes probably meant that it is only once we involve ourselves in serious play that we become full participants in the economic life. The role of play in organisational learning has recently been forcefully advocated.

Back to my description of the trip through the shopping mall. I am just out for the necessities of life – the trip is pure duty. The markets in the shopping centre are exclusively oriented towards consumption and are not stimulating in the same way as, for example, a conference at which you can exchange skills, meet interesting people and cross frontiers into the unknown. I reel when faced with racks and racks of goods, knocked out by my own inability to find any joy in the pure efficiency of these markets. The relationship between the seller and me is crowded out by the products' glaring monologue: 'Buy me! Buy me!' across the over-filled racks. Instead of dialogue, exchange and gossip, what remain is a mechanical smile from the cashier lady which prompts an equally forced smile from me. Other people perhaps find a little networking and sociability at shopping centres, but I do not succeed in that – I am affected by shop-neurosis. I go stiff, get absentminded and only wish to get out of there. This market is becoming lifeless and soulless in all of its colourful but fully controlled profusion. I just cannot play there or be at ease with myself. I have to go through and past the cash desk and out. The invisible spirit of the market is gone, even if its invisible hand is still taking care of efficient allocation.

I like to believe that Hermes would hardly feel well there either. He wouldn't find anything of the excitement, enthralment, crowding, shouting, seduction, haggling, loud laughter and often coarse humour that traditional markets have had and still have. I remember my encounters with the marketplaces of Zanzibar. The immediate impression is not of the food or other goods for sale. No, the lasting impression is of people in all sorts of conversation with one another. A profusion of people and goods in a small space. Many of the people there have no intention of buying or selling anything. They look, talk, share gossip and enjoy taking part in the great theatre of the market. The attraction of it is the participation, with the broad network of relationships that markets create and intensify.

Between price and story

Two related things weaken participation in modern markets: fixed prices with the associated standardisation of the sales process, and a purely quantitative approach to transactions. Having fixed prices on all goods in shops is a relatively new invention. It became widespread from the 1890s onwards. Before that hardly any prices were fixed. This prevents any adjustment of the price based on the relationship that exists between buyer and seller. In modern shops, an employee does not have permission to change the sales price. Only the manager, or maybe the owner, can do that.

To the extent that the seller has no personal involvement in the sales situation, it gets mechanised. Bureaucracy surrounding prices set centrally within the organisation weakens the intensity and liveliness that has been the traditional hallmark of the relationship between buyer and seller. Shop employees are disempowered, and this transfers to the buyer. The transaction has to be carried out with the minimum possible involvement of human relationships, thereby becoming dehumanised.[31] The meeting between the seller and buyer dissolves into mechanised pricing, standardised payment systems, one-way communication in advertising, and monitoring by video cameras.

When the fixed price tag defines the transaction, the quantity of money also becomes the most important feature of the relationship between buyer and seller. This isolates the moment of purchasing from the great network of relationships that the transaction would otherwise have been interwoven into. The sum does not say anything about how the goods travelled or where they originated. The contents declaration only tells us what the contents are now.

Apollo asks Hermes if he was given the lyre by the gods or by people. In the same way, many people today are starting to ask about the *story of the product.*[32] For a long time, marketing theory and the development of branded goods have been working on spinning stories about the product. More information than just price is needed if the transaction is to be perceived to have any meaning. Therefore stories have been made about the product's identity and origins. But in the last decade or so these stories have been generic stories about the product brand as such, and have not had much to say about the individual product.

But markets have always been changing. If more of Hermes' qualities are to participate in the markets again, perhaps the next change will be that much richer stories can be told about every individual product. It might be information such as how and when a cod was caught. Where the fish grew up and how fat it is. Has the shirt been produced by underpaid child labour in Sri Lanka, or has it been sewn by a lady who also studies English in the evenings? Is the cotton grown using irrigation systems that lower the groundwater level and pesticides that are harmful to workers and the natural environment, or is it from locally adapted or organic agriculture?

To be given stories like that is no longer a technological impossibility. We will be able to get such a rich story by pointing our mobile device towards the product. We could see – or maybe even speak – with its maker at work, provided that suppliers make such information available. Both money and goods need a story in order to belong somewhere and in order to convey meaning.

Every exchange is also a gift

The perception in economics that everyone ought primarily to pursue their own self-interest has given the markets a strong stamp of individualism and competition. But an exchange can also be seen in a different light. For example, take a purchase of apples. I go into a shop and give maybe £1.50 for a pack of three apples. When I say give, I mean give, and not that I am paying. Giving involves respect for the recipient and the situation in which the transaction is taking place. Giving implies a gift.

But what and to whom am I giving something? A whole network of relationships. Not just the shop I am standing in, not just the assistant I am standing face to face with, but also the company that owns the shop, the community of employees in that company, the cooperative that bought the apples from the grower, the grower who cultivated the apple tree, the apple tree itself which produced these wonders of apples, the soil that bears the tree and allowed it to germinate and grow, the rain that moistened the soil, the clouds that ensured there was rain and, not least, the sun that with its warm, daily kisses nurtured that lovely red colour. There is the potential for all of this to be present at the time of the purchase, but all too soon the only thing I see is the sum of money. The price is there as an anonymous, deaf-and-dumb representative of a world that is being hidden behind it.

There is also a network on the buyer's side. The exchange starts right enough with my desire for apples, with the image of a juicy, red apple and the imagined act of sinking my teeth into it and sensing the pleasant, exciting, sweet-sour feeling on my tongue and in my throat. However, my family is also involved, because I am going to share the rest of the apples with them. When I am able to *give* the money, it is because I myself have been *given* it. In that way, my *employer* is present, as is the payroll office who had the money transferred into my account. In addition, the employer's products and services, plus the customers who are willing to purchase them, have all made the payment to me possible. If I look at the receipt, I can detect that some of this money goes back to the State as VAT, so that the State is able to contribute to maintaining the entire society converging around this transaction concerning three apples bought in a shop.

It is impossible to make all of this visible for every market transaction. But a little more transparency and story exposing the underlying network of relationships could contribute greater meaning and presence at the moment of purchase. Now we are limited to a 'thank you' when we take the apples from the assistant and a 'thank you' in return and perhaps a quick smile once she has the money in her hand.

A little more image and storytelling could deepen the give-and-take relationship that frames each purchase and thus provide a link to the much older, archaic traditions of the gift economy. The anthropologist Marcel Mauss wrote about a spiritual bond in many non-Western cultures that arose between people and objects through the circulation of money and gift objects. Gifts and money expressed and strengthened relationships between people.[33] Mauss found three types of obligations that characterised the gift economy: the obligation to give, the obligation to receive, and the obligation to return the gift when the time came. All forms of trading transactions were and still are variations of this logic.

In principle, this is just as applicable in today's markets as it was in the gift economies of earlier times. It is just a matter of looking at buying and selling a little differently. It is just as difficult for us to opt out of market relationships, to refuse to participate in the giving and receiving as it was in the gift economies that Mauss describes. Rather than wishing to opt out of markets altogether we could, through the give-and-take circles, recognise that, through participation in the markets, we belong more profoundly also to one another. When we receive goods, we pay at the cash desk and say 'Thank you very much', we are participating in an ancient ritual practice in which everyone receives and everyone gives in turn, although to extremely different degrees.[34]

However, in a standardised transaction the sale is so efficiently mechanised that the soul's participation in that relationship is almost totally removed. It is usually done as quickly as possible, and it then becomes difficult to be present in the relationship with one another and with the rest of the network that is affected by the transaction. We lose the psychic capacity of being fully present and fall into a zombie state of psychic numbness and absence, a state that, mythically speaking, is reminiscent of Hell. The market also becomes a hell then, which is exactly where Apollo first threatened to throw Hermes: into the dusty, burnt-out Tartarus.

Hermes' dark sides and the market's destructiveness

The pre-Socratic Greeks were not blind god-worshippers. They were *sceptics*.[35] They were constantly suspicious about the gods and their capriciousness. Every god had its dark sides, and the Greeks ensured they reminded one another of this through songs and rituals: Do not forget that you are a mortal who will quickly become a pawn in the divine game. Disregard or hubris towards the gods could bring a terrible payback. Therefore they had to keep in contact with the gods, but not have blind faith in them.

So, what are Hermes' dark sides? What are the side-effects if someone becomes a fundamentalist worshiper of free choice, absolutely free markets and a quick-flowing market system with increasingly few barriers?[36]

In economic analysis, the concept of market failures has been central. This applies to situations where the market does not function effectively when left to its own devices. The four most important of these failures are externalities, lack of competition, income differences and deficiencies in public benefits. The first of these, *externalities*, revolve around market activities that spill over and inflict negative changes on some parts of society that are not involved in the exchange. The economic activities have, in other words, harmful side-effects. The classic example of this is pollution. If it does not cost anything for a factory to release toxic substances, it will not clean up and the costs will have to be borne by society and the ecosystem.

The second, *lack of competition,* is what we get when there is only one dominant player (monopoly) or only a few strong players (oligopoly) in the market. The distribution of power in market societies then becomes skewed, with the possibility of prices being set rigidly too high. The dominant company or companies then gain a great deal of power, which allows them to squeeze other companies dry, buy them up or force them into bankruptcy. Even customers have to put up with poor service and fewer options.

The third, *income inequality,* in simple terms means that markets make the rich richer and the poor poorer. With no intervention or regulation, the results can be unsustainable for societies as a whole.

The fourth and last in our list is the market's inability to provide *public goods*. Left to their own devices, markets would not be able to attend to or produce shared benefits such as fresh air, national defence, basic research, law and justice, street lighting or lighthouses for safe navigation. Markets are great at providing private goods to those who can purchase them. Government is necessary to provide public goods and regulate their availability.

If appropriate regulations are not forthcoming at the right time to handle the market failures above, this could be called government failures.

Many people's hostility to markets has its roots in the effects that are brought about as a result of market failures. For that reason, action needs to be taken by government, with regulations that can make best use of what the markets have to offer. Markets are never free, even if there is freedom of choice within the market. Economics has always recommended intervention by government in order to prevent and resolve problems – typically in the form of fees, subsidies, competition supervision and appropriate tax arrangements. Economics has a long and comprehensive tradition of research in order to counteract distorted fluctuations of the market in the most efficient manner possible. Every market always has a dark side, but *how* dark it becomes depends on how well the State manages to regulate it. Efficient, good markets therefore need a brisk, just State. Not at all easy.

That is as far as conventional theory on market failure goes. The rational Apollos of this world are definitely not always capable of reining in the swift Hermeses. But what psychological characteristics do we actually find in Hermes' shadow side?

First, Hermes is quick and cunning. He is always on the go between one place and another. He does not need to sleep, and is always on the way to a new deal. But he is an immortal god and we are mortal humans. No human can live always on the run, as if being Hermes himself, for any extended period. When we are always taking work home with us, working on the train and after the evening news prog-ramme, we are participants in *hyperculture,* a culture that is possessed by Hermes' capabilities and opportunities. If we follow these, we have to be flexible and adaptable; changes and adjustments are intended to be fun. We have to think of the next reorganisation as a positive thing – changes come increasingly rapidly, and if we are to retain our customers we have to be faster than our competitors at adjusting. Meetings in faraway countries are fun; new technology has to be mastered and put to use – the faster the better.

Living the full pulse of the markets means that we have to be on our toes twenty-four hours a day, speed always increasing; more and more has to be fitted into every minute. Anyone trying to live like Hermes will finally suffer from stress and burnout. Books on stress management are selling well because they are dealing with something that most people are experiencing: the feeling of constantly having to participate in labour markets and consumer markets at superhuman speed. Those who get dizzy from the speed are tempted to jump off the whole market merry-go-round. Then trends like *slow food, slow cities* and *simple living* become popular – simply because life in the market has become so complex and hectic that we just don't see the point in keeping up. We react to an overdose, an inflation of Hermes.

Hermes is, further, the god of messengers and communications. With the Internet, TV, radio and wireless computer networks, he is spreading an always-on, mushrooming cloud of virtual information. As if we were not already drowning in newspapers, magazines, journals and books we ought to have read. We are also always available for messages that are picked up by our mobile phones with their distracting rings, or invisible messages that travel right around the world in an instant and land in our digital inboxes. Information, information, information. Knowledge, knowledge, knowledge – right up until it flashes Error! Error! in both our eyes. Society is possessed. Stress changes the bodily functions. Information overload makes us want to switch off. These costs of living in a network and market economy (they might be called 'externalities') will not be mentioned in any economic theories.[37]

Hermes is also the first communications guru, the first *spin doctor* – he knows all there is to know about how to spin a profile and an image, a brand and a façade, and how to seduce the audience into believing what he says. Hermes is often personal, although showing only the features of himself that he knows will serve his purpose, such as when he says he's born yesterday and calls Zeus his father. Also traceable back to Hermes is the politics of the personal and media intimacy. Personal, close-up images of politicians and other celebrities displace logical, historical or analytical knowledge.

In line with Hermes' philosophy, *how* you say something is much more important than *what* you are saying. It might lead to facts and statistics presented rather irresponsibly, and to the logic faltering. But as long as you can charm people, it *seems* right. Then lots of people 'buy' the message. And that is what counts in Hermes' world – that is, the market. Many people detest this side of Hermes, in particular rationalists who have more sympathy with Apollo's clear differentiation between right and wrong; truth and lies. 'Tabloidisation!' snort the true Apollonians disdainfully; they call the message irresponsible 'low culture', and feel strengthened in their self-image as rational people, raised above the gullible masses.

More frightening and worse for the planet are the many market fundamentalists. They forget about the Greeks' *skepsis* and become believers, almost fanatical

Hermes-worshippers of the 'free market'. Markets are best for organising everything with the least possible involvement: If a market is good, more market
exposure and market competition are better. If local markets are good, globalisation and global markets are supreme – no matter what. After the collapse of
the Soviet Union, the 1990s were not just an era of economic prosperity in Western countries but also a prosperous time for the belief in globalisation, liberali-
sation and the rule of new communication technologies. In its future scenarios,
the oil company Shell gave this trio the name of TINA: There Is No Alternative.

According to this fundamentalist belief, the markets should be further liber-
alised; they should become more global, finance more pervasive and universal,
so that innovations in financial instruments would flow unstoppably. The consequences are first of all wild fluctuations between booms and busts.

On an organisational level the consequences are what management gurus
have written about in their books since the 1980's: modern organisations must
become faster, more flexible and adaptable. They have to feel comfortable on the
boundary between order and chaos, become more creative and communicate
better with their customers. In other words, quite like Hermes. All of this happens within the global marketplace and in an atmosphere of increasing global
competition. Companies have to learn to innovate more quickly than their competitors, or they will be 'cast into Tartarus' – out of participation.

How should we as participants in the market relate to this story? Should we
believe it? Should it legitimise change and adaptation as *necessary? Must* we
globalise, *must* we liberalise, *must* we adapt, *must* we rush to adopt all new technology? When a myth is taken literally, it locks market participants into rigid
behaviours which are experienced as correct and necessary. Privatisation, liber-
alisation, outsourcing and management share options all become 'natural' phenomena – that is just how things are done.

Organisations and nations are gripped by an image of how the world is a vast
competitive game. Either you win or you lose, and the goal is to avoid losing.
Previously, people played on a national basis; now we compete globally. Here the
thing is not to give in. This attitude can be expressed as follows: we have to be
world class, or there is little or no point to it all. This is a fundamentalist belief in
the market gospel.[38]

But the network of relationships in the market can also be seen as an ecosystem. In it we may see that symbiosis and co-evolution in different niches produce many more opportunities than just win or lose in an universal market.
Universal competition is an image, a story that highlights the need for lean cost-
cutting and harsh organisational change. It omits values such as distinctive cultural features, tacit knowledge, employees' quality of life, innovative business
clusters and network effects.

The classic theory about perfect markets assumes, for example, that everyone has access to the same, valid information.[39] This is obviously a Utopian image, which the Greeks also realised: a lot of what Hermes says is pure manipulation, half is almost true, and the rest sounds fairly good. He hardly knows himself what is what. Fundamentalist belief in the free market gospel is to take Hermes literally as an ideal and close one's eyes to his shadow side.

Some conclusions about markets

The markets' potential for contributing to human development and happiness has hardly been tapped yet by modern market democracies. One important reason for this is that the inherent values of relationships between people and the inherent value of work for one's self-respect are not reflected in the considerations that hold sway on the market. The ideas that dominate the markets are perceptions about efficiency, consumer choice and price. But consumption of goods and experiences are poor substitutes for friends and relationships. Accounting systems reflect this attitude: purchase amounts and people's incomes are recorded with great accuracy, but not efforts made for other people, the deepening of relationships nor our interactions with the natural environment. Markets therefore often end up opposing aims such as human development and happiness.[40]

At the same time, the markets are indispensable. It is difficult to fight against the markets today – it turns into something like Don Quixote's struggle against windmills. Well-functioning markets are efficient, decentralised decision-making systems, extremely well suited to the flexible and optimal allocation of goods and services. The markets can also be exceptional at rewarding innovations, handling risk and reacting to changes in the environment, and in that way increasing wealth for society. Perhaps it would do to be a market adherent, while also retaining our scepticism about a market fundamentalism in which efficiency and growth is the Promised Land, and in which the same market model can be applied everywhere.

The soul of the market, however, does not lie within an efficient distribution of goods, but rather within the social contact networks that it promotes. On this basis, markets are just as much networks of the soul as they are "a mechanism through which buyers and sellers interact to set prices".[41] Market participants who concentrate exclusively on prices and an economy that analyses markets mechanically always run the risk of losing their soul. The stories, people and images disappear behind the price tag and the graphs. The function of money as a facilitator of social relationships will not be realised. For a long time, economics has been analysing the characteristics for *efficient* markets. Now we see that

markets are *conversations*, the important question then becomes: What characterises markets that also strengthens social relationships and doesn't destroy
nature?

Markets can also cast long shadows. Weaker parties can quickly be squeezed
out when another party is much larger and stronger. This is not because they are
less effective, innovative or supply poorer quality; they lose out to power, such as
when Microsoft bulldozed Netscape in the struggle for the Internet in the 1990s;
or when poor developing countries try to compete on a level playing field with
rich and technologically advanced countries; or when stockbrokers and top
managers have special access to information that makes them into vastly better
positioned players than the average investors in shares. Inequality in terms of
power, information, wealth, location and political networks turns the assumption of free markets as an unconditional and universal ideal into an illusion. If
one adheres tightly to this, one joins the fundamentalist worshippers of Hermes
and his invisible hand.

The markets will quickly turn into *the* market in a global world with digital
finance. Even if there are different marketplaces and stock exchanges, today the
money can be moved instantaneously from one market and region to the other.
That happens all the time. So markets can be good assistants, but they are poor
masters – and outright terrible as a world fundamentalism.

One challenge will therefore be to counteract the power that seeks to make
the whole world into a market, based on only one world dimension: global
money. The myth itself offers a clue to help us here: Hermes – as the essence of
the market – is inherently pluralistic and diverse. He introduced the practice of
sacrificing to several gods – to all twelve on Mount Olympus, or so the story
goes. He is the one to engage the other gods and negotiate between them. Some
economists have been arguing for a long time that markets can serve several
purposes – and even balance things out between them. There are markets for
exchanging care and social services. Markets can be created for reducing carbon
emissions, other markets for keeping fishing catches within reasonable total
quotas, and yet others for purifying fresh water and protecting wetlands. It is
quite possible that we may have got started on utilising the markets' potential for
social development and enhancing natural diversity.

The central message of this chapter must be that the markets are actually
something much more than the simple story about a perfect market mechanism
for freedom of choice and efficient distribution based on one-dimensional
money. How markets can be used for several purposes in a pluralistic economy
will be discussed in Part III.

Chapter 7

Riches, milk and honey

Is it a sin to be rich?

Wealth and riches have been central concepts within the economy since Adam Smith's Wealth of Nations. *But what shapes our ideas about wealth? What forms of capital are taken into consideration, and how? This chapter will make a mythical analysis of what might be called 'poverty consciousness' and 'flow consciousness'. This includes an introduction to the glutton Chronos and his wife Rhea, and is rounded off with King Midas's lessons about gold and benefits.*

The Norwegian philosopher Arne Næss lived for several years a very simple life at the Tvergastein cabin high up on the Hallingsskarvet mountain. Here, he enjoyed practicing the art of consuming as little as possible. A match can be used several times. If you have a burning candle, you don't need a new match. The cooking stove can be lit with the same match. His record was seven times using the same match. At Tvergastein, no water has been installed indoors, and in the winter the supply of running water is very limited, usually in the form of melted snow in a kettle on the stove. Næss's experiences of riches then include having two full buckets of water in the house. Imagine two buckets of crystal-clear mountain water ready to use! What a luxury! I can recall at the drop of a hat the memory of that beaming smile on his face at the feeling of being *so* rich.

How are riches defined in economic thinking? One great thing about economics is the precision of the language (even if there are many ways of counting). Wealth can be defined down to several decimal points if wanted. And there are two ways of measuring it: wealth and income. Wealth consists of the net value of all assets owned at a given point in time, something that is normally settled at the end of the year. Income refers to the flow of wages, interest payments, and dividends during a period of time, typically a year.

Wealth is thus a *stock*, like the volume of a lake, while income is a *flow*, like the flow of a river, says economist Paul Samuelson.[1] From an economic point of view, then, being rich can mean one of two things: either a high income, or that you have great assets. And maybe – why not – have both?

There is a widespread scepticism towards the super-rich. In the social demo-cracy of Norway, we are traditionally not terribly happy with multimillionaires. It would probably be preferable if they'd won their money in the lottery or on the horses. When that happens, they are still a sort of *normal, decent people* who have just happened to come into money. We are all overjoyed if a poor mother-of-six in a the desolate valley of Kvinesdal wins 10 million.[2] Other rich who have made a lot of money themselves, perhaps on the stock exchange, are viewed with suspicion. They are either the 'nouveau riche' and heaping up profits, or they are 'ancien riche' and are freeloaders living in luxury just because they happen to have been the child of someone who exploited previous generations. They are suspect, say our democratic prejudices. At the same time we love reading about their sumptuous houses, island retreats and slick cars, in articles with glossy pic-tures. Or we flatter ourselves if we have been in the same class at school or if they say hello when we meet them on the street. And we love to play around with the idea of what we would do if a million or five were to end up in our bank account.

From a purely economic point of view, defining riches is simple, but emo-tionally we harbour some deep-set ambiguous feelings. Wishful thinking is mixed with envy and prejudice. Great wealth arouses conflicting feelings. Greed versus sobriety. Commercialism versus idealism. Swaying between rejection and admiration. The split between money and soul perhaps emerges most clearly when we have to socialise or collaborate with someone whom we know to be much wealthier than we are. Our culturally inherited suspicion of money makes it difficult to remain unaffected. For very wealthy people this can mean social isolation; it is more difficult to socialise with 'ordinary people'. They end up almost ghettoed in the company of only other rich people.

Studies from the UK and Australia show that between 70 and 80 per cent of the population believe that the wealthy have too much and that the difference between rich and poor is unjust.[3] Most people recognise the necessity of having differences in income and wealth on the basis of the functions people have and their work contribution. But that necessity does not cover the perceived differ-ence. And the actual difference is even greater than the perceived difference: the poorer classes consistently appear to undervalue how much the very rich actu-ally earn. It seems as if the sums are beyond their comprehension.[4] The paradox is there, statistically documented: we would all like to be rich, while the rich have far too much. If the wealthy are not themselves directly suspect, the situation is unfair anyway. Wealth is attractive and wealth is filthy.

In his book *The Secret Life of Money,* the Jungian psychologist Tad Crawford differentiates between internal and external wealth.[5] What we do not like, he says, is great external wealth without the corresponding internal growth. Spiritual values must be cultivated in parallel to cultivation of the external world of money. Investments in the internal world are often forgotten. Crawford points to the camel and the eye of the needle, and interprets this image to mean that Jesus warns against great external wealth because it becomes difficult to enter into and discover the riches in our internal life. External wealth needs internal development or else it leads to perdition. To avoid this, Crawford recommends the cultivation of spiritual development in the individual.

This interpretation however, is still caught in the split where internal soul and external money are separate spheres. I believe it is useful to abandon this way of thinking when we study wealth. It is hardly sinful to have external wealth, even if you do not have a particularly rich inner life; nor is it sinful or particularly noble to be poor. Overall, a too-moral reading of capital and money can easily backfire, as the catastrophic consequences of Karl Marx's philosophy have shown. I prefer an attitude of psychological wonder rather than a moral judgement to economic conditions and concepts here.

This is a book about reconnecting the ideas and concepts of economics with the imagination of the soul and its emotions. The question then becomes: What are the images that shape our relationship to wealth? How do they make us feel and think about our own wealth and that of others? Are there other ways of thinking that could change our actions?

One starting point for investigating this could be the metaphor used by Paul Samuelson: Do you imagine your riches as a large lake, or are they more of a cascading river? What is the situation: a lot of water in the lake, but a dwindling flow? Or is there a large inflow, but with an even larger drain? Maybe in the middle of a drought? With just a few trickles in a mire in the middle of the riverbed? Money and water have a lot in common, something I will come back to under credit and liquidity (Chapter 9).

It's interesting to note that economists use metaphors from nature, of rivers and lakes, when understanding and explaining wealth. Wealth is thus originally placed in the context of something wider than money. The economic magic usually works in one way only: all physical assets such as houses, cars, computers and tracts of land, even rivers and lakes, are translated into amounts and prices. But if we read the metaphor closely, we can note a difference: In the economic view maximising wealth is probably always good, but lakes and rivers have *optimum* levels. More than a certain volume of water causes a crisis, flooding and breakdown, perhaps a repositioning of the entire riverbed. Is there an optimum of wealth and income equivalent to an optimal flow of water in a watershed? Is there a level of profusion, at which the flow of money destroys the course of life? Paying close attention to the concepts and metaphors of economics, we can start reconnecting the economic ideas with the imagination of the soul as well as with nature.

'There's no such thing as a free lunch!'

As we saw in Chapter 5, 'New welfare', income levels have never been higher in Western countries. The river flows of money are greater than ever before. Nevertheless, many are experiencing it as form of drought. The flows are perceived as too small and the satisfaction with life is low. How is it that we do not feel rich, when statistically and historically we are now richer than ever before? There are others who live in a materially simple way, like Arne Næss, and feel rich nevertheless. The point must be that richness is a *state of mind,* not a numerical level of wealth and income. Wealth becomes *a mode of being in the world,* a relationship between the world and me, and not something that is reserved for those upper five-to-ten per cent who are the ultra-rich.

'Wealth is . . . munching a handful of nuts while I put an extra log onto the crackling fire and the snow is falling outside and the aroma of freshly made coffee wafts around the room from the coffee pot.' – Per E. Stoknes

---

A trip in the mountains on a misty October day. Suddenly an eagle glides in front of me, letting itself be borne up by the air currents around the steep mountain peak I am standing on. I walk on, and am struck by the reddish-yellow highlights in the grass around a misty, dank marsh. A dying pine tree, with woodpecker holes in several places, is pointing a few long light grey fingers towards the neighbouring peak while a bracket fungus sits comfortably right in the middle of the trunk. I bend my way through some bushes, and my nose is hit by the bittersweet smell of autumn leaves on the ground. I step on an old, decayed branch that snaps with a hollow, muffled crack. I am hiking among gold, gilded leaves which scatter around me, all backlit by the sun which breaks through the cloud cover. I am sitting still on a stone in the marsh and sensing beauty ahead of me, beauty behind me, beauty to the west and beauty to the east. If anyone has ever had reason to feel rich, it must be me here and now. Me, who can hike around here in all this sumptuousness. Drinking as much water as I can and wading through gold and bright colours all day long.

Every morning, the sun rises and gives us the daylight. We can breathe in an abundance of air all day. And when we sit and look at the sunset, we can meditate on the wealth of our relationship with the Earth, the sun, the moon and the stars. Every atom in our bodies has been gifted at some time from one star or another which managed, via pressure and intensity, to produce carbon, oxygen, nitrogen and the other elements – before the star itself exploded and sent its riches out to us. We bathe in the elements, drink them, eat them – they are completely free in almost infinite numbers. One of the favourite expressions in economics – *there's no such thing as a free lunch* – is completely insane. We will not survive until the next lunch without these free gifts, this never-ending flow of riches from the Earth and the sun, the air and the water.

We might call this flow of blessings – whether they be blueberries, birdsong, green grass underfoot or fresh water in the lakes – *natural capital*. If capital comes from heads in a herd, natural capital relates to all of these more-than-human multitudes – to trees and fish, squirrels and elk, algae and rivers, ants and bogs, which every day make their own contribution to keeping our planet alive. Natural capital yields a flow of gifts that we humans can live on, as long as the capital is not depleted. Without this flow of 'goods', there would be no human life either. Natural capital is the foundation of all other forms of capital sold on the markets. However, in standard economic practice it has been undetected because it has had no price and thus has not been entered into the books. How these riches can be made visible to economics will be the topic of Part III of this book.

How can it be that this natural capital, which forms the essential wealth for our lives and for the Earth itself, has been of so little value in the market system that it is seen as free-for-all, a 'free lunch'? How is it that fresh water, which we are totally dependent on and which is an absolutely vital necessity, has a low market value, while diamonds and gold, which are hardly of any benefit to us, fetch high prices on the market and have represented wealth throughout the ages?

This paradox of value was something that Adam Smith struggled with in 1776.[6] The later, elegant solution that emerged much later from economical theory was called 'marginal utility'. It is not the total usefulness of diamonds or water that matters, but the usefulness of *each extra* unit of water or diamonds. It is true that the total utility of water to people is tremendous, because they need it to survive. However, since water is in such large supply in the world, the marginal utility of water is low. It is how much people are willing to pay for another litre that matters, compared to how much they are willing to pay for yet another diamond. Thus it is the *last glass,* towards the limits of supply, that determines the price and therefore the value of all water in this market. The person who is about to die of thirst in the desert would gladly give a whole bag of diamonds for the last bottle of water in the vicinity. *The intensity of the experience of scarcity thus determines the price on the market*, and therefore what is given economic value, as measured in money.

So it is only when we reach the limit of supply in relation to demand that the prices quickly go up. Money does not measure the total utility of anything. The price relates only how much most people would be willing to pay to obtain one more. So, to put it bluntly, today's markets don't see an item's real value until it has almost all been used up. For that reason, water has been cheap and the clean air free up until now. Unlike in Adam Smith's time, in the twenty-first century we will probably see fresh water and the air itself becoming extremely important 'goods'.[7]

Golden insanity

just gold, or an ....
high seemingly regardless of supp...

If we are to try to understand riches, we ca........
and psyche appear to meet in the magic of gold. But just what is it that makes
gold so attractive? What is it that makes people go off the rails just to get a *little*
more of it?

Gold is radiant, shiny and extremely malleable. It has always been linked with
things that are royal, glorious and superhuman. Gold is rare. If we were to gather
together all of the gold discovered and refined since the dawn of time up to the
year 1900, it would only be around 30,000 tonnes. Since then, around five times
as much has been produced.[8] If we were to melt it all down into ingots and stack
them up into a cube, it would be no more than around 20 metres in height, depth
and width. The cube would easily fit into a large sports hall.

Gold is permanent. Neither acid, alkali nor rust will break it down. All of the
gold that has ever come to light exists still in one place or another, even the dust
that is consumed or scattered around in a ritual gesture. Since gold is so malleable it can be hammered out into incredibly thin leaf, only a few atoms thick,
and still stay together. In nano-format, it gains a number of new characteristics,
from disinfecting to catalysing.

The symbolic power of gold lives on in our fantasies about money. Subcon-
sciously, this is mixed up into a psychic complex, *gold-money*, which is always a
motivating factor in our fantasies and our actions as economic players. Gold is
the archetypal expression for lasting values. When we give each other wedding
rings of gold, we are giving the marriage a symbolic envelope of something eternal. Neither good wine, cattle nor corn has been able to fill this role.

But like everything else, gold has its dark side, and gold has cast long shadows into our civilisation's history.

For a long time, attempts were made to use gold as an anchor for the value of
money. But this gold standard was abandoned because the supply of gold was
insufficient to provide for the money needs of the rapidly growing markets.
There was *never* enough gold. Just ask conquistadors Cortés and Pizarro, who
annihilated the Aztec and Inca empires perhaps especially for the sake of gold.
The yearning for gold is self-reinforcing. The lustre of gold stirs a desire that
awakens rather than quenches the thirst for more. Gold allures with a promise
of permanent wealth and access to the Earth's, sun's and the universe's profusions
– if only we are able to capture it and keep it under our control.

- $ -

The question again is: even if we are surrounded by the abundance of the Earth – and some even by money and gold – why do we not feel rich?

Perhaps we can make further gains on this question by looking more closely at the experience of poverty. This is a feeling that arises from being shut off from goods that others have. The world denies you access even to necessities like water, food and warmth, because you lack money. If this is a life that you – as opposed to Arne Næss – have not chosen voluntarily, it will feel like a poverty trap. Destitution can bring both the bodily pains of undernourishment and the gnawing pain of the soul of having to make tragic choices like distributing too little food among household members. This relates to absolute poverty. In the following I will focus mainly on the psychological aspects of poverty.

The whole international development aid system is set with the intention of richer countries to help poorer countries. But at the same time the recipient countries are being defined as poor, helpless and passive recipients that have to comply with certain conditions. It is not an partnership for development, but these countries are placed in a subordinate position, based on a Western definition of capital and wealth. These countries' own traditional experience of wealth – based on family, ancestors, language, traditions, air, water, forest and land – is shoved to one side, considered inferior. The rich party knows best what the poor really need. This adds insult to injury in the experience of poverty.

I remember a crowd of around thirty small street children who were following my partner and me in Nairobi, Kenya, with outstretched hands. They had practised at how to look sad, hollowed-out and lame to get more out of the white passers-by. But several of the smallest just could not manage to stop smiling among themselves at how the cleverest actors of the band managed to appeared to be suffering so terribly as they stretched their hands out to us. Incredibly, there was some kind of dignity and humour in their show, their ability to play with destitution that I will never forget.

More than a billion people live on less than a dollar a day, often with ostentatious displays of great wealth in their close vicinity. It is not remarkable that these people are preoccupied by what *they do not have*. Many rich people, on the other hand, have more money, food, cars, and access to more services and opportunities than they will ever be able to use. Still, in the middle of all this bounty their attention and their conversations too are dominated by what they *do not have*. Coming home to Norway from travels in poorer countries one very striking thing from picking up news and discussing with colleagues is that we dwell more on what we lack than what we have, as if we belonged to the world's poor. When put into focus this phenomenon is quite astounding. Perhaps we can

...the experience of poverty in the widespread and

enough. Soon my thoughts wandered to the bundle of bills I would have to pay.
I don't really earn enough money. I am not getting enough of my manuscript
written. I don't get enough exercise. I don't have the right shoes. There is not
enough time to do even half of what's on my to-do list. There is not enough . . .
I hardly get out of bed before having thought and felt several times that I am
lacking something, that there is a whole heap of things that there are not enough
of. Regardless of actually circumstance, this *mode of thinking* has affected me
before I notice it, let alone freed myself from it.

If I thumb through the papers or go to work, I am surrounded by similar
impressions: There is not enough wilderness left. We do not have the right skills.
We are lagging behind in international competition. The surplus is too small.
Turnover is not growing enough. We have lost power and influence. We neither
have the time nor the money to resolve the tasks we have been given. We do not
get enough rest. The holidays were too short. We do not have enough energy.
There are too few days in a week and too few weekends in a month. And, obviously, we never, never, never have enough money – ever! We feel insufficient
even before we have sat up in bed in the morning, before our feet have even
reached the ground. We feel constrained by scarcity on all sides. And, late in the
evening, before we are overcome by sleep, we race through the list of what we
have not managed or accomplished, or of what we ought to have arranged that
day.[9]

This mode of thinking tells us a lot about how a deep-seated feeling of *too* little, of deficiencies and scarcity, is strongly and closely intertwined in our relationships with other people. Habit and automatic responses are part of this; the
assumption of scarcity becomes the premise of my ideas about myself and the
rest of society. There is no room for sufficiency or generosity. Imperceptibly,
focus and input shifts to how I can procure things for myself. The basic rule is
the same as in the classic game of musical chairs where there are more children
than chairs. Someone will always be squeezed out. And it is not going to be me!
The problem is just that this is not a game but played out in society at large,
where it becomes a grim indubitable truth that sets an iron cage around our lives.
If the mindset does not change then, regardless of what I have, the feeling
remains that it is just not enough.

In economics, the idea of scarcity has been elevated into the first principle of the field. Economic textbooks and dictionaries define economics as "the study of how societies use scarce resources to produce valuable commodities and distrib ute them among different people"[10] Thinking economically and becoming an economist requires that we start from the premise of scarcity, and then look for maximisation within given constraints. Economic analysis thus begins on the basis of the premise that there is not enough.

The assumption of scarcity throws a shadow on the economy. We are cast into a struggle for goods, in which the rational thing is to grab on to our own share, so that we are never the one left standing without the chair. If we lose, in the logic of this game, we are thrown out of the market altogether. *You lost*; the shadow of scarcity wheezes, and rattles the fetters of death.

You would think that people who belong to the higher echelons of wealth and income, who are surrounded and encircled by money and possessions, would also *feel* wealthy. They don't have to fear deficiencies, or worry about being duped out of everything they own. But in conversations with rich people, with managers and investors, I've learned that the mind-set of scarcity is often just as prominent among them as among people who have a tiny fraction of their resources.[11]

Regardless of whether we are in the upper or lower sectors of the wealth distribution, it seems that the way we behave in the world is based on a fundamental assumption of scarcity. That is what we are used to. That is what we are trained for. As individual people and as a culture, we have learned that there is a scarcity of things in the world. According to economic theory this is logical and correct: the world does not contain enough to cover all our needs and desires. If there really was enough of everything, economics says, all prices would go down to zero and the markets would come to a standstill because no one would have any needs that were not yet catered for. It is exactly the idea of scarcity that gives us an economic system and makes more efficiency imperative.

In addition to being a modern economic concept, scarcity is also a kind of archetypal idea. It can have an emotionally possessive effect. We can imagine it to originate deep in the reptilian, evolutionarily ancient parts of our bodies. We do not have control over ideas like that. What we can do, however, is to take a step back and distance ourselves a little from it. This allows us to keep an eye on how the idea captivates us. Like other indigenous peoples, the Greeks personified such archetypal ideas in the form of gods and related myths about them so that we mortals would not forget how easily we are bedazzled by their power.

When we see the world through the idea of scarcity, with whose eyes are we looking? When we see that there will not be enough for everyone; when we start suspecting deficiencies, destitution and deprivation? When we feel the need to

Krono... ....
the sky, whom he envied. He therefore castrated his father and became ....
the universe, but was later overthrown by his own son Zeus.

Kronos is the master of harvest and hoarding. He is one of the masters of the underworld, of darkness, night and black winters. His metals are lead and gold. In his world, things are cold, dull and dry. The Romans called him Saturn, and *saturnalia* was a harvest festival. We can recognise him as 'the man with the scythe' who harvests both people and crops when the time comes. How did Kronos come to be like that?

The original period of Kronos's rule was called the Golden Age, as the people of the time had abundance and no need for laws or rules. Both Kronos and Saturn are gods of riches, Wise Old Kings, and not just greedy monsters. But then,

the myth tells, Kronos heard of an ancient prophesy. It was said that if Kronos had children with his wife, Rhea, daughter of the Earth goddess, Gaia, one of the children would force him off his throne and take all of his wealth. He therefore swallowed all of his children as soon as they were born. However, Rhea finally managed to fool him. She wrapped a stone in a cloth and gave it to Kronos instead of the newborn baby Zeus. Kronos did not notice anything, just swallowed the stone in a huge gulp. When Zeus grew up, he tore his father down from his throne and made him disgorge the other immortal gods. This is how Zeus became master of the Universe, and Kronos was sent away to the Earth's core, to the realm of death. From that time, this old-man god ensures that the days and time keep to their rhythm.[12]

Kronos (Greek) or Saturn (Roman) swallowed all his children. Francisco Goya, 1819.

As a psychological fe...
ways of thinking tha...
experiences. Kron...
opportunities for...
thing, Kronos i...
the more we try to o...

The main character in Char... Scrooge. He is a rich old miser who 'swallow... chest. In this way, he personifies this basic attitude, like a ... Saturn. Dickens writes that when Scrooge came walking down the street, he spread such a coldness around him that the guide dogs led their blind masters out of the way in order to avoid meeting him. Disney further developed the stereotype into Duckville's Uncle Scrooge. In similarity with Kronos, Uncle Scrooge never gets enough and is always missing a million or two. Dickens was probably right when he hinted that we are all like Scrooge as long as we operate on the basis of the economy's fundamental assumption about self-interest and scarce resources.[14]

Kronos personifies what we might call a *persistent poverty-consciousness* – based on the perception of deficiency. The mythical image of the glutton Kronos can be understood as personifying this never-ending craving for more. To enter into a culture, organisation or conversation in which scarcity is an basic premise, where employees mainly struggle for higher wages while management struggles to cut costs, is to enter into the mindset of Kronos-Saturn. The important thing is to eke things out to enhance one's own position and interest. The feeling of not-enough can overrule reason and any suggestions for win-win solutions. The voice of Kronos is capable of creating distorted attitudes to money among both rich and poor. Better a chunk extra for me than a little more for the many.

Kronos gains power and rules our minds through fear of decline and loss. Research into economic psychology has shown that there is a much greater aversion to losing £1,000 on an investment, for example, than the corresponding feeling of happiness attained at winning the same sum. Some studies suggest that losses are twice as powerful, psychologically, as gains. Loss aversion is far more widespread than is logical among investors and other players in the markets.[15]

The inherent fear of loss that most people have can therefore be manipulated. In political and economic debate, Kronos's voice easily becomes dominating by playing on this fear of ourselves and our nearest and dearest not having enough to live a good, happy life. Those others will come and grab what is ours. We must keep hold of it. He himself is without any joy and without the capacity for enjoyment, say the Greeks. Regardless of how much he has swallowed up, the goods remain unused, so that they are lost to this world.

The golden cornucopia

The golden horn of plenty contrasts with Kronos's gaping shortage. When Zeus was saved from the mouth of Kronos, Rhea placed him in a golden cradle which was hanging from a tree in the fertile land of Arcadia. He was able to eat honey and drink milk supplied by the celestial goat-nymph Amaltheia.[16] Zeus was also given one of her horns, and this is what we know as the cornucopia or horn of plenty. It is always filled with any food or drink that its owner may wish for.

The goddesses Gaia, her daughter Rhea and granddaughter Demeter are goddesses of fertility. The myth tells us they are in conflict with Kronos. This can be understood as their living by a cyclical principle rather than linearity and shortage. They let things flow, they provide milk, nectar and golden honey to all of their children. Gaia, Rhea and Demeter are open to the air and the warmth of the sun and make infinite benefits flow out, time and time again. Their riches lie not in what they gather in, but in what they give away. They dry up only when their partner male gods such as Kronos or Hades cram their children into their own bellies and keep them there without giving anything back. Then Rhea gets her son Zeus to overthrow Kronos and thereby re-establish balance in the cosmos. Correspondingly, Demeter forces Hades to release her daughter Persephone, to allow Spring to arrive once more.

Here we have an early mythical version of economics. The theme is wealth and scarcity versus abundance and sufficiency. So, where a Kronos-inspired economy grabs and stores wealth, a Rhea-inspired economy will go for cyclical renewal. In her book *The Soul of Money,* poverty campaigner Lynne Twist makes the concept of *sufficiency* her primary point. The feeling of sufficiency is an alternative to the feeling of scarcity. When looking through the eyes of Kronos, we see scarcity and the need for hoarding. When looking through the eyes of Rhea, we see flow and sufficiency, if not always abundance. The spectacles we are wearing determine what we see. In her world there is always *sufficient*.

The myths about Rhea and Demeter relate that if we link up to the flows of life and to the Earth's major and minor cycles, there is enough for everyone. In this way, it is possible to create a you-*and*-me world rather than a you-*or*-me-world.[17] The visionary American designer Buckminster Fuller maintained that, technologically, this was fully possible, as early as in the 1970s. It is society's linear, non-systemic mentality which obstructs us. However, if we hook up to Rhea's approach, we will find it natural to pass on the resources that flow through our lives – time, money, knowledge and energy – regardless of the absolute level of the flow at the moment.

This does not have to happen on the basis of idealism or altruism. We do it rather on the basis of a deep recognition of the Earth's natural cycles and on the basis that wealth exists in participating in these, not in strangling, swallowing, stemming and storing them. There is no sacrifice in this change of perspective. There is satisfaction. If Kronos represents poverty-consciousness, we might say that Rhea personifies a flow-consciousness – where Nature's elements exist in an eternal circle-dance with one another, where everything is linked to everything else. We feel that the Earth allows a stream of gifts to flow to us and through us, absolutely free. The only thing we need to do is to be open and participate. There are riches around us and inside us, in all directions.

Today's economy, however, sees scarcity of goods wherever it directs its gaze: unmet needs, shrinking resources, insufficient competition, under-investment, lack of growth. This is how Paul Samuelson and William Nordhaus define the situation in their classic economic textbook:

> Ours is a world of **scarcity**, full of **economic goods**. A situation of scarcity is one in which goods are limited relative to desires. An objective observer would have to agree that, even after two centuries of rapid economic growth, production in the United States is simply not high enough to meet everyone's desires.[18]

So even after two centuries of rapid growth, and people swallowing all they can in the biggest economy in the world, there is still "simply not enough". Economic theory is based on the utilisation of Rhea's gifts, while nevertheless retaining the mindset of Kronos. It may be that we need to rediscover a type of economy in which sufficiency is the basic assumption: in which we start thinking from an understanding that the Earth, with all of its limitations, is sufficiently abundant; in which we take as our starting point a flow economy rather than a scarcity economy; in which we think psychologically just as much as materially, about growth and riches.

Milk and honey

The two richest men in the world in 2005 were called Bill Gates and Warren Buffett. They were then worth around US$55 billion each. How did they feel about their wealth? Did they have enough, or was the important thing to double their fortune as quickly as possible? They have been friends for years. One September afternoon they met up in Nebraska for what *Fortune* magazine called The $91 Billion Conversation, in front of 2,000 students. Bill Gates' image in the Internet world is quite like that of Kronos-Saturn in the classical era: an insatiable titan who swallowed competitive companies and fleeced poor people to increase his own vast fortune. For many IT people, he has been the man with the scythe in real life. What does he want to amass so much money for? What ideas does he have?

"In 1998, I was just getting started [in philanthropy] and back then I would have said, 'Look it's too confusing and distracting to be making money and giving money away at the same time,' said Bill to *Fortune*. "As my dad encouraged me to jump in, as Melinda weighed in on that side, and both of them were willing to put time into it. . . . I'd always thought that I would wait until I was done working full-time. But it's worked amazingly well to be able to do some of both."

"Do you two [Warren Buffett and Bill Gates] talk together about this?" *Fortune's* interviewer wanted to know.

They both answered in the affirmative, before Bill went into more detail about not trying to convince Warren to become more active as a philanthropist. "But I share [with Warren] the enjoyment I get out of it and some of the fun dynamics, the dynamics of what works and doesn't work." He explained that he had been inspired by what Warren had written in a previous *Fortune* article about not giving wealth to his own children and drowning them in money, but that "it should all go back to society. Warren influenced me dramatically on that . . . It is a bit like Robin Hood – you circulate money back down from the top."[19]

So they are both saying that they want to pass the money on and no longer hold on to it themselves. They have clearly had a change of perspective: from being driven by a shortage-consciousness in which a miserable billion or four is not enough, they appear to understand wealth as part of a greater flow and bigger cycles. "A development is taking place within me," expands Warren. "If I had done this in my forties, it might have been $20 million. Now I've got a sum that

can do something significant. It is no longer certain that I will wait until I die before I give away what I have." This expresses a fundamental change in consciousness, from one mythical pattern to another. And, as they themselves say, at first it seems confusing and distracting.

Based on the *Fortune* interview, it might seem that the Rhea-Gaia ideas are gradually gaining ground and that the Kronos-ideas are being dethroned by these two financial giants, just as the myth tells us. Strangely enough, that report ends with a picture of Bill and Warren each licking their ice creams, more or less in the same way as the growing Zeus is suckling on Rhea's horn of plenty filled with milk and honey, or as *senex* is portrayed by the painters Peter Rubens and Deshays Cimons.[20]

Peter Rubens' rendering of 'the senex' in the painting *Caritas Romana*, 1625.

We can only hope that most of us do not have to pocket a net worth of US$45 billion before a corresponding change in consciousness can take place. The essential difference does not lie in whether it is 450,000 or 45 billion, but in what guiding images we hold of it. Regardless of how high or low the financial sum is, it is the images through which we understand these sums that gives them importance to the soul.

Some conclusions about riches – the secret of King Midas

There is a simple reason for the rich still being rich: they use less money than they possess or earn. The money piles up; it doesn't all flow away. The assets and goods are swallowed up and stored, just like Kronos's children in his great belly.

I believe that true riches lie neither in personal inner growth nor in an eight-digit sum of money. When I dare use such a pretentious expression as 'true riches', it is because it points to another way of being in the world. The riches of the soul consist of increased sensitivity, not in accumulating possessions, says Carl G. Jung.[21] With an increased sensitivity to riches, perhaps it then becomes possible to find gold in everything?

The Greeks gave us the famous story of King Midas, which has mainly been read as a moral warning against greed. The myth says that Midas was so absorbed by wealth that when he once was to have a wish fulfilled by the god Dionysus, without thinking about it, he wished that everything he touched should turn to gold. "Granted," said Dionysus, and began to amuse himself with the thought of what he knew would happen. Midas used his first day to touch everything he could. Stones, horses and chairs immediately turned to solid gold. He was blissfully happy and multiplied his wealth each hour. But the problems began when evening came and he wanted to eat. Wine, meat and vegetables turned to metal as soon as they entered his mouth. He became terribly hungry, and it dawned on him that he had made a dreadful blunder. Luckily, he managed to get hold of Dionysus again before the god travelled away, and he begged on his knees that this gift should be taken from him again. Dionysus said that he should go and wash himself in a river. Midas hurried away and did as Dionysus said. Then the gift was 'washed' off him. Since then, gold has been found in river sand and riverbeds.

As mentioned above, the story is naturally used as a warning against greed: Gold is not worth anything in itself. You can't eat money. We must not become like Midas. Some read the story in a more positive vein. Then his name is used admiringly about people who succeed in creating business from everything they touch – they have 'the Midas touch'.

A third reading of the myth would be to imagine this applies to everyone; that *we are all like Midas*. This implies that there really *is* gold in everything. And it is significant that the god who provides this gift is Dionysus, the god of joy, intoxication and hedonism. Everything can turn to gold for the person who lets go of the urge to hoard, instead valuing the unique sensuous richness of things. Then it will be possible to discover the full value inherent in every tree, in every glass of water, in each head of broccoli and every egg in the way they already offer themselves to us. And we will become really rich when we let go and allow the gold to flow away, when we see that gold belongs in the river, in the sand and in the major cycles of the seasons. Everyone who rediscovers this is already richer than Croesus and Bill Gates together.

I look forward to seeing a Midas principle from this perspective discussed in an economics textbook. I would be very pleased if that happened, but it is unlikely as long as economic theory holds on to the Kronos logic, with the struggle for ever-more-efficient production of always-scarce goods, right up to the end of time when GNP will be a thousand times greater than today, and when we will have amassed increasingly large hoards of consumer goods – even then, dissatisfied souls will brood on their holdings and make plans about where the next consignment is going to come from.

Kronos is a deep-seated, ancient power. Our tendency to stuff as much as possible into our own bellies and to keep holding on to gold and old ideas will not be the first thing to go away. Riches are not without their advantages and the case to the contrary, although it has often been made, has never proved widely persuasive, as the economist John Galbraith pointed out in his book *The affluent society*. There is little reason to believe that miracles of self-development will suddenly create some general overstepping of the little ego's huge desires.

But just perhaps, other ways in which to think and measure wealth can turn the conversation away from scarcity and deficiency. In Part III of this book, we will look at the possibilities of bringing to light sources of wealth that are based on other forms of capital, such as social capital and natural capital. These are based more on Rhea's and Gaia's forms of wealth than those of Kronos. To get any further with this requires a more detailed study of the way we keep account of riches.

Chapter 8

Accounts and bookkeeping
What story does money tell?

Money flows through the markets according to the choices we continually make. Money's enigmatic routes can only be tracked afterwards, however, through the accounts. Accounts provide money with memory, and weave stories about the movements it has made. In them we can see how far there is conformity between the values we talk about and those we live by. Changes in bookkeeping practice will be imperative if other forms of capital and dimensions of value are to be included in the markets of the future.

The language of business

A manager for a major organisation was going to appoint a new auditor. He interviewed three people from three different firms of chartered accountants and asked them this question: "How much is two plus two?" The first answered "Four." The second answered "It is in the range three to five." The third asked "How much would you like it to be?" Guess who got the job?[1]

At the start of a course in bookkeeping, students are told that accounting is the language of business. Sums that are moved from debit to credit and vice versa tell the story of how money moves about, how physical items change owner, and about services that are carried out. Making a single bookkeeping entry thus constitutes something like a few characters in the sentences of the long story of what an organisation is engaged in, what it has accomplished in the year the accounts book covers. First in the books comes the summary, going under the heading Profit & Loss Account and Balance Sheet. Being able to read a profit & loss account and a balance sheet is all part of mastering the language of business.

However, experienced businesspeople and accountants find it easy to forget that this actually is a *language,* a way of talking. Many have not spent time reflecting on the way language and words actually function. It is easy to believe that bookkeeping is simply a matter of writing down what happened 'out there' in the market in the appropriate accounts, and that this is a passive registration of the external economic reality. This way of understanding language has a long tradition. This traditional perspective implies that a spoken word refers or points to something real out there in the world, somehow outside of language. Applying this method, the word 'table' represents the material table I am sitting at. Correspondingly, a sales entry in the accounts will be only a representation of a transaction that has already taken place in the market.

But today we know that language and the world are more intimately linked than that. There is an extensive philosophical tradition indicating that the language speaks us, just as much as we speak the language.[2] The way the language works is not, primarily, to reflect an objective world outside. No, the language *co-creates* the world. By speaking the language, we are also creating new understandings and new realities; we are linking ourselves to things and to one another.[3] New terms – such as 'cyber-space', 'website', 'share issue', 'stock option' or 'level of shareholders' equity' – put us in a position to participate and join in with co-creating the reality that we call the Internet, and the reality that we call finance. Language is not secondary in importance to these worlds – it produces them.

This also means that we do not talk about what we are seeing, but that *we talk about the things that the language allows us to say.* Until we have language for something, we are unable to understand it, and it does not then exist in our consciousness. Before Pasteur, for instance, we could not talk about bacteria. So they did not exist for us, and humans were thus oblivious to their existence. The reason for my mentioning this in a chapter about accounting is that – with bookkeeping as the language of economic life – it is only when something has been entered into the account books that it can be perceived and understood as reality in organisational and economic life. Anything that does not end up in the books and in the accounts becomes ephemeral to organisations and authorities. When the bottom line is marked with a double underline, anything not included in the accounts is of lesser importance. It has not been recorded, you will not find it in the documents presented to the board of directors, and the owners do not become aware of it.

When a regional health trust was to reduce the costs of patient transport, they put the taxi services out to tender to various taxi companies. A company from a nearby town won the bidding competition because their rates per kilometre were a slight fraction lower than the local taxi company. Viewed in economic terms these are useful decision-making processes: they empower the purchaser in relation to the bidders and increase the economic efficiency. The competition is tightened and costs go down. There is less waste of 'tax-payers' money'. The economic language emphasises that part of reality that comprises the number of patients that are entitled reimbursement for transport, the number of patient kilometres driven and the kilometre rate.

But the things that have not been entered into the books include items such as the social capital in the relationship between taxi driver and patient. The fact that the driver knows who lives where, that the patient knows and trusts the driver, that they have acquaintances in common and a pleasant conversation during the journey. When drivers come from the neighbouring town and do not know road markings and addresses, in particular in rural districts where the signage is not good, insecurity increases, as does the number of misunderstandings. This weakens established relationships for anxious patients who may already be halfway to isolation. No ledgers would make social facts like this clear. Accountants do not account for them, and managers therefore do not know how to talk about them. The shared language of established bookkeeping has no words for these areas. They will not appear in the basic decision-making data.

After the turn of the millennium, stringent economic principles were introduced in the operation of the health service in Norway. Personal and social conditions that used to be built in to the network (known as silent knowledge) no longer held the same weight. Costs were cut as if this was a production plant. People were reorganised and functions moved around to where economies of scale could be gained. This may have led to economic efficiencies, but has it also improved health or strengthened the social capital?

'What you measure is what you get!' is a slogan from organisational life. There are measurement systems other than conventional bookkeeping, such as a balanced scorecard, management by objectives, intellectual capital or environmental accounting. But financial accounts are primarily the ones being constructed, covering things that are actual and essential. If something has an effect on the top line or the bottom line, then it is counted. If it is not *counted* anywhere, it will not be found anywhere either. The reason for things being this way is not that business managers have personalities that are fixated on figures and obsessed with quarterly totals. The reason is that what we choose to measure silently determines what we talk about and how we talk about it. It is easier to talk in a persistent, structured way and to make decisions about those things for which there are clear key figures.

There is something remarkable about numbers. They seem to be so concrete, factual, indisputable. However, figures do not relate to an objective world out there. They are primarily a language. Key economic figures are an effective form of speech: counting things and entering them into the ledgers is known, linguistically, as 'speech acts'. Speech acts like 'Can I help you?' or 'I'll take this dress' are not 'just words', but are in fact joint actions. They contribute to how we relate to each other. Likewise, the figures are not 'just numbers' but they construct reality, and we therefore get what we measure. The figures obtain the power we give them, and they speak back to us using that power.

There is a fascinating double meaning to the word *accounting*. While the word *count* means to translate some series into a number, *to account for* means to explain or report on the background of something.[4] When we create an *account* for something, this implies telling the story of how something came about. Its meaning is also linked to the word *accountable* – being responsible. The specific extent of liabilities and assets are expressed in the balance sheet. The balance sheet thus – in principle – tells the status of how the company relates to the world, at any point in time. This, surprisingly, expresses the company's soul – because the soul exists primarily in the relationships, as discussed in Chapter 4.

However, for many people it is difficult to understand or get to grips with the company's economic soul just through the sums indicated for assets and liabilities in the balance sheet. To make the story more complete requires footnotes, addenda and explanation. All of this has to come together in a tale – a detailed account of – all the challenges, defeats and victories, trading results and changes. Previously things were like that; now they are like this. A good yearly report tells that story of what has been achieved eloquently.

The goat kid who could to count to ten

The other animals got uneasy when the little kid started counting them:
- "One for the calf, two for the cow and three for the bull," said the kid.
- "Oooh, now he's counted you too!" cried the calf.
- "I'll teach him," said the bull.
- "Come on, let's get him."

– Alf Prøysen

Alf Prøysen's goat kid suffers the consequences because of the power of definition that figures have.

Much of the problem we have with bookkeeping today is that, like many other systems created with the best of intentions, it starts to take on a life of its own. It grows big and strong and becomes a monster. It devours anything it can lay its big hands on and stuffs it in to its mechanical mouth. Out of its digestion comes long columns of figures, which are difficult to interpret and make meaning out of for both stakeholders and employees. Bookkeeping systems become a sort of Frankenstein – a human construction that turns against its creators. The output numbers gradually acquire an air of truth that seems difficult to deny – as inescapable as fate. The figures' trundling story drowns out the fact that this is something that we ourselves have constructed because someone once discovered that this was one way of doing it. After a while we stop asking why: this is the method that must be applied. And that's that. A standard was born, and we organise ourselves and comply with its requirements, regardless of what business we are in.

One institutional executive I know was suddenly required to do an tax audit one rainy autumn day. The organisation in question is one of Norway's leading institutions in the use of art and expression within psychotherapy. It trains psychotherapists and teachers of art, holds lectures and arranges workshops and seminars. However, it has to follow precisely the same accounting template as an industrial company or a hot-dog stall at the side of the road. When accounts are reviewed, it is totally irrelevant what your business is – the language of accounts has to be spoken correctly and literally. In this case, certain words on the invoice were wrong (for example, 'administration' or 'seminar' instead of 'teaching'); long meetings were held and there were discussions about value-added tax and surtax. All vouchers had to be studied again, the costs of bookkeeping services went sky-high, and there was hardly enough time for professional development, creative workshops or extra guidance for psychotherapists. The creative, innovatively entrepreneurial institution manager had to spend a lot of time struggling against this monster. Many long sessions later, the only thing to come out of all of this was that the tax authorities shelved the matter. The dark sides of bookkeeping systems are made very evident in cases such as this.

There is huge power in the way something is defined and how it is counted. But when society changes, terms and methods of counting also have to change. This makes the need for reforms in bookkeeping increasingly pressing if its procedures for accounting are to keep their relevance into the future of the twenty-first century.

The past of accounting, and the future as accounted for

Let us return to the medieval markets of 1305, which we visited in Chapter 6, and move along the stalls as we see before us the traders involved in intense trading, haggling and exchanging. At the end of the day, if we go back to the tables and thumb through the merchants' books, we would find a little of everything that would have given the auditors of today hiccups. Here there are no neat columns, just separate annotations. A merchant enters the following: "Owed ten gulder by a man since Whitsuntide. I forgot his name."[5] Calculations are made largely in Roman numerals, and sums are often wrong; long division is reckoned as something of a mystery, and the use of zero is not clearly understood. What they make and lose money on, and what products are more profitable than others, are about as clear as the fog on a rainy November morning.

The revolution within bookkeeping came along in 1494, and it had a power to gradually shape society that can hardly be overestimated. It was the Franciscan monk, Luca Pacioli, in the Italy of that time who published one of the best-sellers of the Middle Ages – a book about double-entry bookkeeping. It became available in French, English and Dutch during the course of only two generations. Since then, it has been added to with decrees, regulations, principles and laws in every country in the world. In Norway, it is the Private Limited Companies Act, the Accounting Act and the Tax Act that dictate how things are to be entered. Without this discipline, this technology, this language, the development of major organisations, companies and markets would not be possible. Neither would capitalism in its Western form.

The founding father of sociology, Max Weber, pointed out that both capitalism and capitalist companies existed in China, India, Babylon, Egypt and Europe before the modern era.[6] But the calculating *rational capitalism* that developed in the West was dependent on double-entry bookkeeping. A trial balance can be drawn up both at the beginning and at the end of a transaction. The opening balance is entered, then successively all transactions are inserted into the debit and credit sides. The totals on the left and right sides must always be equal, with a difference of zero. You can check for errors and draw up the trial balance at any time, so that you keep things under control. Once the closing balance is calculated, the size and basis of the surplus is determined precisely on the basis of the previous voucher entries.

The Romans, for instance, kept detailed lists of real estate and other possessions, but had no precise method of valuing capital and earnings. Only the later Western form of capitalism was built upon a rational system which included the opportunity to calculate profit for every deal. Perhaps rather paradoxically, it was the God-fearing Franciscan who provided the West with this worldly tool. However, he challenged everyone to start keeping books in a Christian manner: "The objective and purpose of every businessman is to create a legal, satisfactory surplus, to ensure that he is able to maintain himself. So, he ought to begin with God's name," was what he wrote in his bestseller. This was in an era when business life was still under the influence of the Church.[7]

Gradually, business life has torn itself away in order to rely upon guidance from its own books rather than on *the* Book. Obedience to the Bible has been replaced with obedience to the bookkeeping tradition and calculation of profits and earnings. A modern equivalent of sin is not having one's books in order, like in the accounting scandals of Enron and others. Therefore the infamous

Sarbanes-Oxley act was introduced in the US to require that senior executives take individual responsibility for the accuracy and completeness of corporate financial accounting.

What guides the most important decisions in the economic life of today? What decides whether an oilfield should be developed or if the natural world should remain undisturbed? What decides if property should be bought, houses demolished and new hotel complexes with spas set up on the sites? What decides if the interest rate is to be put up or down? The answer to all four questions is neither God's name, the Pope nor the Bible, but is given as the outcome of calculations based on figures from the ledgers.

Today, investment decisions are made on the basis of trust in concepts such as ROI, EBITDA and ROCE.[8] Different companies use slightly different definitions as a foundation, but the pieces of arithmetic and the manner in which they are set up determine which companies invest where, with what type of technology and with how much capital. Together these concepts make up a language that constructs the decision-makers' minds. Key indicators from the ledgers, such as annual turnover, operating profits and shareholders' equity, have had an elevated, almost sacred status. Managers can try to turn, stretch and embellish the figures so that the efforts appear as positive as possible. However, *which* figures are to be used is much harder to manipulate. The pieces of arithmetic are the determining factors. Figures with associated concepts have become the guiding stars of the modern era. These are the guiding stars that dynamic companies navigate by when they are going to build 1,500-ft-high buildings, send satellites up into orbit, construct gigantic oil installations on the seabed, or introduce new pharmaceuticals on to the world market. Investments are shifted systematically in the direction of those things that can be accounted for so that profits can be calculated.

This has had wide-ranging consequences for our society, and for the planet we all live on. What can be activated as assets? Buildings, cars and boats can be on the balance sheet. However, values such as the beauty of product design, investments in local communities, fairness in agreements with weaker partners, social reliability or taking care of biodiversity cannot easily be entered into the accounts and will not be included in the profit and loss account or balance sheet. Investment in new skills for employees manifest in the accounts as costs and not investments. Investment in the integrity of soil and ecosystems also registers as costs. Five hundred years of bookkeeping practice enters bricks, metal and machinery onto the assets side of the ledgers, while knowledge, fairness, beauty and consideration for the environment become costs that are not reflected in the summary of the assets that the organisation creates and possesses.

Here is an example: a company takes out a loan from the bank against the security of the building in which the company is based. However, the most important factor for value creation is often the skills of the employees, and not the building. Those competencies are what constitutes the most valuable feature of the company. How can a financial institution have realistic figures about a company's worth when its most important asset is not properly entered into the accounts, and even walks in and out of the doors each day? [9]

Since the 1990s, therefore, extensive efforts have been made to include the development of skills and knowledge in the accounts. This is what is known as intellectual capital. The object is to straighten out some systemic biases that have accompanied traditional bookkeeping since the Renaissance. So far, no common standard has been established, but quite a lot of annual reports include a genuine effort to balance the normal financial annual report with a presentation of an intellectual capital annual report. There are also attempts to enter other types of value into the accounts such as fairness (corporate social responsibility) and beauty (the value of a company's aesthetic capital, such as design and branding), as well as consideration for the environment (environmental accounting).

However, investors do not take these other figures as seriously as the things they see as the bottom-line realities – in other words, the financial accounts. So, – 500 years after Pacioli's work – it becomes increasingly clear that fundamental reforms in accounting practice are necessary, if the full story of modern organisations is to be taken into account. Perhaps a new Pacioli is needed, who can provide the twenty-first century with a sorely needed renaissance of business language. From the year 2100 and beyond, we will probably look back on the bookkeeping of today with the same large measure of amusement and wonder with which we today view the trading ledgers of the fourteenth century.

Even within the confines of traditional accounting, not all stories told are as serious and factual as they present themselves. Since the turn of the millennium, we have also seen modern financial accounts that have been guided mainly by fantasy and spin, as for instance the scandals with Enron, Worldcom and complex credit derivatives. That first scandal dealt the chartered accountancy giant, Arthur Andersen, a single knockout blow. The last toppled the entire world economy in 2008. These cases illustrate to what degree accounting constructs an economic story, rather than represents reality objectively.

We are not able to grasp or understand economic life without a language that does justice to the actual complexity of the world. When reality changes as a result of new technology, new cultural values and new natural circumstances, there also have to be changes in the language and the method in which we document our business.

To grasp what money actually does, it has to be held on to for a moment and entered into an accounts ledger. It must be remembered. The traces of money movements are memories of human interaction, even when the deal has been carried out digitally. Bookkeeping gives money memory, expands the moment's monetary events into a documented transaction in a specific situation of human relationships. A single transaction bears witness to the occasion when I was there, at that hour, in that store, bought an item there and it cost exactly £39.95.

As mentioned in Chapter 3, money, in addition to being a means of exchange, also consists of social relationships. This social dimension of money is not made explicit in today's accounting. Bookkeeping thus only *indirectly* documents relationships between people by focusing only on the amount traded. One idea for a change to the accounting system will be presented in Part III – it might perhaps be relevant in future to make selected social relationships apparent and to enter them into the books directly with a new type of money.

The account statement as life story

'All this is of no relevance to me, I am neither a manager nor an accountant,' you might complain. 'I am a creative person and can't cope with accounts. I make my decisions based on other considerations.' Does keeping accounts have any meaning other than for commercial life; for example, at individual level? Can anything as dry as keeping accounts have anything at all to do with our personal lives and the state of our souls?

In the golden age of psychotherapy (from around 1910 to 2000), sexuality, neuroses, dependency and family relationships were the principal topics of millions of therapy sessions. People worked on themselves by uncompromisingly telling their story to a therapist, who listened empathically. Their internal private life was laid bare, but money was excluded. The economic sphere was often limited, in the therapy sessions, to discreet envelopes, bills or deductibles. If we are to take seriously what we maintain in the Introduction – that in the twenty-first century people live primarily through the economy – we ought perhaps to start analysing our account statements instead of our childhoods!

Can I see this account statement of mine, this monthly report with two columns of figures and some totals at the bottom, as the story of my life? It perhaps looks unbearably dull, with all of its dates and long lists of transactions. It is not even real double-entry bookkeeping, since the transactions are not recorded in different accounts. Nevertheless, what story do the figures actually tell about my actions, my relationships with the Earth, the world and society? How do I express my deeper self through the flow of money?

Account statements give a summary of what has been happening in my life on Earth over a month: through deductions for car and house, I have nevertheless maintained part of my obligations to the monetary system. Money has also flowed in, thank goodness – this month, the transfer from my employer also came at the agreed time. This is the basic rhythm, the pulse in my economic bloodstream, my exchange with the world. In and out, expenditure and income, like the heartbeat and the breath themselves. The balance between right and left is not just an accounting arrangement. It has its parallel in the body's balancing of left and right, as well as between breathing in and out. This is something that all body-oriented therapists know, that without backbone and breath in balance we lose some vitality and grounding. We need a certain economic balance too, in the same way that we need to have our breath and body in balance.

'Last month you travelled to Copenhagen,' the account statement from the bank tells me. The journey was evident via a series of small testimonies down the page. It is down there in black and white about where I ate, how much I paid for meals and where I paid for overnight accommodation. I also bought books and gave flowers to some good friends – they were paid for at seven o'clock in the morning in the Flora shop on the corner. Other transactions are perhaps so private that they are not suitable for publication, but ought to remain hidden in the private ring binder on the shelf.

This is the detailed, concrete level. I can easily access memories to the various items, totals and names. But the account statement can tell even more, because it follows me over a period of time. If, for example, I take twelve subsequent account statements and read them like a chapter in the book of my life, I can start seeing patterns: They tell the story of how illness affects me (repeated treatments, large pharmacy fees), which major decisions I have taken, and which patterns repeat themselves in my life.

The two columns of the account statement modestly tell the story of the actual balance sheet within my life. The values that guide my actions are disclosed by the accounts. The columns show my priorities and the types of relationship I consider important.

The debit columns (in other words, 'account withdrawals') can be particularly merciless in their direct speech, because they do not listen to all of my fine words about ideal values but bear witness to the values that I *actually* base my actions on. Prioritisation between ethical products, organic goods, health foods, home, alcohol and fashionable clothes are made evident by the story the figures tell. A survey of eco-friendliness among consumers found that nearly a third said that they preferred to buy products from companies that exhibit responsibility for the environment or for social conditions. The same survey found that only three per cent actually shopped in the store on the basis of that same set of values.[10]

The key question is: in which direction do I direct the flow of money? This is a moral question – I am responsible for the values my use of money reflects, regardless of scale. This is exactly where soul and money meet: what images guide the flow of my funds? Which voices calls the loudest for my hard-earned cash, and to which do I listen? Which sirens sing so beautifully that I ought to be tied to the mast, like an Odysseus, not to be sucked dry of strength and liquidity? *We express who we are through how we let our money flow.* Account statements are therefore also testimonials about identity, understood as the relationships we have to the world. If I draw up a personal balance sheet, it provides me with a clearer picture of my economic Self. And it says something about my soul.

What can be read from this kind of economic balance sheet?

Some people find it hard hard to value themselves. A new sofa or the massage that does so much good is never to be seen on the account statement. My economic superego would cry out 'You cannot afford it!' Or, maybe it reminds me gently, 'Saving is more important than satisfaction.' And it can be difficult to treat yourself when there are so many other worthy people in need. However, using money to 'care for the soul' can be a good investment.[11] For other people the opposite prevails, as they invariably treat themselves with one thing or another – their credit cards run hot. Why not treat yourself to the goods now, and preferably pay later? In ways such as these your self speaks loud and clear through the statements of your account.

Things that are psychologically suppressed are nevertheless present on the account statement, but perhaps more has to be read between the lines. What and who is it that does not get economic attention from me? Or, perhaps it is certain individual relationships, grown-up children for instance, that drain me disproportionately in relation to what ought to be the case. It can be easy to be generous while suppressing important aims. Someone may always be owing me money, or we may have relationships that are not in balance. Our accounts are not balanced: we have some outstanding items with one another. Perhaps we start avoiding one another in daily life. In this way we see that feelings are awakened when we relate to our different accounts. There are complex images in the simple figures.

Financial phobia?

Double-entry bookkeeping provides the option of control and consciousness about the flows of money, on both company and private levels. But many people do not see the link between income and expenditure, and how the costs are distributed. Then a thorough economic clean-up might be required. There is a lot of surplus and unhealthy 'fat' around, both in bodies and budgets, and the potential for cost-cutting can be huge. Often this means reorganising and processing information that already exists in the financial accounts and presenting this in new ways. We obtain a new or revised language that helps us remove leaks, such that money flows where it is needed most and vitalises the things that are most important.

Many people resist taking control of their own cashflows. We prefer to continue to consume. We continue to borrow and use our credit cards way over the limit of what we can stand. We 'mislay' receipts. We cannot afford charity. We rarely sit down and count our own consumption. We have a bad conscience about something we bought last week. We do not open envelopes that contain bills, as we are nervous about seeing the amount. We put off paying. Account statements are left lying at the bottom of a thick bundle of papers. And we do not worry about whether our cashflow is going to products and services that are harmful to the environment or society.[12]

Some economic psychologists call this 'financial phobia', and they believe that one in five people today shows signs of this.[13] With Carl Jung, the psychiatrist, we could call this the 'economic shadow'; the part of our economic life that we cannot bring ourselves to shed light on or look straight in the eye. Money is a taboo. Secrets abound wherever money gains the upper hand in people's lives.

Not much is written in economics textbooks or the how-to-get-rich-and-happy-quickly books about what happens to people who end up in financial distress. When someone is under pressure regarding liquidity and credit, powerful emotions can be stirred up. We might start to panic, or end up in a state of deep anxiety and a quagmire of sinking emotions when we have lost our way through the financial labyrinth. Everyone who has been through a financial crisis at work or in his or her private life knows that this can be overwhelming. The British economist and psychologist William Bloom calls this the black hole of monetary anxiety.[14] Those of us who have been there know why that term is so apt.

The first and most important step is to become aware. Know how money flows: look, observe, count, add. Money in and money out. It is the ancient art of being able to keep note of something, to retain something in memory. It does not necessarily mean immediately changing course by making a huge effort to get one's act together. Rather, 'Thanks, I am just looking,' as we say in shops. We must simply dare to look closely without judgement. It starts with a consciousness of habits – overcoming an often mundane automatic action that turns the spending of money into an automatic process. If the spending of money is automated, who then does the power lie with? With the money or us?

In an interview, the founder of a successful business tells of how she made it a ritual every evening to check her company account, so that she always knew what effect the day's trading had had on the bank balance. This helped her to keep solvent even through the difficult start-up years. Her consciousness of the cash flow was fresh and new each morning.

When we know where the money is going, the next question comes along by itself: is the flow moving in the direction of the values I believe in? Is the money being put to good use? Or does it tell a story about deep values on short rations? Maybe I've got some personal black holes – economic parallels to the galactic ones – that are sucking in most of the my cash flow. I believe most of us suspect where these drains on resources are, but how much vital energy they actually drain away is something that I for one refused to acknowledge for a long period. However, when I first start to ask these questions, I get back on the path of life again: How do I align my monetary values with the deeper values of my life? Or will the money continue to be the enemy of the soul, sending me on eternal detours – such as when I believe I will have to wait ten to twelve years until those student loans and mortgages are paid off, before I can allow the use of money to follow my heart.

In the twenty-first century psychotherapy, for the economically neurotic among us, must involve going through the totals to see what they are doing to us. We thus bring some light to unconscious parts of our lives, so that changes can start taking place. Then we can enter into an active psychological relationship with that most dynamic, potent and crucial factor in our times: money. In the same way as we might treat fear of flying, of large gatherings of people or of spiders, we must first become acquainted with the beast. Only then can change happen.[15]

It is remarkable, perhaps even surprising at first glance, but bookkeeping can help us reconnect our daily lives with the deeper issues: What do I want out of life? What is the purpose of my life? And what state is it in *right now*? Account statements actually tell an essential story about the balance of the soul, but we must acquaint ourselves with them before we are able to hear the story they tell.

Solvency and solidity – the warm, glowing core

If we do not have our personal economies in order, nor any reserves, the feeling of security in our lives easily evaporates. We have to live with uncertainty, and sometimes from hand to mouth, perhaps in fear of receiving a sudden extra bill. But, as we have seen, it is not sufficient with financial wealth alone. The feeling of security does not automatically follow from having large reserves to rely on. Many wealthy people feel insecure regardless of how solvent they are on paper. Others have very small means but still feel very secure of life's providence. The actual feeling of security needs to be based on something else – and more – than the sums in the accounts. If the feeling of security lives a life of its own, independent of the amounts of money, where does it come from? What is the source of feelings of security and serenity in the psyche?

Similarly, at the corporate level, banks and investors go through profit and loss accounts and balance sheets very carefully to see what the situation is regarding security. Is this company solvent? Economic solvency means that the company has to have sufficient book values to be able to pay creditors and owners what they have to be paid in future. But what makes people feel secure about the company, apart from what is stated on the balance sheet? To find that, a study must be made of the core of the company that provides the basis for its sustained existence.

Perhaps the Greeks' goddess of security and reliability can teach us something about internal peace and confidence. Hestia was the goddess of the hearth, of warmth and embers, the very centre of the house. Hestia was the firstborn daughter of Chronos and Rhea, whom we met earlier in the chapter about wealth.

There are few images and sculptures of Hestia, but when she is portrayed she is usually in pure, long clothing and in a straight-backed, discreet posture. Sitting or standing, she never shows any form of agitation, but radiates calmness and dignity.[16] If the pursued sought refuge in Hestia's fire, they could not be captured as long as they stayed there. In Rome (where they called her Vesta) a person condemned to death could even be released if he met a vestal virgin, as Vesta's priestesses were called, on the way to the place of execution.[17] For a long time, the Greek city states had a city flame consecrated to Hestia at their centre, with people commonly congregating around it.[18] Hestia did not travel around like the other gods. So people were able to spend time with her in peace and quiet. The English classicist Robert Graves describes her as the mildest, most honest and kind of all of the Olympic gods.[19] She never took part in the bickering and wars of the other gods. Dependably, she stuck to her post on Mount Olympus. In Latin, the word *focus* means a hearth or central point. Similarly, Hestia was the warm, safe centre that people could gather around. In economic life, people talk about focusing organisational activities, defining core skills and cultivating core business. This way of thinking reflects the Hestia tendency within ourselves: the desire to withdraw to the core and tend the fire there.

When we find safety within ourselves, alone or in relation to others, a feeling arrives which *is* Hestia. She *is* the hearth and feeling of security, the solid being right to the core, unadorned substance, with pure, sober congregation around warmth, the thing that supports and maintains core values. Those who believe in a company have 'seen' that there is a crackling fire at its core.

Unadorned admissions from companies on the analysis couch

However, it is rare to find a pure and sober representation of the company core. Accounts are embellished and adorned in order to mislead the outside world, says economics journalist Finn Øystein Bergh.[20] And the make-up box is deep indeed, with a wide selection of lipstick, mascara and powder. In general, accounts that show weak profit and loss accounts and/or weak balance sheets will hide much worse circumstances. They have been made up for the media lights. That is not difficult to understand: wanting to be seen as better than you are is a deeply human characteristic. On the other hand, good accounts are probably even better than they appear. There is a desire to camouflage the surplus for various reasons, not least to reduce the amount of tax due.

On this basis, financial analysis is similar to psychoanalysis: the 'hermeneutics of suspicion' are needed when we are going to read the stories provided by the accounts. Psychoanalysis tries to remove pretence or distortion that people carry out to trick themselves and others into believing they are something other than they are. The goal of the analysis is to get to the core of self-respect and vitality. Perhaps the flame has to be lit afresh inside, with painstaking rituals, if it is to reignite the hearth.

Correspondingly, balance sheets must be read with a large pinch of salt. Financial analyses try to remove any applied mascara and several layers of face paint to get to the core of production and value creation, to clarify where the flame is burning and where values are created or wasted. Perhaps the company will have to be restructured and renewed to get the flame going again, with a new focus on core competencies and core processes. This is what accounting and company analysis is all about, viewed from a mythical perspective.

Some conclusions about accounts and bookkeeping

Accounts and bookkeeping are more fundamental to who we are and the way we act than many people realise. They are the very foundation of the economy. They provide both the primary data and the overview and thus become both the ground and the horizon for economic decisions.

It is therefore far from insignificant what kind of names we give to the figures that track the flow of money and goods in the markets. Language is power – that is acknowledged by philosophers, sociologists, psychologists, feminists and people carrying out research into power in the last half of the twentieth century. If you win the battle for terminology, you can win the battle for power. The economic power lies in defining the accounts. This is probably the reason for the miserably slow pace of progress in the work to reform bookkeeping practices. They give names to the targets we aim at (top line or bottom line growth), and give us figures to choose from (ROI, P/E, operating profits, capital expenditure, etc.) that tell us something about how we get there.[21]

Figures and targets become more real the more we use them. Decision-makers from all professions can use figures from business economics, such as turnover and quarterly results; and macro-economic indicators, such as GNP, inflation and interest rates; as a form of 'newspeak' for guiding others into the future. Most people do not understand the possibilities of – and the magic behind – organisational or national bookkeeping. By selecting certain figures and excluding others, as, for example, the export surplus including oil, GNP, growth in productivity per hour, wage growth index in relation to competitive countries, poverty quartile, etc., those who master the language can send out exactly the message they want.

- $ -

Marx wanted to have armed insurrection, the proletariat's revolution. Personally, I believe we can make more progress by having a revolution in accounting and auditing practices. It is these that run the machinery inside the economic jugger-naut. If we change the information at the core of the system, completely differ-ent decisions will be made, and completely different effects will follow. Holistic decision-making requires good figures for social and environmental effects – in addition to good financial figures. Making changes to key economic and social indicators can assist us in seeing the world with different eyes, providing fertile soils for new thoughts and new creativity. This is the basic idea for profound change that will be explored in Part III, Chapter 12.

To many people, accounting and bookkeeping epitomises everything that is tedious, dull, monotonous and uninspiring. But, paradoxically, this may be where the greatest potential for change lies. If the 'revolution' ever comes, it probably starts with the – bookkeeping.

Accountants of the world, unite!

Chapter 9

Money as credit

Faust's dark secret

Goethe's principal figure, Faust, entered into a pact with the Devil: in return for knowledge of the black arts and becoming thoroughly familiar with the magic of alchemy, the Devil would be able to come and take Faust's soul in twenty years' time. This wish was fulfilled, and Faust then went out and became successively a businessman and then a pillar of society. Faust's pact is precisely what you and I do when we flourish our credit cards or take out a bank loan. This chapter discloses the innermost 'secret' of the money markets – how money is made – and highlights some disadvantages of this pact.

What is credit?

The origin of a word often gives a pointer towards the content and wealth of meaning that has been lost over time. Once it becomes automatic in usage, a word is exposed to wear and tear. It loses contact with those images and feelings with which it had been charged when it was coined. Over the years, the word also acquires new meanings. This is the case with the word 'credit'. Where does this come from?

Credit entered the English language in the mid-sixteenth century – in other words in the late Renaissance period – and probably in conjunction with the emergence of bookkeeping. The word is rooted in the Latin word *credere,* to have belief in; confidence in. Originally it was a matter of something being trust-worthy and present for the *senses.*[1] The story about the boy who cries 'Wolf, wolf' until eventually no one bothers to come and help him is the story of someone who loses his social credit. When in past times you were able to make purchases on credit it was because the local merchant knew your face and your family and had confidence that you would pay him back. Today, losing your financial credit is perhaps even worse than losing your social credit.

Credit is thus an expression of confidence or trustworthiness. It is worth noting that the word was originally linked to tangible presence. Something that is in credit is in its place, available, permanent and trustworthy. It is concrete, and not a bluff. This has consequences for the way we should understand debit, the opposite of credit. Debit is a more abstract concept, and consists of invisible obligations and ties. The Latin word *debere* thus also means to owe something, and it must be possible to document this in order for it to be valid, such as in a promissory note.

The principle of credit is not new. It is probably one of humanity's most important inventions, one of the most potent social technologies along with writing, trade and money. It seems that some of the first writings we know about, the stone tablets from Babylon, are mostly about credit relations. This man owes six barrels of wheat, another owes two oxen. Nevertheless, European countries needed the whole of the seventeenth, eighteenth and nineteenth centuries for debate, experiments and social upheavals before money in the form of credit found its current form. There are still relatively few people who really understand this almost magical technology on which we base our lives. In about 1930, John M. Keynes is said to have stated that he knew only four or five people who really understood what money and credit are. All the same, it is hardly possible to imagine modern life without credit. It is something close to all of us. As with electricity, computer software or video players, a lack of understanding about the inner workings of technology is no obstacle to using it. Still, the lack of understanding leaves us even more vulnerable when this technology suddenly stops working, as in a credit crisis and economic depression.

The long road from gold to bank money

To understand money as credit, gold offers a good starting point. For a long time, money was the same as a certain amount of gold or silver. It was linked to the weight of the metal, which was something solid that the senses could perceive. You could touch it and feel the weight of the money in your hand. You could melt it down and still hold the equivalent value in your hand. Money had substance, could be weighed – and there was a limited quantity of it. Gold kept its value because it was universally attractive and at the same time scarce. Only a limited amount of it has ever been found throughout history.

But limitation of available gold inhibited economic activity. Trade was sluggish because of the lack of liquidity. The flow of money stopped when it ended up in the bottom of wealthy people's money chests. Most people had to resort to bartering to generate any wealth-creating turnover. However, bartering is much

more laborious than using money. Gradually, kings, banks and the king's treas-
urers tried to mix gold with other metals to get a greater number of coins out of
the same gold – not particularly confidence-inspiring.

Goldsmithing was not just a profession in the Middle Ages. It also involved
having a solid vault in which people could store their precious metals. When
they delivered their gold to the goldsmith, people were given a slip of paper on
which was written the amount they had deposited with him. This slip of paper
began gradually to function like a bond. Instead of running to the goldsmith's
house and withdrawing the gold to give it to someone else, gradually the slip of
paper itself became used as payment. The new owner could go and fetch the
gold, or sell the paper security to someone else.

The goldsmiths discovered gradually that their vaults were never totally emptied of gold. The majority of it remained in the vault because it was easier to pay
with the notes. Even if someone did take out his or her gold, there were always others who deposited some and left it there. A golden light lit up for the goldsmiths:
'I can issue paper securities for more gold than I have received! And the paper is
still as good as gold!' It was a reliable security, as long as their secret was not
revealed. Credit was thereby (re)invented, and the prototype of the banking business was created. If someone was uncertain about the validity of the paper, they
could just go to the goldsmith and he would show them that the gold was being
safely stored. The next day the goldsmith might point to the same gold and convince the next customer that the gold was his too. The reserves in the vault could
be noted down several times on paper; no one would notice the difference – as
long as not all of the customers wanted to have their gold back at the same time.

The origin of the word *bank* comes from the goldsmith's business *bench*
[Middle English: banke].[2] And the word *bankrupt* comes from those cases in
which everyone actually did want to have their gold back at the same time. When
the vault was empty, and there were still furious customers standing in the
queue, they broke the goldsmith's bench to show that this was fraud and deception. This story does not say much about how things went for the goldsmith
himself, but he – and his family – was probably crushed and disgraced for life, if
he survived the mob.

The receipts, or 'gold certificates', were gradually linked to the understanding
that coins could be stamped with the same amount, even if they just contained
half as much gold. The idea that money was something different and more than
just precious metal was then staring people in the face: money is the *belief* in
notes and coins, not the actual notes and coins themselves.

During that period several of the European kings were constantly at war.
They needed to be able to finance their armies, and this was another crucial
impetus for the emergence of money as credit. Many courts in the sixteenth and

seventeenth centuries employed alchemists who attempted to create gold out of lead and other less precious metals for their king. The Midas dream was strong – taken literally here as the art of producing physical gold.

For a long time, these court alchemists had very well-paid posts and fine laboratories complete with steaming cauldrons. However, this type of alchemy was widespread only until the first finance and banking people understood that no one really *needed* to make gold. It is enough for people to have a degree of faith and actually *believe* that there is gold in the vault. And why be content with the gold in the vault? Why not give promises about the gold lying in veins deep in the mountain rock, which will be dug out at some time in future years? Is it really of any importance whether it is lying in a vault or inside the rock? And why not equally well use the entire mountain, or the country itself with forests and land and rivers and game, as a guarantee for the figure that exists on the paper money? A new type of alchemy emerged in individual courts. The old alchemy was hard work. Why get caught up with physical gold, when the *belief* in gold is just as good? The new 'credit' alchemists were extremely successful.

Among the most famous and colourful figures in the history of money was the Scotsman John Law. He had experimented with the idea of a national bank in Scotland. In a essay in 1705 he wrote: "By this credit Money the People may be employed, the Country improved, Manufacture advanced, Trade be carried on, and Wealth and Power attained." His ideas didn't meet with much enthusiasm in his own country. But he saw a new opportunity when he came to Paris in 1715 and met advisors to King Louis XV, who was almost bankrupt at the time. Law convinced the king that if he was allowed to establish a national bank under the king's protection, he could issue notes with State security and buy up the State's debt. Paper replaced gold. With that, the old alchemists became unemployed at court.[3]

Armed with this insight into the magic of credit – and a large helping of self-confidence – Law's bank the Banque Générale became a huge successs during the years 1716 to 1720. The new notes gave a strong boost to production and trade. Both the bank and the nation, as well as the speculators, prospered. The sky seemed to be the limit. Law's success, however, was also his downfall. He was too enthusiastic, and because of over-issue of notes the system collapsed in a terrible bust in May 1720. John Law had to flee from France and died in poverty.[4]

Alchemy has been called 'the black art', and most famous of all among the alchemists is the figure that Goethe had playing the principal role in his masterpiece, *Faust*. John Law's progress and success in Paris in 1716 was a clear source of inspiration for the second part of the drama.

In the first part, Faust enters into a pact with the devil figure Mephistopheles. The pact states that Mephistopheles should do everything that Faust asks of him for twenty years. Once this period is over, Mephistopheles would obtain Faust's soul in return. One of Faust's greatest desires is to learn the magic black art thoroughly. With that, he mortgages his soul for the ability to be able to produce money and for the power money brings. In one central scene, Mephistopheles explains to the king how Faust has mastered the secret of credit. With it Faust is able to convert all assets in the country into paper money, thereby making it possible for the king to pay his way out of all debt. The only thing he needs to do is to put himself and his crown forward as a guarantee for the value of the paper money. He does that with his signature and his official seal.

The king allows himself to be convinced and signs away the notes willingly. And – hey presto! – paper based on a form of credit becomes money proper, which spreads throughout the land. There it lubricates all trade, something that increases both demand and supply, and thus also wealth creation. The assets of the land have become liquid funds. Gold does not need to be extracted from the mines. Now gold, silver and other assets can circulate in the form of paper, moving from one hand to the other at markets and taverns throughout the country.

Natural resources such as timber, fish and grain no longer need first to be produced, transported and sold to customers. Now we can financially issue papers based on a *future harvesting* of the assets. The king or the State puts up land and the reputation of the king's office as a guarantee of the notes' value. Natural resources become just as good as gold – even more so, for they become paper which is much more easily handled than gold. Finally, the resources become just figures and, as we know, figures in a digital age fly from one end of the world to another in a fraction of a second. Now all the world's assets have become liquid funds. And the process has put us in a situation to liquidate the world in a darker meaning of that term: eliminate, wind up, do away with.

A modern example comes from the Philippines: some businesspeople, having the right political connections, obtained exclusive rights to the mahogany trees in the country's rainforests. The licence gave entitlement to cut down trees for the production of expensive desks, tables and chairs that could be sold on global luxury markets. But why struggle with all of that logistics and manual production yourself when you can set up companies that own these rights, and 'float' them – in other words, introduce them on to the Bangkok Stock Exchange? Analysts in financial centres such as the City of London and Wall Street in New York did calculations that concluded that these companies were now sitting on such valuable licences that they were clearly underpriced. A golden investment opportunity! Investors and shareholders could therefore buy shares in the company, to capture the profits that the rights would later provide. The assets constituted by the trees thereby end up with investors in London and New York, instead of the population of the Philippines, *even before the trees have been cut down.* And once investors have gone in with money, you can be certain that they will do all they can to realise the anticipated yield regardless of any 'nonsense' such as the inherent value of the trees, the rights of the local population, or the forest as a habitat for rare species.[5] The mahogany has been purchased by investors, and they have a claim on it!

The only thing needed immediately to extract value out of rainforests, goldmines and oilfields is that someone *believes* that certain papers containing numbers – notes, shares, bills of exchange, share options, bonds – will have a value in the future. We saw that *credere* meant trustworthiness and confidence; that is to say, confidence that the papers really are equivalent to – and in many people's eyes actually *are* – material assets. Modern money therefore means a type of transference of the more fundamental assets of land, capital, work and new technologies.

Under the gold standard, every pound, dollar and other currency type was worth a certain weight of gold. The gold standard crawled its way up through the centuries, at best contributing to controlling the growth of credit and avoiding escalating waves of inflation. However, in 1971, partly as a result of the extremely expensive Vietnam War and speculation against the US dollar, President Nixon dealt the final death-blow to the system where money represents a specific physical value. The Americans renounced the option of being able to exchange dollars for pure gold.[6] Money was no longer a representative of some real commodity value. Since then, money has been backed only by legal and credit systems. It is called 'fiat money', i.e. money made by decree. Very few people then understood the long-term effect of a decision like this.

Since then, money and currency rates have been in free flow, with only central banks attempting to regulate them. This reconfirms that money is now valued at what people *believe* it is worth. In the final analysis, money is a construct that lives off belief and trust. It relies on a conviction about the reality of our images and expectations. In this way, we get one of the fundamental outcomes of international finance: if the general trust in a currency is weakened, people will quickly move into other investments. The belief becomes self-fulfilling. The entire economic structure maintained by this currency can be undermined and, at worst, collapse.[7]

- € -

The modern economic world can seem overwhelming in its wealth, manifested in the shape of high-rise buildings, wide roads, gigantic shopping centres, marbled bank façades and shiny jumbo jets. It appears so fundamentally solid, so unbreakably real and utterly robust. Psychical images, beliefs and confidence correspondingly appear helplessly soft and ephemeral. It brings to mind the suspicion that maybe symbols of money such as buildings and financial institutions present themselves as something hard, precisely to hide the fact that money is lighter than air. It is not even as substantial as the thin paper notes we may still have between our hands. In the twenty-first century, money has become invisible bits on magnetic surfaces, cursory traces on a hard disk, and mainly a purely psychological expectation among citizens. This is an precarious expectation that certain figures on certain magnetic fields on certain hard disks kept hidden at an unknown location controlled by the banks have equivalent value in the retail store. And that these figures will magically provide us bread, water, shelter and clothing and everything we might otherwise wish for in the future.

This is, as we'll soon see, all built on the idea of credit – an invention that has changed all civilisations and the fate of the Earth itself. Modern capitalism would be impossible without the idea of credit.[8] Nevertheless, it is fully possible to imagine monetary systems that do not have credit and debt as a foundation. If we become aware of how we have come to build a monetary system based on credit, it becomes easier to imagine monetary systems based on other ideas. In Part III we shall use this insight to sketch a few alternatives.

Money as circulation

Water and blood often crop up as images for money. Otherwise dry economics textbooks use metaphors such as the circulation of the blood when they want to describe money.[9] Why are these images chosen? Just as the blood has to flow to all cells in the body, and flow evenly between skin and heart, cells and lungs, money has to be in movement in order to function in the optimum way. The blood brings with it oxygen from the lungs and nutrients from the walls of the intestines, taking it to the body's tissues and nerves, joints and organs, in order then to bring other substances back to the starting point.

If the blood stops flowing and starts to coagulate, the entire body becomes sick – equivalent to when water is blocked in a depression or a backwater. It comes to a standstill and gradually becomes foul, depleted of oxygen and toxic. Collecting and withholding large amounts of money can have the same fouling, toxic effect as coagulating blood or stagnant water. The nature of money is to be in motion. When it is stuffed into the mattress, gathered into piles or guarded in Uncle Scrooge's money bin, it loses its real nature as money. Most people with more money than they can manage or want to use therefore put it away in the form of investments. In that way, the money remains in movement.

The velocity of money is central to monetary policy. This figure expresses how many times during the course of the year the average pound is used to pay for goods or services. The more times a pound moves from one hand or account to another, the higher the velocity. At low rates, as was the case in the 1930s during the Great Depression and in the US's recession after 1980,[10] the economy becomes stagnant and depleted of oxygen. Those who had money wanted to keep it in their purses and accounts. Both bodies and economies depend on a free-flowing circulation in order to stay healthy.

In the Middle Ages it was a widespread metaphor to compare the whole of society to a body. If we view money as its blood supply, it's easy to see that today some body parts get only a tiny part of the total blood supply, whereas others get a disproportionately large amount. The bloodstream is far from even: some toes and fingers go blue with the cold, while there is coagulation both in the shoulders and the knees. In other locations it rushes around increasingly quickly. If we had been doctors and modern society our patient, this uneven blood supply would have made us seriously concerned about the patient's health. However, this type of elaboration on the blood metaphor is unfortunately not seen in economics textbooks, even if economic theory is genuinely concerned with equity and regional development.

Every pound we have in income is there because someone else has spent it. They have paid for your services; handed over their money in exchange for your time and your attention. And you will send the money further on to someone who has what you might want. It is this flow of money from one cell to another, from hand to hand, from account to account, that is constantly revitalising our economy. Your consumption, your needs and desires, become my livelihood. Your livelihood becomes my consumption. The money unites us in the same flow.

The English seventeenth century philosopher Francis Bacon thought of money as muck. Not because he despised money and thought it was something filthy, but rather because it needs to be spread about like muck for us to have the benefit of it. If there is too much muck in the same place, it stinks. Good economic policy is therefore about ensuring that the money circulates and is spread widely. Then new nourishment is supplied to the economy's green meadows, and new value creation becomes possible.

A simple method

Now we are beginning to get a handle on the magic of money, on finance as alchemy: imagine a triangle containing land and natural resources in one corner, public authorities with power to act as guarantor in the next one, and the willingness of citizens to believe in paper figures in the third one. Money as immaterial credit arises from this type of magic triangle. Paper notes can be printed and as soon as they start their critical circulation in society they increase economic activity and wealth through the mutual trade. The making of modern gold became as easy as child's play: it was just a matter of printing numbers on paper and producing them in suitably large quantities. And, no less magically, this increased supply of money stimulated greater economic activity and wealth creation in society.[11]

Note that when money is understood as credit, as something created by governmental decree and which is widely believed in, then money becomes closely related to the soul. The soul's imagination is an actual *prerequisite* for the belief in money. As previously mentioned, credit involves relying on the senses. We have to be able to imagine the values in a sensuous way. Paper money would not have been possible if the soul wasn't already predisposed to become fascinated by it. Mephistopheles knew this – it was he that taught Faust and the king. He also knew that once the soul was stuck on the power of money (like a fly on flypaper), victory was certain: he wanted finally to get Faust's soul and to win the wager.

- £ -

But the history of money is not at an end here. Gradually, an even more canny way to create money emerged, independent of natural resources and governmental guarantees – private bank credit. Today, it is not only government and central banks that create money; it is mainly privately owned banks. Since the nineteenth century the banks have been entitled to create money in the form of loans to citizens. How this is carried out is the topic of the next section.

Summing up, we have so far seen how money has developed from 1) commodities such as cattle, knives, kettles and spices, to 2) metals and coins, more or less regardless of their weight, and to 3) paper money guaranteed by national institutions of power. Now we will look at the fourth step, how money becomes figures in bank accounts. This fourth step is really the most radical shift. The basic entitlement to make money by issuing credit has moved from natural assets via national authorities and now to independent economic credit institutions.

The process by which banks create money is so simple that the mind is repelled, writes the economist John Kenneth Galbraith in his 1975 book *Money*. Where something so important is involved, a deeper mystery seems only decent. In the 1960s, Mr George Ball, an eminently successful lawyer, politician and diplomat, left public office to become a partner of the great Wall Street house of Lehman Brothers. "Why", he was heard to ask a little later, "didn't someone tell me about banking before?"

And the banks have not been lazy, particularly in the last forty years. They have happily taken on the job of creating and issuing money in a big way.[12] It is so easy: the bank official signs an agreement with a customer and, hey presto, new money has come into existence and can move around in the outside world. Today, the proportion of money issued by authorities is only a few per cent – and shrinking – in relation to the volume of money that originates in credit from the banks.

Money, more than anything, has become a belief that the customer will be able to repay the bank at some time in the future. This belief – to differentiate it from pure fantasy – is linked to a paper on which there are some figures, something about repayment and security, and some strokes of the pen in the form of signatures at the bottom. The money has been created in this way and now emerges from this social contract, formalised in loan documents. Essentially, it says only I owe you X pounds – or IOU for short. This was the scheme that was operational in the Western world's housing boom in the first decade of the twenty-first century. The infamous subprime lending schemes in the US, where anybody could get a loan to buy a house at high prices, was a means by which some banks could make huge volumes of IOU money.

Thus, the new alchemy introduced by John Law and Faust continues to work its black magic in new ways. Gold, land and natural resources are no longer necessary, they have simply become background security for money. Even national governments are no longer necessary to guarantee its value,[13] and we are left with an agreement between two parties to believe in repayment to be made in the future. Credit thus makes money into a legitimate child of the soul. Money does not exist outside psychic reality. Rather, money is born in the soul's imagination when a desire to acquire something is mixed with a mutual belief in the future resulting in an IOU arrangement. Let's take a closer look at the inner workings of this alchemy.

Modern alchemists

One day you wake up and the dream has come true: your lottery ticket has come good. You've won £10,000. The prize is paid to you in real, Bank of England notes. You now stand holding twenty £50 notes in your hand. Wow. Spend them all at once? On champagne! Stuff them in the mattress? Put them in the bank? You regain control over your impulses and choose the sensible option. Not long after, the money is lying on the counter in the bank. The bank official and you sign a slip of paper confirming that £10,000 has been deposited in your account. The bank promises to take good care of it. In return you will receive a few hundred pounds a year because you let the bank take care of them for you.

Next day, someone else comes into the bank. She sits down with the bank official and requests a loan of £9,000. The two draw up an agreement, in which she undertakes to pay back the money with interest at some time in the future. But she wants to have the money in notes – now! OK, says the official, and takes out £9,000 from the notes you deposited yesterday. The bank retains a tenth as a reserve, because that is what has been promised to the central bank when they make loans. She leaves the bank building and spends the money on a horse, a holiday or whatever it might be. The lottery money you won yesterday is circulated back into society again.

However, you have no idea your money has secretly left the vault! You will not get a letter telling you that £9,000 of your own funds are now unavailable, given away to someone else, and that you cannot use them until they are given back to the bank. No, you can still use as much as you want of the £10,000 by means of your bank card, cheque book, Internet banking or similar technology. You can buy goods or you can withdraw money in cash. What does this mean? It means that two people can use exactly the same money at the same time in sums that in total constitute approximately £19,000! And what has the bank done? What black art, what secret lies behind this? If I had made some copies of the £50 notes on a high-quality colour photocopier before I handed them to the bank and had distributed just a few score of them round about, I would soon have ended up behind bars. But the banks do this with impunity and with the blessing of the State.[14]

It does not stop here: the farmer who sold the woman the horse, or the travel agency that sold her the holiday, also deposit the money they have taken to the bank at the end of the day. The bank does not know where that money comes from, it is just happy to receive £9,000 of 'fresh' currency. Next day, your neighbour comes into the bank. He wants to borrow £8,100 for a new car. Well, yes, says the bank and lends exactly the same money that they took in yesterday. For a second time! Now nine-tenths of the £9,000, that is £8,100, again is used as new fresh money. Your neighbour signs an agreement with the bank in which he promises to pay the money back at some time in the future.

Three people are now using the same money at the same time, without knowing one another. They may even buy and sell to one another. There is a lot we simply don't know about how money comes into existence, where it goes, and who is using it. Only access to everyone's bookkeeping can give us any knowledge about what is happening. And that, in practice, is something no one has.

Nevertheless, what we are now seeing is that the banking system can continue recirculating the easily flowing money again and again, if people bring the money back and do not stuff it under their mattresses or send it abroad. Gradually, as the banks over and over again issue in the form of loans up to nine-tenths of the sums they have taken in – and the majority of which they have created themselves – the money supply can be blown up into an hugely inflated balloon of agreements. The sum can be up to ten times the size of the original amount (assuming that the average reserve requirement for the banks is one tenth).[15] My £10,000 of happy new lottery money numerically turns into up to £100,000 in the banking system books. And 90,000 of that provides income to the banking system in the form of interest, at the same time as the bank pays you interest of only ten thousand. Fresh deposits makes it possible for them to hugely expand their business. It should be no surprise then, why the banks are eager to get hold of your savings. And every pound of the £100,000 has equally strong purchasing power on the market. For everyone buying and selling, such new money is just as solid and real as the original tenth in notes.

Economists call this system the 'endogenous money supply' – that is, money generated from within the system itself. The money multiplier (see Figure below) shows how large an increase we obtain in the volume of bank-money when the basic money supply increases by a set amount.

"But I thought that the banks could only lend out what they had received, and that the money they earned was the difference between interest on the deposits and the interest on loans!" you might interject. It is an idea that inspires confidence, and that might be what the bank system most wants us to have. The

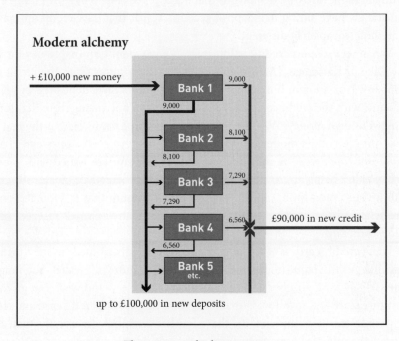

The money multiplier in action

question is whether we fully accept that the banks not only lend out your money again, but that they have created several times as much in the form of bank credit – in other words as new loans to customers. This is ghost money and *doppelgänger* money. It resides in a psychic and social reality – arising in an invisible space *between* the recipient of the loan and the bank.

The tracks from the multiplication of the money can be found in the form of promises to repay in the future, distributing it around in different banks, noted down on paper and filed in ring binders and computer indexes. But there is next to no cash involved anymore. So it should be no surprise that the bank vaults are usually quite empty of physical money and valuables. The banks never store the money given to them. Anyone who has lived through runs on banks or banks not having public guarantees and going bankrupt has felt this emptiness physically. In Scandinavia, there has not been a run on a bank for more than 60 years, and until the financial crisis of 2008 most people had forgotten even the possibility of that happening. This is also due to the fact that the State is the guarantor of last resort for small savers.

The credit card as bank-note printing press

Ordinary bank cards are debit cards that make it possible to pay with money that you already have sitting in a deposit account. Cards that have credit options are something completely different.

When you swipe a credit card through the payment terminal to pay for your new bike or flatscreen TV, you are not borrowing money from the credit card company. Nor are you borrowing money that others have deposited in savings accounts with the credit card company. Nor are you borrowing from the store or using your own money. Where does this money come from? Here is the real surprise, the core of the modern financial system: *You create the money once the terminal says 'approved'.* A magical moment! When you are issued with a credit card, you are being approved as a printer or, more correctly, a creator of money within your credit limit. Only a fraction of the amount that is deducted on the card is already in existence, in the form of the relatively small reserves of the credit company.

Your credit card is therefore an approved, distributed money-printing machine. A mini bank-note printing press that fits into your wallet. You imagine a new lovely king-size bed in order to sleep really deep and well. You go to the furniture store and say: 'I want that one.' You fish out your credit card and let the strip slide through the slot on the payment terminal. In exactly that same second, the miracle happens. Just like in the folk tale about the genie in the lamp, or Mephistopheles in Faust. Rub gently on the lamp and invisible, powerful helpers stream out and give you exactly what you want. Money which did not exist arises out of thin air, and your desire is fulfilled. The imagined goods manifest themselves as actual consumer goods that can flow out of the store to your house.

But if credit cards can print money, why do people not use them all the time? There is, as has been mentioned, a credit limit on the card. But there are two other, more profound reasons that are not particularly salient in that magical moment of making the purchase. The first is that the money you create does not belong to you. It is the bank that owns it, and the bank demands it back. The bank now has a claim on you. In return for using your lovely mini bank-note printing press, the bank now owns a bit of you and your time. It is not interested in the bed. The bed and millions of other goods are means for getting you to print money on behalf of the bank. Banks cannot grow just by printing money by themselves. The bank needs the help of customers who want to own a little gadget – or five. To achieve their goal of growing and earning money, the banks and credit-card companies must have willing customers.

In addition to getting back the money you created for them, there is a price on the money. When the credit-card account is repaid, the credit is cancelled and the money returns to the genie in the lamp. However, both the shop and you have to pay a little for using your mini bank-note printing press. Not all that much each time. But the larger the sums you make purchases for, the more the bank earns. And the bank is pleased to see repayments being made late. The later you make a repayment, the more the bank earns. It is actually the most expensive money it is possible to get. Credit-card interest is the highest rate of all types of interest. That is why the banks think credit cards are so great. And they are only too pleased to allow the first use of the card to be interest-free. Nothing is as profitable for the banks as credit via credit cards. Up until the financial crisis of 2008, the credit-card industry was hugely profitable as Americans were charging around 1.5 trillion dollars on their credit cards a year, and about half of them habitually carrying a negative balance on their credit-card account.[16]

Credit-card use thus has a shadow, just like all other credit. The genie in the lamp has a claim on you. Every time new money arises via a credit-card purchase, *a debt too is created.* Liquid funds are made instantaneously available, but only at the cost of potential future pressure and belt-tightening. For the system to work, there has to be growth in future disposable income. Then we can start to sense the actual cost of money. Strictly speaking, a credit card ought to be called a debt card, lending machine or future-thief. 'Temporary on-loan money printing press' or 'automatic debt generator' might be other alternatives. However, they don't seem quite so attractive, do they? Negative associations can nevertheless be avoided by issuing gold-class credit cards. Who would not want to be among the chosen few, the exclusive recipients of 'Gold' or 'Platinum' credit cards?

Some conclusions about credit

Mephistopheles tempted Faust with taverns and revelry, with falling in love and sex, with wealth and power. But it was finally with the magic of credit that he got Faust's soul on the hook. Credit is invigorating and intoxicating: it allows dreams to come true and raises the pulse rate of economic life. More credit is to the soul what adrenalin is to the body. We can bring dreams to life here and now. We can live faster and avoid having to wait until we have saved up the money at some time in the future, and only then buy what we dreamed of. Why postpone to tomorrow the purchase of what I can have today?

Today, people acting on the economic stage are largely unaware of the nature of money.[17] Most of us perceive money as something substantial, an objective asset in the material sphere. But, as we have seen, money today is mainly bank credit, which again is based on mutual trust and confidence in the future.

Other cultures have believed in honour, gods, the forces of ancestors or nature. We believe in credit. The monetary philosopher James Buchan points out: "Belief in God (in the eighteenth and nineteenth centuries) was replaced by belief in credit".[18] The miracles of credit were much more potent than those of the Church and God put together.

With increased credit, the liquid flow of money in society increases. This at first seems to vitalise economic life, similar to how the state of psychological *flow*[19] has a vitalising effect on the creative psyche. When in psychological flow we feel fully immersed in what we are doing and enjoy an energized focus, full involvement, and an expectation of success when in the process of the activity. When in economic flow, the activity level rises, exchanges increase, arrows start pointing up and everyone swarms around like busy ants on a hot sunny day. Does this mean that credit contributes to more vitality, regardless?

Assets such as property, shares and other securities become more valuable when the amount of credit grows without any corresponding inflation (measured by the consumer price index). Housing loans go up, but the house prices climb even further. Apparently we are all becoming richer. The problem is that with a credit-based monetary system we have, like Faust, sold our soul to the money magician, Mephistopheles; also known as the banking system. All credit triggers a debt that has to be serviced in the future. This is possible only if real economic growth continues, profitability increases and confidence in future growth continues; otherwise the system crashes, creating recession and depression. That is particularly unpleasant for the creditors, but even worse for the poorest debtors and perhaps worst of all for natural resources: ever larger amounts must be sold at low prices to service the same debt that was made when prices were high.

Maybe Goethe wasn't just writing about the individual character Faust. Could he already in 1820 have seen something in the very mechanism of credit that would entail a Faustian bargain for the whole of society? As our monetary system currently functions, more and more resources, energy and biomass must therefore be pushed into the real economy to maintain this growth. The growth of credit must be followed up with real economic growth, and the entire planet is in danger of being sucked in.

With a credit system, the money supply can quickly grow exponentially. But the Earth does not undergo corresponding growth. Exponential credit-financed growth in purchasing power in a limited world is a combination that sits uneasy with the long view. Very soon several Earth-like planets will be needed to remove all waste and to supply the growing real economy with sufficient resources and cleaning capacity.[20] But the supply of new planets appears to be severely limited. Credit is inherently exponential and, unfettered by restraints, quickly climbs towards infinite heights. The credit must therefore, sooner or later, be delimited by periodic crashes or stabilising regulations, or complemented by other systems with overall quotas for the withdrawal of natural capital and for climate-changing emissions. The way the existing credit money market could be curbed or delimited by other markets is the topic of Part III.

Chapter 10

Debt and interest
The prison of the soul

Debt and interest is the warp that holds the giant economic cloth together. Usually debt is analysed in purely technical and economic terms. However, greater attention needs to be paid to the social and psychological effects of debt. This chapter therefore looks at debt in a metaphorical and mythical way, to re-imagine it within a new framework of understanding. Finally, I question the entire nature of the current debt system.

"Last Friday my bank account was subject to a compulsory withdrawal due to debt and a child support payment. I have 43 cents left in the account. I have nothing left to live on. I do not have any money for food or petrol to allow me to get to work. The employer will only pay my salary into a bank account, but since this money does not get to me, in real terms I am not in paid work. I have talked to the social security office, but because they recorded an income of more than 520 dollars last month, I do not qualify for any support.

"I now have no family, friends, food or paid work, just a bleak future. So, I have decided that there is no point in continuing to live. I now drive to a peaceful area, close to where I live, lead the exhaust fumes into the car, take some sleeping pills and use the little petrol I have to end my life. I would have preferred to have died with more dignity. It is my last desire that this letter should be published so that everyone is able to read it."

Signed A. Trenouf, Thursday 5 November 1998, published in The Daily Press.[1]

True or not, the above captures the exact experience people can get into when the chains of debt are gradually tightened. Finally, death seems the only way out.

A major study from the UK shows a clear link between increased debt and a reduced quality of life. This applies in particular to consumer debt for lower-income households.[2] Other researchers have documented that there is a tendency towards 'unrealistic optimism' among credit-card users, leading to systemic levels of excessive debt.[3] Attitudes to debt and credit cards, however, have become increasingly positive over the last fifty years, particularly among younger people. For people with low or unstable incomes, this quickly becomes a serious problem, and therefore also a major social problem.[4]

The International Monetary Fund (IMF) also has a type of understanding of this, if not exactly in empathic or comparably emotional language. In its terminology, it says "Debt gives rise to future payment obligations. As a consequence, debt liabilities have the potential to create circumstances that render an institutional unit, a sector, and even the whole economy vulnerable to liquidity and sustainability problems. For these reasons, there is analytical interest in debt measures."[5]

The phenomenon of debt thus has many different faces: one directed towards the individual under the pressure of debt, and another towards the economist's analytical key measures. Here, too, it seems that soul and money are very far apart. Human beings in heavy debt face demands for money all around them; they experience the yoke, and squirm as the chains tighten. When chained down the soul is filled with a ever-stronger longing for movement and freedom. The monetary, banking and taxation systems deal only with figures, and are indifferent from emotions connected with debt and how it shapes the lives of borrowers. With a shrug of the shoulders, the analytical attitude simply just points out the fact that it is the individual's own responsibility for having got him- or herself into this situation.

Debt is the shadow of credit

As was shown in the previous chapter, money is created as credit and has debt as its counterpart. Virtually all of the money in circulation today has come into existence because someone has taken out a loan. For some loans, home and property have been put up as security for the debt; other money (such as via credit cards) has come about on the basis of only a promise to pay back the money in the future. Only coins and bank notes issued and printed by the State do not have debt as a counterpart.[6] This is debt-free money: no interest accrues on it. However, it now constitutes only four per cent of the entire money supply.[7]

All other new money (i.e. 96 per cent) comes about in the form of credit. When the money first comes into circulation, there is no difference between what has substantial backing and what has not. All money looks alike. In economic theory, this is called the supply side in the market for money. It covers the demand for money for consumption and new investments. The banks ensure that people who need money for something – and are able to repay with interest

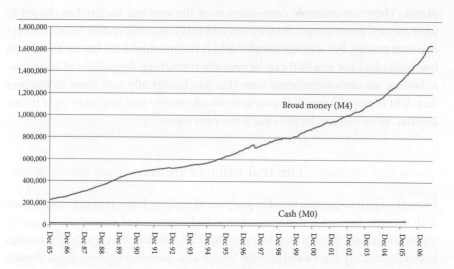

The relationship between cash and broad money (notes and coins together with money held in bank accounts) in the UK, in £ million. *Source: Bank of England*

in the future – get it now. New money thus becomes credit, viewed from the bank's perspective and, at the same time, debt from the money-holder's perspective.[8]

When the principal on the loan is paid back, that money goes out of the bank's accounts and dies. It disappears back to nothingness, just as it previously came into existence from nothing when the bank issued it – a rather disconcerting thought, perhaps! To ensure that the money supply is maintained, there must always be other people and organisations that are willing to enter into new debt. Otherwise, the steady stream of principal repaid will kill off all of our money.

Debt is the shadow of modern bank money. The Norwegian word for debt is *gjeld*, and comes from the Old Norse *gelda*, which also means to geld or castrate. Fortunately, the banking system does not do this physically, by way of debt collectors, if you default on the debt. But it is still possible to set debt collection companies on to you, to reduce your creditworthiness or force you into personal bankruptcy. Then you have been 'neutered' as an economic player. You are no longer a respected participant in financial circles. "You ain't got no money, you just ain't no good" is what the lady sings to Ray Charles in the song *Hit the road, Jack*. The point of living in a society that has economics as its prevailing religion has been taken away. That is when thoughts such as feeding the car exhaust in through the window can come to the surface.

Just as the invisible hand, the invisible bond of the debt has actual – emotional, physical, tangible, concrete – effects on human life and the life of the planet. There are systemic consequences of the way our society has chosen to issue money. Everything is interwoven into this ingenious system because everyone uses money. For wealthy people, debt is not much of a tie, but for those with low individual net worth it can be severely restricting. Regardless of social distribution, we can nevertheless view this psychologically and come to discover that debt is actually one of the areas in which money and soul draw near to one another. How this can be the case is the next topic.

The real price of money

From the lender's perspective, the purpose of making loans is to get money back with interest. Interest is therefore often called 'the price of money'. As we saw in the Introduction, throughout the entire Middle Ages there were strong warnings from Christianity (and also from the Jewish and Islamic religions), bans, threats, judgements and punishments applied to people who lent money for interest. No Jew was permitted to lend money with interest to another Jew but, as this ban was interpreted, Jews were able to make loans to non-Jews. This greatly added to the unpopularity of Jews and their subsequent persecution.

Nowadays, loans, interest and compound interest are quite simply the way we do business. However, within Christendom, asking for interest on debt was, for hundreds of years, regarded as one of the seven deadly sins. It was considered to be equivalent to greed, and high rates of interest were a special variant of greed called usury. It meant giving in to the lowest, most inconsiderate, greedy and raw emotions from the lowest levels of human nature. Throughout medieval times, violent uprisings against price rises and expensive loans were constantly occurring. As early as 1520, Martin Luther thought it was time "to put a bit in the mouth of the holy company of the Fuggers." [9] The Fuggers family were the Citigroup, Microsoft, General Electric and CocaCola of those days – all rolled into one. Other Protestant reformers, like Calvin, Zwingli and a number of others, contributed to a flood of pamphlets against interest during the sixteenth century. Shakespeare's *Merchant of Venice* deals with the moneylender Shylock's unavoidable claim: he has the right to cut a pound of flesh from the merchant's body if the debt is not paid on time. The merchant's future is completely in Shylock's hands.

Islamic tradition too forbids interest. The Koran says: "Those who devour usury will not stand except as stands one whom the Evil One by his touch has driven to madness. That is because they say, 'trade is like usury', but Allah has permitted trade and has forbidden usury." [10] Grounded in the Koran, Islam wishes to eliminate the exploitation it sees as intrinsic to the institution of interest. Many Western Muslims come under moral pressure because it is a breach of Islamic law to take out loans in ordinary banks. Islamic banks must find other sources of income, such as fees, dividends from share capital or the distribution of any surplus, to cover their risk and expenses.

When Napoleon, at the height of his powers, had the effect of compound interest explained to him, he exclaimed "Strange that this beast called *interest* has not already swallowed up all of humanity. Only bankruptcy and revolution have prevented that so far." And in 1815, after the Battle of Waterloo, he said: "When a government becomes dependent on banks for procuring money, it is the leaders of the banks and not the government who are in control of the situation. For the hand that gives holds sway over the hand that receives (. . .) Money has no homeland, finance people have no patriotism and no decency; their only objective is gain." [11]

A positive function of interest is that it acts as an incentive to increase savings. Without interest, it would not be worthwhile laying aside your funds and postponing your consumption. However, as a side-effect of this, interest actively contributes to an increasing gap between poor and rich. The interest ensures a steady transfer of wealth from the poor – who need (expensive) loans, and have no capital to invest – to the most wealthy. The reason is that the richest people own the majority of the world's most income-generating and interest-bearing assets. On the top, if they need loans, they get lower rates because they have higher credit ratings. The differences between the many poor and the few wealthy is maintained and increased in this way – between net debtors and net creditors.

A German study illustrates this effect. [12] Households were subdivided according to income into equal-sized groups, with 2.5 million people in each. The interest rate was 5.5 per cent. In total, in that year, DM270 billion were paid and received in interest. The Figure opposite shows those who were net recipients and those who were net payers. Thanks to their investments, via the finance system, the wealthiest 10 per cent of the households received large indirect transfers from the lower-income groups. This type of transfer was due exclusively to the debt system that society uses, and has nothing to do with the degree of competence or the amount of effort put in within the different income groups. Differences in competence is the strongest argument for justifying existing differences in income. However, these sums show only the systemic flow of interest expenditure and interest income, and have nothing to do with competence.

It is nothing new for people and ideologues of all shades of opinion to rage at the finance system and the wealthy, or to rebel against repressive burdens of debt. In his 1920 book about religion and capitalism, Richard Tawney, the Oxford Professor of Economic History, sighs, "If the world could be saved by

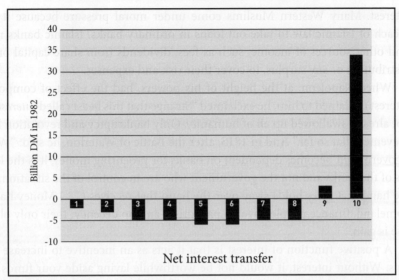

Net transfers between income groups in Germany, 1982. Source: Margrit Kennedy, 1995

sermons and pamphlets, it would long ago have been turned into a true Paradise."[13]

We see the same pattern in the international arena as we do in the national one. A lot of pointed and well-researched criticism has been penned in recent decades about the unjust system regulating poor countries' burdens of debt. The international monetary system's interest claims become a form of structural violence exercised against these populations.[14] Ask landless Mexican smallholders, or Argentinians who lost their restaurants, what they feel about financial restructuring in order to pay the national debt to foreign countries. The collective debt continued to rise, regardless of the increase in exports and GNP. Between 1946 and 1986, for example, the Latin American countries' GNP rose by 4.6 per cent per annum. But despite more rapid growth than the rich countries, forty years of restructuring (including numerous cuts in healthcare and education) and a steadily stronger move towards exports, they just fell deeper into debt to the IMF, the World Bank and the Western banking system. Constant new rounds of long-drawn-out negotiations about cancelling debt were initiated, but twenty years later many of the countries are still deep in debt.

This has been called, by some, *aid to industrialised countries*: a steady transfer from countries that do not have to the countries that have most. 'Charity' in the form of development aid is peanuts in relation to this systemic flow of money from poor to rich countries. To date, with development aid having had a limited impact, it can for a large part be explained as being like a minor relaxation of the economic iron grip in which these countries are already tightly held via the international debt and interest system.

What is it about debt that will not let go of its grip, despite all of the well-meaning and constructive individuals, organisations and prominent officials in the world who have criticised the arrangements over the centuries? Rebellion and pamphlets have clearly had little effect. Interest will not be chased away by rebuking and berating it at length. There must probably be solid social structures and emotional bonds behind its iron grip on our culture.

Goddess of bonds – Ananke

This is a book about the relationship between economic ideas and deep-seated emotions in the psyche. And it uses mythic images to make such links come alive. In the market ideas about 'truck, barter and exchange' we found Hermes, behind the welfare ideas about security and order we found Zeus, Midas came up in the ideas about wealth, the feeling of scarcity is expressed in the image of all-devouring Chronos, and the ideas of morally just and incorruptible book-keeping have a lot in common with Hestia and the Vestales.

But who lives within the conception of debt? And interest?

Debt involves being under a obligation for something, usually money. The feeling of indebtedness is something we recognise. It restricts us. Many people with a feeling of obligation to someone lose their spontaneity. The inflexibility comes from the feeling of being restricted, from the bonds of something we would prefer to be rid of. Being indebted to someone for something is therefore a form of enslavement. It is therefore often a bad idea to borrow money from friends. Friendship entangled by debt and credit can easily break. Many people have experienced the embarrassing and disturbing impact of money matters that have not been settled between friends. Invisible bonds push and pull at us and prevent spontaneity and freedom. We no longer phone one another; we turn away from the other person.

The words used to describe debt point to the way it is perceived psychologically. We are *under* an obligation. We are *tied into* a mortgage. The company issues *bonds*. The word 'obligation' derives from the Latin *ligare*, which literally means to bind. Debt is then connected with being fixed into something, and it imposes restrictions. Free movement becomes inhibited.

When we take out a loan, particularly for houses and other real estate, we have to put something up as security. In English, the word most often used for this is *mortgage*. It is a fascinating word, because it is made up of *mort*, which has something to do with death, and *gage,* a promise or pledge – thus it is a 'dead pledge'. *Gage* or *gauge* can also mean a set of pincers, an instrument or a device for measuring a dimension.[15] Originating in Old French, the word *mortgage* means that we pledge to put ourselves under tight restrictions until the death of the pledge – once the obligation has been fulfilled or the property taken through foreclosure. In a mortgage deed, according to the word itself, you are swearing to the creditor that you have submitted to the constraint to repay everything with interest, at the risk of losing even your life. You do not own your house with a mortgage until the debt is 'dead' or paid off.[16]

In the previous chapter, we saw that credit came from the word *credere* – trustworthy for the senses, whereas debt comes from the word *debere* – to owe something that is not 'on hand'. That means a deficiency, an absence that must be filled. We thereby have invisible obligations and restrictions placed on our future. This leads us in the direction of some central figures in the emotional landscape mapped out by the Greek myths. The goddess of bonds and necessity was called Ananke.

Ananke is the powerful deity that rules compulsion, constraint, restraint and coercion, and presides over all forms of slavery and bonds. Consequently, when someone is cast into prison, or fastened by chains, her name is evoked. For she is behind all bonds, and has a share even in the ties of kinship, friendship and love. She is called Necessity, since once the attachment is established there cannot but follow what necessarily is derived from it, her might allowing no resistance.[17]

Her domains are bonds of every kind; from *having to* eat and drink to yielding to someone else's will. Many forms of ties are necessary – no one can live a totally free life. Ananke is therefore also present in ties of friendship, family and affection.

Some classical quotations from the realm of Ananke:

"Ah! But there's no such thing as a free man! All men are slaves, Agamemnon! Slaves to money, to Fate, to the cries of the masses, to the written laws! They all stop him from doing what he wants!" – Hekabe to Agamemnon

"We men are in a prison all that time which we choose to call life. For this soul of ours, being bound and fettered in a perishable body, has to endure many things, and be the slave of all the affections which visit humanity." – Philostratus

Sources: 1) Euripides (424 BC) Hekabe, 864. 2) Philostratus (approx 250 BC) Life of Apollonius Tyana, 7.26.

The word Ananke was synonymous with necessity – that is, ties that it is pointless to resist. It is the feeling of a wild animal when it is imprisoned in a cage and realises there is no possibility of escape. The beginning of anxiety and the death of freedom. Ananke was the mother of the three Moirae, or Fates, who weave the thread of life for one and all.18 Today, 'Anancasms' are a collective psychiatric term for all sorts of compulsive behaviour and thoughts.

"Don't worry, be happy" was what the artist Bobby McFerrin sang in his lively hit, but that is surely easier said than done in the realm of Ananke. Once you have been entwined in her chains, it feels impossible to escape. Once, the god of metalworking and smiths, Hephaistos, was forced to take on the job of putting the rebellious Prometheus into metal fetters. He found the task very distasteful. It is not difficult to recognise Hephaistos's complaint:

Hephaistos: Oh handicraft that I hate so much!

Cratos: Why do you hate it? Your art is, in short,
                Not beholden to any of the hardships that are now ahead.

Hephaistos: Nevertheless, it ought to have fallen to someone else.

Cratos: All work is troublesome, except that of ruling over gods. Because no
                one is free except Zeus.19

Hephaistos' complaints echo those of modern debtors: 'Oh, I hate this job. If it had not been for the mortgage or obligations to the kids, I would have done something completely different, something meaningful. I would have written a book, travelled to Peru to do voluntary work, moved to live on the land, started up my own café, tended a herb garden . . . I would have quit this job right now. No question!' If it wasn't just because of . . . then I would have . . . These are the thoughts that express the timeless power of Ananke' bonds in which the soul is bound.

In economic society, Ananke rules primarily through debt. If your income for some reason is no longer sufficient to cover repayments of debt as well as basic needs, the bonds start to tighten. Stress and obsessive compulsive thoughts of ruin may come uninvited in. Degrading feelings of failure and of being a loser threaten. Quality of life goes down the drain, along with one's self-respect. In a credit-based society, difficulties with debt are a sign that there is something wrong with your economic self. It is like having a kind of symptom, only with no proper diagnosis. You then ought to get an economic advisor, or apply for re-financing your loans. It can feel as if your life has to be realigned with the ideals of the successful economic man in order to be set straight.

Symptoms, however, are not necessarily something altogether bad. One radical move Carl Jung made was in relation to our society's negative view of symptoms and feelings of inferiority. He pointed out that the gods from myths and religions have not disappeared in modern times, even if we no longer believe in them. Instead, they have taken up residence in our worries and symptoms, in back complaints, in heart complaints or in money worries. In a modern society in which people prefer to regard themselves as rational agents, the gods will have to relocate themselves where we are the least rational and in that in which we have the least control over: our symptoms.

"We are still as much possessed by autonomous psychic contents as if they were Olympians. Today they are called phobias, obsessions, and so forth. In a word, neurotic symptoms. The gods have become diseases: Zeus no longer rules Olympus but rather the solar plexus, and produces curious specimens for the doctor's consulting room, or disorders the brains of politicians and journalists who unwittingly let loose psychic epidemics on the world." – Carl Jung

If we can recognise what gods live in our symptoms, we may discover that we are not suffering from any detestable failure – but, on the contrary, that through that very symptom we are in the service of a god. If you find it grandiose to use the word 'god', one can also call it an archetypal pattern or an evolutionary, emotional predisposition of our human bodies. The point is that this goes beyond the purely individual.

If we can see that in our symptoms we are serving a god through tending to our troubles, we also serve something that is greater than ourselves. Those afflictions can then be seen in a larger context, perhaps even filled with meaning and dignity. They will no longer be experienced as only degrading and detestable, even if Ananke's fetters hinder the life that our ego would like to bring about.

This way of thinking can also be applied to our ties of debt: many people see a high burden of debt and interest as proof of failure. We are not free and on top of the world as we 'ought' to be. We live in a society possessed by ideas of everyone being economic winners, in which there is an expectation that everyone will be self-supporting, hold down a good job and become debt-free. On top of this, we shall release ourselves from all shackles, travel around the world and realise our dreams. "You can if you really want to!" say our self-development gurus and life coaches. But the debt makes us completely stuck, in a 'safe' job, for example.

The experience of getting caught up in debt and obligations can, however, be viewed as a form of initiation into Ananke's world: that being human is also to allow yourself to be bound by strong ties to a greater society. The fact is that we are all part of the chain gang: we are *of necessity* bound to one another. This is socially unavoidable, but at the same time there is a darker side that makes us potentially vulnerable, exposed to the dominance of others.

Being a 'slave to debt' has elements that are similar to other types of slavery. Through this experience we can connect ourselves with psychological images and emotions connected with being a slave a few thousand years ago, or with

Latin American coffee pickers in debt over their homes; an Eastern European woman deeply in debt who is encouraged into prostitution by a pimp who takes 80 per cent of the income; fishermen in the eighteenth century who sink deeper into debt; to the Native American beaver hunters who would never be free of their indebtedness to the white man as soon as they started to borrow money to buy rifles and ammunition. Psychologically speaking, these situations have something in common. We are initiated into an ancient shared human mode of being in the world; bound together by seemingly unbreakable ties.

The most ancient writing discovered in the world, from Babylon, seems to be the totals of lending records. Perhaps it was money owed that caused writing to be developed in the first place: who owes whom, and how much![20] Having these invisible bonds written down in a clear way may have been so important that it forced the development of alphabet and numbers. The chains of debt are therefore nothing new. Fair or not, we are initiated into Ananke's realm, as millions and millions have been before us. We can experience the world through the eyes of the captive. And the energy is spent tending to the imagination of what we would have done, if only . . .

It was particularly common to link Ananke's domain with the material, practical world. That was where she had her greatest impact – and a little of the contempt for the body's weakness, which we retain from the classical Greek era, comes from here. Plato perceived the body as a prison in which the soul was kept in place by the body's demands for food, heat, drink, sex and so on. The spirit endeavours to lift us up to the higher world, the home of light and pure ideas, and of which the material world is merely a pale shadow, but we are constantly being forced back to the imperfect everyday physical world. There is no full escape into that higher, freer world. Our obligations drag us down again – the first of the next month will probably be a due date for paying an instalment on the loan. The money *has to* be there then. So, in the morning, I *have to* go to work.

The money itself may today be intangible symbols that race through computers throughout the world. It is in free flow. However, for all members of Ananke's huge band of sworn slaves (that is, all net debtors) only more toil and drudgery can procure income to meet her unavoidable claims for interest and principal repayments. You have chosen between paying or ending up outside society.

Who likes a goddess like that? No one loves her, and everyone forgets to make sacrifices to her. The Greeks shuddered just to think of the name. With incontrovertible power, with or without worship, she remains in a superior position within life's situations. Given that she must be obeyed, the Greeks gave the following advice for enduring her: "If a man endeavours to . . . persuade himself to accept of his own accord what needs must befall him, he will have a very reasonable and harmonious life"[21]

In other words: be satisfied with what you have, instead of grinding your teeth over what you do not have. There is some liberation in that. A similar thought finally occurred to the rebellious Prometheus where he lay, chained fast to Mount Caucasus at the end of the world. "No sharp surprise of pain shall overtake me. What's determined, bear as I can I must, knowing the might of strong Necessity is unconquerable."[22]

Debt, depression, death

Perhaps some other god too is active within this debt phenomenon. Debt is not just the feeling of being bonded. There is also a feeling of being totally exhausted, anaemic, drained of the spark of life. We are weighed down with thinking about our obligations, the endless duties at work, debt and the money we don't have. The darkness descends over us, while we grumble about how we are to earn what we need for the future. It seems hopeless; perhaps we might just as well choose that exhaust pipe . . . We do not do it though. We think about our children, brothers and sisters, parents. But the *thought* might occur to us. Perhaps in despair over the pay increase we had been counting on but which never came. Or the investments that went wrong; that we were tricked; that we went into the market at its top and sold at the bottom. Most things can seem to be going downward, apart from the debt which never seems to reduce.

Sometimes it seems as if death is the only escape, as Shakespeare writes in *The Tempest:* "He that dies pays all debts." Thomas Jefferson, President of the US in the early nineteenth century, struggled with huge personal debt throughout his life. As an elderly man, he wrote in a letter to a friend that "the torment of mind I endure till the moment shall arrive when I shall owe not a shilling on earth is such really as to render life of little value." He never managed it. When he died in 1827 he left behind a debt of 100,000 dollars, an enormous sum at that time.[23]

Such feelings of depression – which also inhabit the concept of debt – brings us to the god the Greeks called Hades. He has been mentioned previously, but now may be a place for a more detailed presentation. Hades ruled over the Greek underworld on the far side of the River Styx. The Greeks believed it was dangerous to say his name, so he was often called The Invisible One, or *Plouton* – The Rich One. The Romans called him Pluto, and both Hades and Pluto were therefore linked with great wealth in addition to having dominion over the souls of the dead.

However, we must not confuse Hades with Satan in Christianity.[24] Certainly, Hades is dark, strict, inescapable and makes irrevocable decisions about the destiny of souls. But he is not evil. He is not an enemy of human beings, not a snake who tempts people and lures them to a fall. Nor is he a despot who tries to get the whole world under his control as Satan has been portrayed by Christian fire-and-brimstone preachers, nor like the empire-building Sauron from Tolkien's *Lord of the Rings*.

Ruler of the underworld: Hades or Pluto – the Rich One.

He rules over and lives in what we call death consciousness, that dark area at the bottom of the soul. The feeling of dying, like at the end of a relationship, or like the end of a phase of life or of an aim for which you have been struggling for a long time; all of these produce the meeting with Hades. This becomes particularly evident in the feeling of being anaemic, exhausted and depressed.

When Odysseus, on his journey home after the battle of Troy, sought advice from the underworld, the souls of the dead stepped out in front of him. They all wanted part of his blood sacrifice. Their bodily lives were over; they lived on only as shadows in the underworld. In particular, they longed for fresh blood. We can understand that to be a longing for a rigorous, full-blooded life. These shadows of the underworld lack vitality, circulating blood and 'meat on their bones'. We could go over to economic language and say that they lack cash flow and liquidity. They are insolvent. Only liabilities – no assets. Economic ghosts slowly on the road to oblivion.

A large net burden of debt can produce similar mental states to the images linked to Hades: the burden sucks the marrow out of our time, our strength and our vitality. We all experience a little bit of Hell when our attention is drained by daily economic worries, when our good moods are ground to pieces by claims that exceed what we can handle.

Being beset by feelings of not having money, and the requirement to acquire more, can, psychologically, be like ending up in Hades. We lose the ability to be fully present in the here and now. We become absentminded, and we are mentally absorbed by work and troubles even outside working hours. Ghosts like those that Odysseus meets, are not fully present either. In a way, we also become like ghosts: we are there in a way, and yet not entirely. The shortage of liquid funds and blood circulation sucks the vitality out of us. However, like all other gods (and emotions) Hades has both positive and negative sides. The journey to the world of shadows is also the journey away from the world of actions, where the blood rushes around in ever-quick and decisive acting, to the world of images and thoughtfulness, writes James Hillman.[25] Depression, despondency or despair as a result of economic worries may give us the advantage of being able to let go of our ambitions to some degree. It may be painful, but could just as well be an initiation to something new. It may lead to contact with other sides of life. Let me name a few of them.

Depression is a good antidote to high-tempo living and long-term stress. When depression kicks in, the tempo drops, and you get a chance to think through the life you are leading. Your values can be turned upside down: the things you have been struggling for, and believed were worthwhile, suddenly seem pointless. If you dare to trust it, depression can set you free from compulsion and obligations. Many ruthlessly exploit their own strengths, and the soul's resources are regarded as free for exploitation. A bout of depression can stop this, and give us an opportunity to change direction.

Questions such as 'What is the point?' and 'Why am I alive?' begin to swirl around the head. Depression offers a golden (or leaden?) opportunity to engage with the existential questions. Perhaps we get absorbed with questions about death, which might in the long term make life deeper and more meaningful. Below is the direction towards Hades, but also towards the depths. We are invited to a deeper relationship with ourselves.

An economic depression can paradoxically enough make you richer, if the soul is given occasion to digest and expand upon this event to find lasting meaning. It is riches of another kind, Hades' riches. You now know that life also means slowness, darkness and vulnerability. If you accept the way down, instead of suppressing or fleeing from it, you can experience a new solidity and depth. Hades *is* the depth, the underworld. A journey through his realm can teach us to see, even in the dark. It is a meeting without superficiality; instead, it is a hard-earned gift that becomes ours when we permit Hades to become part of life.

Some people try to flee from debt and Hades: rather some desperate caper or financial acrobatics than to go down there in the dark. And some succeed: through violent effort and desperate activity they struggle free from the realm of Hades, in more or less the same way as when Hercules was there and fought his way free with his enormous club. With a few successful blows – a clever refinancing scheme or ingenious high-risk investment – they can suddenly be on top again financially. But they may not have taken with them any of Hades' riches, which exist in the deepening of their own soul; nor the certainty that living a life for the sake of soul entails more than success in the form of economic profits. Instead of fighting *against,* it is therefore possible to move *with* an economic downturn, accepting it as a dark companion, dismal but perhaps inescapable in order to make the necessary emotional changes.

Is the time ripe for debt reform?

Why are we all so busy? Not because we prefer stress and pressure, or because we love to dash around like consumer junkies, buying ever more things. It does not properly hit the mark if we morally criticise people who hold several jobs or are working ever-longer hours, because this overlooks the systemic effect that an increasing number of people have to borrow more than their income actually permits.[26] Collectively, we are more indebted than before, despite increased levels of income and wealth. It then follows with inherent necessity that income *must* increase in order to service the debt.

The collective debt, particularly in the form of home mortgages, has increased for most households in the rich world over the last twenty years – often increasing more rapidly than income.[27] Values in the housing market have been increasing too, but this does not change the fact that many people end up running faster and faster to service debts linked to education, ever-better housing, family expenditures, the car, a new boat, or just plain conspicuous consumption.

People often say that time is money, but perhaps not in the way that the American politician of the eighteenth century, Benjamin Franklin, originally meant: that it was shameful to 'waste' time – i.e. time that is not used for productive work. Time is money in a much more profound way than that. When credit is created, the debt that comes along with it means that we now owe productive time to the financial system. The debt makes claims on our future work. And the interest rate determines how much of my future time is pledged. We could thus say that money is monetisation of the future, in the way that today's money comes about. We have borrowed away, mortgaged, our future to the financial system, with interest and compound interest. No wonder we're all busily running around.

- € -

It is obvious that too many poor people in the world do not have enough purchasing power to allow them to be heard in the market. On the other hand, many
people, even in rich countries, feel that they cannot afford either to work or live
in the ways they would like to. Depression and dissatisfaction seem to be
increasing in rich countries too.28 Money is kept scarce and debt levels are growing. The chronic shortage of money prevents movement and room for manoeu-
vre. Not just human time and life energy, but the world's natural resources are
also being tapped at an increasing rate in order to fill the gap, with the result that
many people believe we 'cannot afford' to do anything either about the debt traps
for the poor or the problems of climate change.

We are in the process of turning the entire world – fish stocks, farmland, cars,
houses, estates, minerals, everything! – into liquid assets for feeding the insatiable, exponentially growing financial-debt monster that we ourselves have created. By some sort of black magic, ever-more resources are transformed into
ever-higher levels of debt. Here, we are at a core point in this book. Based on
Tolkien's mythology, it might seem that the Earth's rivers, trees, groundwater,
glaciers, oilfields, the air itself and millions of human hands are fodder for the
power of 'Sauron', Tolkien's dark lord. At the same time, we could, like Frodo,
find an opportunity to cast the ring (of debt) into the Cracks of Doom.

The metaphor may not be particularly far-fetched. Tolkien subscribed to a
conservative English magazine called *Candour*. He took care of all twenty annual
volumes, and faithfully underlined statements he wanted to note. These include:
"Throned above all, in a manner without parallel in all past, is the veiled prophet
of finance, swaying all men living by a sort of magic, and delivering oracles in a
language not understood by the people"[29] and "it has always been and still is our
contention that the prerogative of creating and issuing the money of the nation
should be restored to the State."[30]

In other words, Tolkien was concerned with debt and monetary reform. It is
not inconceivable that he associated the most powerful ring, forged in the
Chasm of Doom, with the modern fairy ring of debt money and compound
interest – a central element in the system that is gradually absorbing all the
world's resources into its huge economic empire. In a survey carried out by the
Folio Society in 1997 (before the films were released), *Lord of the Rings* emerged
as the 'best-loved book of all time'. If Tolkien had published a pamphlet about the
reform of political economy, it would probably have had a very limited print run.

The ring – debt money with compound interest – cannot be destroyed or dissolved with physical power. However, by not putting the ring on and still bearing it to its final destination, the world can be released from the bonds in which

debt-based monetary systems have ensnared the world (to the advantage of the richest few). The debt system is hardly a conspiracy, but it is based on a specific set of ideas that became dominant in the West in the eighteenth and nineteenth centuries.

Some conclusions about the debt system

We have a debt-based monetary system. Debt and interest is the warp around which the economic system is woven, It is what bind all participants in the great financial network together. The system intertwines everyone in the bonds of debt, although to various degrees. But debt has major and permanent effects on the choices people make and the way they live their lives, both in their working and private lives. We are barely conscious of these long-term effects at that euphoric moment in which money is created as credit along with its dark twin of debt.

The arrangement has been passed down from past centuries when money was precious metal and the supply was limited by gold. Then, credit was needed to increase the money supply sufficiently. Now, money has become a purely psychic phenomenon, an information product with fewer and fewer physical limitations. There are therefore valid questions about whether, for the sake of society and human quality of life, it is appropriate to continue perpetually with this current debt-based money system.

Among the strengths of the system are: 1) stimulating people to save, 2) creating money by a fairly decentralised decision system for those who need it for (good?) investments, and therefore 3) contributing to social change by supplying entrepreneurs with the necessary capital to implement innovations.[31]

It also has a huge shadow. These include: 1) it contributes to systematic unfair distribution through interest, 2) it brings about reduced quality of life because of a generally increasing burden of debt in society, 3) it generates an increased level of taxation in society in order to service rising public debt, 4) it rewards banks for the greatest possible growth in loans in periods of prosperity, 5) it contributes to greater fluctuations in the business cycle, and 6) it requires an exponential increase in real economic activity and material throughput to keep the system growing at the pace of the money supply. And if not, 7) busts follow.

However, building a non-debt-based economic monetary system is quite feasible.[32] It would also be possible to build an monetary system that would not enforce exponential real economic growth together with continued growth also of resource consumption and harmful emissions. It would mean our having to change both our ideas about what money is and the way the supply of money might look. This thread will be picked up again in Chapter 12.

Part III

Towards a pluralist capitalism

Chapter 11

Powerful economic myths
About economic ideology in practice

Previous chapters have delved into different economic concepts. This chapter deals with economic theory as a whole, and how the field appraises itself. Using mythical analysis, the field's 'self-image', along with the shadow side of economism, are viewed through the myth of Apollo. This chapter is analytical and critical, whereas the next one is more constructive and includes concrete proposals for future change.

Every spring, here we go again: next year's budget. Who is going to get more, and who less? What is an efficient and fair distribution of scarce resources? All kinds of economic arguments swarm when the government's budget is settled. Plans for investments and changes in taxation and subsidies are discussed. Political parties present their alternative budgets. Newspaper front pages try to predict what the changes will mean for you and your wallet. Spreadsheets and macroeconomic models project the effects of cuts and weigh things up to see whether different political parties' election potential is affected. And the parties attack one another with 'there is no money for . . .'. On both sides of the traditional dividing lines between the political parties, money and economic methods of calculation are accepted as being crucial to the process and final decisions.

Different groups use slightly different models and methods of calculations, but the entire discourse takes place within the same basic economic mindset. Interestingly enough, only a few percentage points of the budget totals take up 90 per cent of the discussion – marginal, as economists would say. What is discussed is usually small ripples on top of a vast sea of unquestioned economic reasoning.

A consequence of this ubiquitous acceptance of economic reasoning is that we allow economic figures to a large extent to determine what we can and cannot do. Some calculations tells us, for instance, that we cannot capture CO_2 and store it in aquifers deep in the ground because this is currently too expensive. Therefore the greenhouse gas must be released.[1] There are economic conventions that say we ought to be able to expect a minimum yield, in real terms, of 7 per cent of invested capital per annum, regardless of industry and geography. Others maintain that when everyone pursues their own interests, it will benefit the entire system.[2] They say that large differences in wealth between people is economically efficient.[3] They say that it is stupid to meddle with the market – because, as a rule, the market knows best.

How has it come to be like this? What is it that gives such ideas the dogmatic status they get, and the impact they have? To give a reasonably nuanced answer, it is important to distinguish between three very different areas of the economic field: academic economic *research*, economic *textbooks*, and what might be called economic *ideology in practice*.

Current economic *research frontiers* are very diverse, and cover an huge number of perspectives. There are many competing research approaches within economics – both on macro and micro levels – which have relatively little in common with each other. The question is whether it is at all possible today to talk about a unified professional discipline. It might have been so about twenty or thirty years ago, when the 'neoclassical tradition' was at its zenith, dominating the main current within the profession.[4] Within this tradition, central ideas include rational actors, rational expectations, maximisation of utility, efficient markets and general equilibrium. Since then, theoretical and experimental research have regularly been questioning all of this.

In the economic *textbooks*, however, the diversity, contrasts and divergences of opinion within the profession are easily lost. Most textbooks still portray economics as if it had a clear core and unified conceptual structure. Once the student has mastered this, she or he will have become an economist.

Economic *ideology in practice* appears to be even more disconnected from current research than the textbooks are. The ideals and concepts from long-gone textbooks, lectures and exams of previous decades have today taken firm hold inside managers', policymakers' and practitioners' minds. Those widespread ideas have become part and parcel of just about any current economic decision-making process. There they are included as building blocks of the prevailing economic ideology, which I call *economism* to distinguish it from economics as the current much more diverse academic research frontier. This chapter is intended to provide a mythical reading of some core ideas in this dominant ideology, and to see what shadows they cast. Here, economism lays itself down on the analysis couch to gain some insight into its own self-image and to confront its shadow.

One starting point might be the way some prominent economists view their own professional field. What do they see when they look in the mirror?

Mirror, mirror on the wall . . .

Paul Samuelson, Nobel laureate in economics and professor at that prestigious institution MIT, has published the most influential economics textbook ever – *Economics*. It has been revised a full eighteen times during the period 1948 to 2005. It has formed generations of economics students. After sales in the millions, it has canonical status.[5] In the introduction about 'the foundations of economics', he and co-author William Nordhaus refer to the nineteenth-century economist Alfred Marshall's statement that the world needs economists with warm hearts and cold heads. Samuelson and Nordhaus takes it further: "The best route to economic success or to fairer distribution of society's production, requires decisions to be made by cold heads, of the type that would be able to weigh up the costs and benefits of various approaches objectively, and try as hard as humanly possible to keep the analysis free of any trace of wishful thinking."[6]

Here, the ideal for the role of economists is clearly drawn. Personal preferences, care and visions may be a motivation for getting involved, but they must not be mixed up with the cool analysis. The work of economists is to ensure that the roles are not mixed, but that the cold head is still in the service of the warm heart. The warm heart is supposed to set the target, and the cold head finds the means of achieving that target.

On the same page, Samuelson introduces a central distinction between *positive economics* and *normative economics*. The first is meant as an empirical and analytical discipline, in which the facts should speak for themselves without mixing in any desires, values or dreams. Normative economics, on the other hand, is more political, and based on ethical balancing that can result in concrete recommendations. The first deals mainly with *is*, while the other deals with *ought*, to apply a differentiation from the eighteenth-century Scottish philosopher David Hume.[7]

The essence of the subject, Samuelson goes on, is to use a scientific approach to understand all economic activity. It means building on empirical data and theories. A theoretical approach makes it possible to make up generalisations that encompass millions of individual facts. With the aid of mathematics and statistics, economists can then go through huge mountains of data and dig out the most important links in the world outside.[8] These are then condensed into a model of reality. Central economists have given Samuelson much of the honour for the comprehensive mathematisation of economics in the post-war period.[9]

Another Nobel laureate in economics, Herbert Simon, compares the economics profession to a large land in which most economists have chosen to set up their residence in the middle. In this central area there are some high peaks that economic theoreticians have had great pleasure in climbing. From there, they can get a clear view of the rest of the world. Researchers such as Walras, Marshall, Samuelson, Schultz and others have formulated theories with a "mathematical elegance that makes even physics contend for precedence in beauty and elegance." At the time, Herbert Simon felt himself to be a little out on the periphery, at a distance from those central peaks, with his research into 'bounded rationality'.[10]

A third, more recent Nobel prizewinner, Josef Stiglitz, is more sceptical about how specialist economics ideas have spread: during the period 1960 to 1990, economists were mostly enthusiastic about models with 'rational expectations', where it was assumed that all participants had access to the same information and behaved in a perfectly rational way. The economists also assumed that markets were perfectly efficient, that there was no unemployment (except as a result of greedy trades unions or peculiar regulations such as national minimum wages), and that there was never any form of credit limitation. "That such models prevailed, especially in America's graduate schools, despite evidence to the contrary, bears testimony to a triumph of ideology over science. Unfortunately, students of these graduate programmes now act as policymakers in many countries," concludes Stiglitz. There they are contributing to implementing programmes based on ideas that some people would label market fundamentalism.[11]

The economist and author Paul Ormerod has looked at the list of Nobel prizewinners to date in the twenty-first century, and has noticed that many of them have been working outside the standard twentieth-century paradigm, with key texts published particularly after around 1980. This means that the research front of economics has changed dramatically.[12] But Ormerod maintains that virtually all economics, in the way it is actually taught and practised, is lying far behind.[13] The economic historian John Davis maintains that even if the research frontier has moved, the main direction of neoclassical economics remains as it is in practice, as long as this is allowed to dominate teaching and instruction as completely as it still does.[14]

What do these admittedly highly selective examples, from some 'core' and some more 'deviant' economists, tell us about the field's self-image? Images that populate its consciousness and field of vision are those such as free trade, competition, rational actors with rational expectations making free rational choices, positive economics, efficiency, cost-benefit analysis and economic growth. All these are concepts that have been close to the core of economic ideology throughout most of the twentieth century. Together, this has become the tradition often called 'neoclassical', even if there is no theoretical consensus about exactly what that term means.[15]

I therefore prefer the term *economism*, which refers more to how these ideas are put into practice, than to the exact theoretical definitions of the terms. This economism, which has been much attacked by recent economic research, continues its dominance based on the attraction of superiority and theoretical elegance with which the models have been presented and adhered to by prominent practitioners. Its mode of thought is characteristically top-down. Models and analysis are made from a set of assumptions and then worked downwards toward the world of data – 'deductively'. The model-makers often perceive themselves as an elite, where heads are kept cool and they do not give in to pressure groups, to tears or to wishful thinking.

Logical, cool and aloof. Are there any mythical patterns that correspond with this mode of thinking and feeling about the world? Or is this something that uniquely arose within the economics profession? I believe that these features of economic thinking have a deeper cultural history than the tradition from Smith, Walras, Marshall, Friedman, Samuelson and Lucas. The Greeks also had a god for reason and logical thinking, for detachment and perspective, for erudition and scholarship. You have already met him in Chapter 6, about markets and in the story about Hermes: he is Apollo.

Apollo is, as the Hermes story showed, quite different from his half-brother. To familiarise ourselves with Apollo, it is worth looking at the myths in which he himself is the main character.

Who is Apollo?

Apollo is the god of light and the sun; truth and prediction; precise archery and fine poetry; He was called Phoibos Apollo, 'the bright one' or 'the brilliant'. He expresses Greek ideals such as balance, harmony and cultivated beauty. He was among the most important of the Greek gods. He was so brilliant that he was occasionally talked about as the sun itself. When, like the sun, he rises every morning with his light, he chases away all darkness, doubt and fear and exposes the clear, daylit world down below.[16]

Apollo was often depicted as ethereally beautiful: tall, slim, beardless and with golden hair. He often wore a crown of laurel leaves and had a lyre in his hand. In many ways, he personified the perfect ideal of masculine elegance and strength. The Homeric hymns describe him like this:

Apollo, the Archer.

He goes through this house of Zeus
And he makes all the gods tremble.
They get up, they all get up from their seats

Tiepolo Giambattista's *Apollo and Diana* fresco, dated 1757. The brilliant Apollo
looks down on the world from his cloud.

When he comes in,
when he pulls back
his bright bow.
(...)

She [Leto] leads him
Over to a seat,
And then she seats him.
It is nectar then
that his father gives him
in a gold cup.
He welcomes his son,
while the other gods
have him sit down there.[17]

This god's behaviour makes a powerful impression: everyone immediately
notices how brilliant and exalted he is. Common epithets of Apollo are 'the
archer' or 'the long-distance archer' – the one who acts at a distance.

Apollo's mother Leto gave birth to him on the island of Delos. This was the
only place on Earth in which she could give birth, since Leto had become preg-
nant by Zeus and the ever-jealous Hera had sent the snake-like dragon Python
after her. Python did not get hold of either Leto or Apollo, so the monster had to

satisfy itself with eating young men and women from the nearby countryside. The situation needed to be dealt with, and before he was very old Apollo asked for a silver bow and arrows. He was given them immediately by Hephaistos, the metalworking god. Apollo then went on a journey towards Mount Parnassus, where he knew that Python would be. Python was a mighty beast, born of the ancient forces of Earth and stronger even than Zeus himself. Ovid describes the meeting as follows:

> Indeed the earth, against her will, produced
> a serpent never known before, the huge,
> Python, a terror to men's new-made tribes,
> So far it sprawled across the mountainside.
> The Archer god, whose shafts till then were used
> only against wild goats and fleeing deer,
> Destroyed the monster with a thousand arrows,
> His quiver almost emptied, and the wounds,
> Black wounds, poured forth their poison.[18]

Python can be compared to ogres of folklore or to the trolls in Norwegian folk tales. Trolls are huge and dangerous man-eaters that prefer to roam around at night. But if trolls are exposed to clear sunlight they crack and turn into stone. Similarly, fearsome delusions and foggy, erratic thinking evaporate when exposed to brilliant light and pointed insights. When chaos is put into order with decisive logic, it dissolves. When clarity spreads into a previously confused human consciousness, it is – mythopoetically speaking – Apollo who is having this effect. Apollo's penetrating arrows bring death to any confusion.

Apollo then flayed Python and took the skin with him to Delphi. There, he took over an ancient oracle site which had previously belonged to Gaia. He had a large new temple built with extravagant colonnades. The ruins are still there today. Above the entrance were the words 'Know yourself!' People could make sacrifices to the Oracle at Delphi and gain answers to their questions. Apollo's prophesies – his insight into the past, present and future – were regarded as being the most reliable, so the Greeks travelled there from throughout wide Hellas whenever they required advice.

Apollo never married, and his relationships with women – and with anything female – were far from successful. He was a distant and cool god. There is a famous story that tells of the time when this brilliant archer was himself hit by Eros's arrows. Apollo lost himself in the nymph Daphne, who was the daughter of a river god and an exceptionally vital nymph, but also very shy. Someone said that she was a descendant of Gaia herself, and that she was one of her chaste priestesses. Unmarried and free, she wandered around the forests without a thought of love or married life.

Apollo sees her from a distance and desire overcomes him, making him dry in the mouth. According to Ovid, love consumes even his reason and dulls his predictive powers. Even brilliant Reason himself can be seduced:

> So love's fire
> Consumed the god, his whole heart was aflame,
> And high the hopes that stoked his fruitless passion.
> He sees the loose disorder of her hair
> And thinks what if it were neat and elegant!
> He sees her eyes shining like stars, her lips -
> But looking's not enough! – her fingers, hands
> Her wrists, her half-bared arms – how exquisite!
> And sure her hidden charms are best! [19]

But when he approaches, she turns aside. He follows and tries to win her over, explaining that she has misunderstood. He tries to call to her to say who he is, but she runs faster and faster, so that even Apollo can hardly keep up. Now they move over stump and stone at a furious pace. He no longer has any breath to speak, but puts all of his energy into catching up with her with one last spurt. As he stretches out his hand to grab her, she calls out in desparation to her father the river god and to mother earth Gaia herself that they might save her. And at the very moment that Apollo lays his hand on the nymph, she is transformed into a laurel tree.

Jean-Etienne Liotard's Apollo tries to embrace Daphne, who is turned into a tree when he touches her.

Her arms become branches, her body is covered with bark, and her feet stretch out like roots down into the soil. Gasping for breath, Apollo is left embracing a tree. He is still in love, and notices that the heart is still beating inside the tree. He kisses it, but the tree even tries to avoid this. Finally, he declares that even if she does not want to have him, he will make the laurel tree his tree and ensure that it remains green all year round. He picks leaves and twigs, and weaves himself a laurel wreath which he bears on his head always thereafter, encircling his long, golden locks. (The term *laureate*, used for people who are eminent scholars within a particular sphere, as in 'Nobel laureate', literally means 'crowned with laurel' and stems from *laurus nobilis*, the laurel of Apollo's wreath.)

After this, Apollo spoke out for moderation in all things. 'Know yourself!' and 'Everything in moderation!' were his watchwords.[20] He would never again allow himself to be tempted into allowing his feelings to run away with him. From now on, he would represent composure and orderliness, balance and equanimity, integrity and high ideals. He became a model of perfection and balanced reason, and has since inspired everyone who wishes to live according to these ideals. Enlightenment is his domain. All of those who work for enlightening society in any way, even now in the twenty-first century, put themselves under his protection and act in his name, even if they do not know the classical story about Apollo. He is inherent in the idea of bringing light to the world. Allowing oneself to be inspired by the idea of enlightenment is to participate in the Apollonian form of consciousness.

Is economic theory Apollonian?

Myths are not about what once was, but about that which always *is*. They can be seen as descriptions of traits of our common psyche and the way it relates to the world, expressed in the images and narratives of the time. The pre-Socratic Greeks did not have any specialist fields such as economics or psychology. The myths were the language for their understanding of the world and of the immutable features of human life. All historical cultures have their own sets of myths, and our Western culture has its roots primarily in the Greek and Judeo-Christian mythical traditions in the way they became interwoven in the Mediterranean area.

My contention is that economic theory, for good and ill, is framed by images related to the Apollonian pattern: cool intellect allows man to raise himself above the world, observe things at a distance, try to acquire perspective via logical methods and seek to shed light on contexts and 'mountains of data', to use Paul Samuelson's metaphor. It is like sitting high on a cloud or up on Herbert Simon's mountain top, looking down on the world from its vantage point. Characteristically enough, the front page of Samuelson's textbook shows an image of the world viewed from space, put together like a jigsaw puzzle. The reader is invited up into the stratosphere. From there, we can do jigsaw puzzles with bits of the world far down below. It becomes tempting to bring out forecasts, like the predictions from the Oracle at Delphi, about how things will go for the economic world.

"Let us assume a world with a stable population . . . Let us imagine an economy that just produces two types of goods: guns and butter," say Samuelson and

Nordhaus in their textbook. So you can settle down on your imaginary cloud and look down at the way things work. What happens, for instance, along the arch of the so-called 'production-possibility frontier' if we now want to produce more guns than butter? Thought experiments that require the reader to assume some highly abstract worlds such as this one are quite common in economic articles and textbooks.

I believe it is worthwhile to step back in order to ask and speculate about what kind of archetypal images and feelings are concealed within such modes of thought. The narrative about Apollo presents him as the One who shoots from afar and works through detachment and distance. Together with the constellation of Apollo comes images of elegance and elevation. Highly abstract curves for the relationship between mundane and lowly things, such as butter and guns, may be just pedagogical tools to bring some 'higher' point across. At the same time they appear to be clearly inspired by that mindset which Greek myth identifies as distinctly Apollonian. Through internalising such modes of thought, the student of economics becomes socialised and initiated into the cult of Apollo.

The Apollonian *form of consciousness* thus invites logical abstraction, universal principles, and distanced observation. Logic and statistical averages become more important than rich detail and the unpredictable individual occurrence. The language of figures means more than that of emotions. Within an Apollonian mindset, we become sceptical of tabloidisation and the superficial art of storytelling employed by the mass media and those who spin 'myths' in the sense of widely held but false belief and notions. We prefer to align ourselves with the balanced archer who calmly aims at the target of truth away in the distance. The key elements are clarity, perspective and control.

Apollonian thinkers are careful to evaluate their data and its validity, as well as the thoroughness, education and reliability of other analysts. These others must be among the select ones if they are to be taken seriously; in all cases they must be university graduates, preferably in mathematics in addition to having a good qualification from an economics institute or recognised university. Analyses that are classed as being high in abstract elegance and explanatory strength are preferred. Theory formulation and model development gain higher status than data acquisition and laboratory and field experiments in which one might get one's 'hands dirty'.

Apollo's style is that of honest, penetrating insight. He is straightforward, an archer. Rambling fantasies and chaos, wishful thinking and hazy talk shrink from his sovereign glance – and his sharp arrows. As the monster, Python, succumbs to his precision shooting, irrational fears also dissipate as soon as we manage to think clearly and sensibly.

This is reminiscent of the situation in which you are standing in front of a large, diverse and complicated market with a bewildering variety of buyers and sellers. How to relate to this chaos? How to know what is the right price for a product? Well, it is in the centre of the target, say the economists with an Apollonian expression on their face: the market is cleared precisely where the supply curve and the demand curve intersect. That is where the market equilibrium lies. The market seeks this out, almost like one of the laws of nature, and just as reliable as the law of gravity.

The root of the word 'equilibrium' is the Latin words *equi* (equal) and *libra* (balance). Equal balance. This is also a concept from the sphere of the soul. In the seventeenth century, long before economic theory started using the term, equilibrium was a word used to describe the mental state of well-balanced people.[21] Apollo's emphasis on balance and the point in the middle of the target crop up again in the post-war dominance of general models of equilibrium.[22]

In another central concept from twentieth-century economics, the one termed *rational expectations* also seems to be crafted in Apollo's image. In a famous article from 1961, the economist John Muth stressed that to date economists had not credited the players in the market with *enough* rationality. He points out that economists are not in any better position to forecast developments in prices or interests than entrepreneurs or consumers. If that had been the case, economists could have been much richer than successful entrepreneurs. And they are not. Ergo, companies that survive and thrive in the market use their intelligence to ensure that, on average and over time, they hit their targets with their assumptions.

The assumption about rational expectations had a powerful impact on economic theory from the 1970s onward. Robert Lucas was rewarded with the Nobel Prize in 1995, for the further development of the concept and its consequences. The central point here is that individuals within the economy do not allow themselves to be deceived by the government's changes in taxation and monetary policies, but ensure that they adapt immediately. In that way, the public authorities cannot trick the people involved, for example, by increasing the money supply or public budget deficit gradually without the people understanding that this will create more inflation, and making arrangements accordingly. If we listen with a mythical ear, the perfect rational expectations of theory reveal that these individuals are created in the image of Apollo: every man (rarely woman in this story) fulfils his precise and rational predictions, regardless of circumstances.

In addition to equilibrium and rational expectations, we find that economic thinking often invites a type of *elite thinking* that is characteristic of Apollo. As is described in the hymn to Apollo about his entrance among the gods, he is in a class of his own. Apollo does not mix with coarse people. In one story he flayed the lowly satyr of Marsyas alive because he dared to challenge Apollo in a contest of music. He is his father's Zeus chosen and favorite advisor, with a radiant outlook and always accurate analyses. It is to him that Zeus turns when good advice is required. If a person is first drilled in Apollonian ways of thinking, it is often accompanied by self-confidence and a feeling of superiority. 'It is not easy to be humble when you know that you are right' might be a fitting expression within this mythical universe. A person who does not understand mathematical formulae, models and abstract market diagrams with several shifted demand-and-supply graphs, strictly speaking is not entitled to give an opinion on economic policy. Anyone who does not know their numbers well enough ought to stay at home and not try to win arguments in the elevated halls of Mount Olympus and the corridors of government ministries.

Former Chief Economist of the World Bank, Josef Stiglitz, depicts a few manifestations of this attitude within the International Monetary Fund (IMF): "The Monetary Fund was the source of all wisdom, the supplier of an orthodoxy that was much too subtle for people in developing countries to grasp. The message was fairly clear: at best, there would be one member of the elite – a finance minister or the head of a central bank – with whom the fund could hold a meaningful dialogue. Outside this circle there was no particular point in trying to talk to anyone."[23]

I once had an assignment at the Norwegian Ministry of Petroleum and Energy, assisting a governmental commission that was going to investigate Norway's power and energy supplies twenty years in the future.[24] My job consisted of assisting in the development of scenarios for the power and energy market, to ensure that the commission could make recommendations on this basis for long-term instruments for energy policy. A team of economists was appointed who were to estimate quantitative extrapolations based on existing models. After a presentation of the model apparatus and central parameters in the model, they asked the members: "Which sensitivity analyses does the commission want us to run?" They appeared here to be acting like purely descriptive economists: based on the best data and the best models, they would undertake the calculations chosen by the commission members.

The problem was that the majority were obviously unfamiliar with the model apparatus and the logic behind it. It was therefore difficult to say anything about which 'sensitivity analyses', whatever they were, the economists team ought to do. As may be expected, the team of economists was not given any clear signals from the commission.[25]

With that, the team could withdraw to their own offices and computers and prepare the analyses that they themselves believed were necessary to influence the Norwegian parliament to move in the 'right' economic direction. This ended in what they called the 'optimal balanced economic growth' model, which implies a harmonisation of the taxation schemes and maximisation of socioeconomic efficiency, and assumes the continuation of past production and consumer patterns. Scientific? Perhaps. Value-neutral? Definitely not.

- £ -

To have elites is neither undemocratic nor undesirable. It is an necessary part of the Apollonian image. Society needs intellectual elites with outstanding skills and centres for eminent research. Without such gifts of Apollonian intellect, we would be lost in the dark.

The risk with the Apollonian is the huge shadow that grows proportionally with the intensity of the light. The shadow easily hides a fundamentalist – and unreasonable – certitude in the superiority of its own form of consciousness. It is forgotten that reason itself is only *one* perspective – and that Apollo is only one god among several. Elitism becomes sinister when it gives sustenance to an often unconscious sense of being the primary guardian of truth. It quite simply *knows*. Other conceptions become inferior and uninformed.

This is the victory of ideology over science, as Stiglitz says. We have then moved from economics as a venture of enlightenment to economism as fundamentalist supremacy. Everything else suffers under this version of rational and masculine superiority: the poor, ignorant, women, forests, the wild, dark, animals and all speechless beings. Everything else becomes inferior – or Dionysian, if we use the Nietzschean dichotomy. We run the danger of unconsciously continuing the tradition of white supremacy in our very economic theory of society.

Economic ideas have migrated into and settled down in our minds. They have become our true masters in the twenty-first century. And Apollo lends his logic, his precision and superiority, to these ideas that can give the impression of being so rational, self-evident and almost incontestable in public debate. Then attitudes like these feel reasonable: only eco-fanatics, economic illiterates, feminists, agitators and troublemakers are going to protest against our balanced recommendation. But they are so unbalanced, extreme and radical that they are not worth listening to.

Let us do some investigation into the backyard of economism. What is that left lying in the shadows? Every idea emphasises something, at the expense of something else. Thus, everything has its shadow side – people, gods and ideas. What is it that ideas of economism places in the background, or *represses*, to use a psychological concept? I would like to call attention to four principles at the core of economism that all throw long shadows.

1. Price is the measure of all values
2. Individuals are utility-maximising
3. Firms are profit-maximising
4. Economic growth first.

Please note that I do not intend to enter into a argument about right and wrong here. Rather, I am trying to describe some central principles of economism while also exploring the shadows they cast. In psychotherapy, when symptoms get troublesome, one tries to see how one's habitual mode of thinking may be contributing to the very symptom one is suffering from. The same applies to the following 'psychoanalysis of economism': how do reasonable first principles build up a shadow that undermines one's original purpose?

Shadow 1: Price is the measure of all values

Perhaps the largest shadow within current economic practice arises through the limitations on what is counted and entered into the accounts. Conventional macro figures relate almost exclusively to items that are priced in markets – goods and services, work, property and capital. This again is subdivided, into the two realms of real economy and financial economy.

The *real economy* refers to wherever on the planet tangible economic activity is taking place. This might be where trees are being felled, fields harvested, fish caught, guests served in restaurants, houses built, cars manufactured, microchips cut in factories – all brought by road vehicles, ships and aircraft. This is the part of the economy that 'delivers the goods'. Here there are also figures about volumes and physical sizes. But it is mainly the value – that is, the volume multiplied by unit price – that is entered in accounting and then aggregated into larger figures.

The *financial economy* operates more on the abstract and mental, but completely quantifiable, medium of money, in which money caters for payment services, required liquidity and credit. There are no physical volumes involved, but in the financial economy vast amounts of global currency and an endless variety of credit and debt forms are being traded.

Standard economic theory has focused so much on setting prices that it has neglected other sides of the economic system, according to Ronald Coase, a Professor of Economics, in his Nobel lecture. He continues: "The concentration on the determination of prices has led to a narrowing of focus which has had as a result the neglect of other aspects of the economic system. Sometimes, indeed, it seems as though economists conceive of their subject as being concerned only with the pricing system, and that anything outside this is considered to be no part of their business."[26]

Anything that does not become visible through pricing within these two realms gradually disappears from economic decision-makers' attention and slides into oblivion and shadow. For example, there are problems with public economic figures when companies move goods between their own departments in different countries without setting a market value on them (also known as 'transfer pricing'). In the same way, the growth in international barter between companies also disappears from the radar, because it is not recorded with prices.[27] This involves huge sums each year, and they are growing rapidly.

The more fundamental issue is that most things in the natural world and society have no price tags, and are therefore also left out. Only prices from purchases and sales fall within the system. Home cooking is out, whereas meals in a restaurant are in; do-it-yourself car and bicycle repairs are out, while workshop repairs are in; care of the elderly by friends and family are out, whereas care of the elderly in care homes is in. Social relationships such as work processes and stress, family and friends, personal challenges and learning, art and health have an enormous impact on people's life and happiness. But they become invisible in the view of what counts in today's monetary economy. When it disappears from the clear light of economic data and calculation, these realities don't cease to exist, but they fall into a more shadowy existence.

Increasing losses of animal species and their habitats, destruction of natural and cultural landscapes, climate change and far-travelled pollution are not given any price either. Over a longer period into the future, when things get really bad, the market will start to notice increasing costs, but again this will be indirectly, and unfortunately the price signals often come much too late.[28] It may be too late to save the last tigers once only thirty are left. It may be too late to increase taxes on CO_2 emissions once the climate has already changed. As we have seen (Chapter 8), such types of value are not entered directly into the accounts and are therefore left out of market decision-making processes.

This applies not only to nature, but also to poor people. If you have very little money, you easily become invisible with your low purchasing power. For example, in many poor countries, illness among poor people has not constituted a market for pharmaceutical companies, since the poor are unable to pay. Therefore these markets do not even register on the companies' radar. It is more profitable to make medicines for those with high purchasing power.

Organisations and society have chosen economic control systems. Through monthly rituals of wages, purchases, bookkeeping and financial reporting, the company's attention is directed, every Monday morning yet again, towards economic figures. Left lying in the shadow, therefore, are other valuable capitals, based on local communities and biological qualities provided by nature. They end up outside all of the financial totals. If, on the other hand, we could extend economic accounting and markets to cover social and ecological capital forms, it would be possible to integrate some of this shadow back into economic consciousness. This will be the topic for the next chapter.

Shadow 2: Individuals are utility-maximising

The early economists created an idealised picture of the way everyman makes his choices, and named this figure Economic Man or *Homo economicus*. This incredible phantom immediately calculates the consequences of every choice. In this way, he (this figure never appeared in a 'she' version) minimises costs at all times. He will not buy the trousers at one place if they are a little cheaper on the other side of town. On the other hand he always maximises the benefit (choosing the work for which he gets the best pay, maybe for the least amount of his time). Economics defines utility as "the ultimate goal of all economic activity". If item X is preferred over item Y, it follows necessarily that X has greater utility for the individual who wants the item. No question can be asked about the consumer's preferences, as they are by definition rational.[29]

Many people have commented that this is a hopelessly unrealistic model of humans. Yes, that is probably correct, economists have said. Sophisticated economists are quite conscious of the empirical limitations of the *Homo economicus* model. But it was not the intention to give a realistic image of what the individual does. It is a very simple model intended for use in developing theories and models based on the fact that, over time, most people generally choose what is good for them. It reflects the reasonable notion that people attempt to do as well as they can for themselves, given the constraints facing them. Not everyone might behave rationally, not all the time and not in all types of choice. But, on average and over time, at least a significant share of people will use most opportunities to serve their own interests. The system as a whole will therefore behave as if everyone acts out of rational self-interest. In this way, *homo economicus* is reminiscent of Apollo: a abstract personification, more god than human. If you and I are not equally perfect, then we are nevertheless created in the same image – we are similar. This has been a useful assumption, says economists, that has contributed significantly to development of economic theory.[30]

Since the image comes from the Apollonian symbolic universe, we understand more easily how this mythical economic man is always a *man*. There is an inherent disregard for the feminine in Apollonian thinking, as illustrated also by the many stories about Apollo's relationship with women.[31]

When the economic psychologist Daniel Kahneman was awarded the Nobel Prize for Economics in 2002, it was a recognition of the long-term work of nuancing the conception of *homo economicus*. Together with hundreds of others, he has been improving economics knowledge of what actually affects economic decision-making in practice, beyond the idealised image of the utility-maximising individual.

The way in which actual people differ from the Apollonian ideal is researched via the discipline of psychological economics, also labelled 'behavioural economics'. Ordinary human decisions are often based on simple cognitive rules of thumb called *heuristics*. These are often useful simplifications, but can easily give false results. For example, they apply when people believe that expensive beer tastes better than cheap beer – which is something that still applies if you do the same test but swap the price tags (the 'expensive-is-good' heuristics). Another example is when people place great emphasis on dramatic or colourful events (to win the lottery, to catch contagious bird-flu), than they do on more normal, grey events (to lose on the lottery, to die of disease from smoking).[32] Another curiosity is that people seem to hate losing money more than they rejoice at winning an equivalent sum. That means that we are more loss-averse than is strictly rational.[33] Correspondingly, I rejoice if I obtain a tax refund, even if it actually means that I previously paid in too much.

There is also proof of a bias towards the status quo: far fewer people choose, for example, to swap power supplier when the prices change than would have been economically optimal. Most people are systematically slower adapters compared with *homo economicus*. They prefer the well known and familiar, firmly basing their decisions on a subjective reference point rather than thinking in absolute terms.[34]

Within economism, the idealised model presupposes that individuals like you and I always know what we need, and make the necessary adjustments to maximise utility . On principle, economists do not then discuss whether the consumers' choices are correct. They take it as given that we, jointly and separately, make purchases based on rational criteria.[35] But Kahneman has documented the fact that people systematically make the 'wrong' choices – according to the model of maximised utility.[36]

That is not all. Worse, it seems that people often simply do not know what gives them greatest long-term utility or happiness. The purchase of a new PC can be more frustrating than beneficial. Moving to a more expensive house can mean a nicer abode, but also eventually turn out to entail more nose-to-tail driving, more time to work, less time with friends and deteriorating neighbourhood relations. The whole lifestyle we build up is sometimes built on what other people – friends, parents or culture – expect of us, more than what our soul really needs.

To begin with, we may perceive this new lifestyle as slightly unpleasant – later on, perhaps after a major crisis in our lives, as more tragic than beneficial. All the same, we continue to consume goods, services and travel in order to maintain a lifestyle believed to be attractive. In the wealthy part of the world, we borrow and over-invest in areas that do not give us what we genuinely want.[37] In marketing theory, nobody ever believed much in *homo economicus*. Marketing is all about how to best manipulate customer choices away from the most rational choice. The marketers are paid to succeed in this. As a result of both inner uncertainty and external pressure, many of us end up living an inauthentic life; what we end up paying for does not match our deeper needs.

The idea that everyone is a rational actor also glosses over the effect of poverty. With very little or no money the idea of a free, rational choice is devoid of meaning. Most of the Earth's population are too poor to participate in the consumer economy. When three billion of us have such a weak voice in the market, free choice becomes an illusion. Similarly, groups such as children, sick and severely disabled people have very little in common with the idea of a rational actor.

How can we model real people's behaviour in the market if we reject *homo economicus*? But why should we stick with just one model to cover all situations? The Swiss Professor of Economics Bruno Frey takes a critical view of this, because developing one all-encompassing model would be extremely complex (in which case, the most important advantage of *homo economicus* – simplicity – is lost). Instead of one *homo economicus* to cover all situations, he recommends developing *several models for human action* for use in different types of analyses. In that case, researchers would first assess the type of problem to be analysed and then choose a suitable model for the purpose. This contrasts with current economism, in which the same model is the starting point and automatically applied to all types of problems.

"To reverse the procedure by putting the problem first, and the choice among various models of human behaviour second, could turn economics from a technique-driven science into an art. The skilful choice among the various types of *Homines Oeconomici* would differentiate masters from simple technicians . . . knowledge of a deeper kind would be valued again," concludes Frey.[38]

Shadow 3: Firms are profit-maximising

Traditional economics assumes that companies have one single target: to maximise shareholder value.[39] This credo is endlessly repeated in statements both in the field of corporate governance and from the management of companies. For example, in Norway the Director of Information for the Hafslund power company states that they have always said that they regard the solar power company REC as being a financial investment: "We have one single target for REC, and that is the best possible return to our owners."[40] If somebody in the company held the conviction that an expansion of solar power can contribute to the goal of combating climate change, this was seemingly not worth mentioning in an interview with financial journalists.

According to economic textbooks, profit maximization is not simply a potential goal; it's the only feasible goal, given the desire of other businesspeople to drive their competitors out of business. If a business faces tough competition, the only way the business can survive is to pay attention to revenues and costs. In addition, the firm is set up as an instrument for its shareholders to get return on investment.

A few years ago, a colleague and I held a management development course for a Norwegian finance corporation. In the programme, we talked about the value of a personal vision and of having a living sense of purpose in the work of being a manager. If this is not clearly stated and understood by employees, you might end up as an effective manager but a poor leader. The basic idea is that you have to know what your vision is and be clear about it, for others to find you worthy of their trust and commitment.

We asked questions such as 'Why did you become a leader?' And, more pointedly, 'Why should your subordinates accept you as a leader?' We invited to individual and group reflection on this. When we opened the group session to share thoughts on these questions, there was silence for a long time. This was an unusual topic – frightening for some people perhaps. Finally, out it came, with authority: "You are a manager to create shareholder value. That is, after all, what a leader's job is all about."

My colleague and I exchanged a brief glance. The group session was allowed to continue without any intervention from us, but during the first break, we agreed to rearrange the rest of the programme. All we had got were 'economically correct' utterances about a non-authentic relationship to their work in the company and about themselves as managers.[41] What subordinate would be inspired enthusiastically to follow the manager on the basis of a personal vision about increasing shareholder value by 15 per cent or more for somebody they did not know and would never see?

At the same time, of course, this young leader was right. He is supporting the overall target as dictated by the current economic system: returns on their investment for the shareholders, i.e. the owners of the company. If the manager in a joint stock company does not work for the shareholders, what is he or she up to? Then the only thing is to get rid of that person and appoint someone who has a better understanding of the real duty of a manager and the responsibility he or she has to the board of directors and to the shareholders.[42]

- € -

The Economist is an influential periodical which promotes a liberal ideology. Its mission is to spread economic information and understanding of the markets' excellence, and it is a world leader in the quality of its analyses. To improve economic understanding, it has taken up what it calls a fashion that has been traversing the business world in recent years: Corporate Social Responsibility (CSR).

CSR has emerged as the result of the discontent with the unadulterated pursuit of profit in which costs are often shifted over to local communities and the natural world. The point of CSR is that companies should have a responsibility to people and the environment in addition to their responsibility to the shareholders. It is an attempt to counter 'turbo-capitalism' or the economics of ruthlessly exploiting social and natural resources.

The Economist complains that concepts like CSR seem to have won the battle of ideas. Big firms nowadays are called upon to be good corporate citizens, and they all want to show that they are. *The Economist* argues, however, that CSR is based on a misunderstanding of how the market economy actually functions.[43] People who evangelise for CSR (that is, ensuring that companies take extra responsibility for society and the natural world) have misunderstood the most fundamental concept within the economics field. What CSR adherents don't get is how the invisible hand turns each company's self-interest into welfare for society. *The Economist* maintains that Smith's book *Wealth of Nations* is actually an instruction manual in CSR. The book indicates precisely that when companies are running at a profit, it is because they are putting resources in motion to create wealth which, sooner or later, will be to the good of *all*: suppliers, customers, employees, the State and the owners.

The fact that someone is willing to pay the price for the products means that he or she is creating value for society. When companies and individuals thus create a surplus from their own rational self-interest, the wealth of the entire nation increases – as we outlined in Chapter 6, about markets. Once the wealth of the nation increases, the State is in a better position to carry out its task, which includes providing for the poor and protecting common goods such as the environment.

Enlightened self-interest, *The Economist* continues, is useful both to the company and to society, for *both* the individual and the polis. Smith's invisible hand resolves any potential opposition. And, it adds, it is important to remember that enlightened self-interest is something other than greed and corruption. Greed, in the ordinary meaning of the word, is not rational nor calculating. Freely indulged, it makes you fat and drives you into bankruptcy. The kind of self-interest that advances the public good is rational and enlightened. Enlightened self-interest looks beyond short-termism and plans ahead – and is therefore already good CSR, concludes *The Economist*.[44] No change is really necessary. Maximising profits is basically a good thing. Back to business as usual.

After having become acquainted with Apollo, it is not difficult to see where such ideas and arguments come from. And, as always, where Apollo reigns there is logic, differentiation and precision. I personally agree with a lot of this. *The Economist* is right in questioning that part of the CSR movement that criticises high profits on the basis of an anti-money attitude. CSR doesn't make its case by being morally indignant and reproving an offensive firm who plays hardball and secures huge financial surpluses when following the rules of the market regulations. *The Economist* is also right to point out that high profits for players in the economic field often increase collective wealth.

At the same time, the CSR side highlights the need to expand the company's reporting of its impact on social and environmental capital in addition to the financial capital.

The core of the problem, as *The Economist* indicates, lies in the term 'enlightened self-interest'. What is enlightened? And what is the 'self' in self-interest? How are we to understand the *self* of the economic actor? Where does this self begin and end? At first glance, it seems simple: the 'self' of the company is identical to its possessions, as described on the assets side of the balance sheet. Everything the company owns and possesses must be included there. And who owns the company and its possessions is made evident from the liabilities side and the register of shareholders.

Legally and economically, this is correct on the basis of current understanding of bookkeeping and business economics. But the central question remains: Is this too narrow? Are we toiling away with antiquated ideas about singular identity from the days of Adam Smith? Are we operating with an understanding in which the boundaries for the firm are set arbitrarily? When a company is viewed as an atomic entity with a hard shell separating it from the rest of society, this conception casts all that to which the firm is related into the shadows. The degree to which a firm is embedded in a network of relationships becomes invisible to the company.

The key question becomes: Is it possible to define the boundaries of a company's responsibility without taking its broader set of constitutive relationships into account?[45] If not, where do the boundaries for the company's relational self go? It can be argued that there are other relationships than those to the owners, customers and employees that are critical for the firm. If that is the case the company should account for and report on this wider field of interaction.

Adam Smith's famous example, his prototype of the firm as an economic entity, was a pin factory he had visited and described in his book. Everyone involved with that company was working in the same building, each person in their limited location, and the owner walked around, checking the efficiency of the division of labour. The company and its workers began and ended the day's work within the same four walls.

Today, most companies comprise a network of activities, people, financial and information processes that, with the Internet, are spread halfway or all the way around the globe: purchasing in China, a web server in California and sales outlets in London, while design takes place in Paris. Where do the company's boundaries lie? A company is a legal person, yes, but does it make any sense to talk about an independent delimited participant? Systemically and philosophically, it probably makes more sense to think of the firm as *interwoven into the network of relationships that sustains it.*

Today, the company is best served by externalising as much of its costs as possible and transferring them to others. Everything it can avoid paying for, such as oil spills, specialist waste, carbon emissions or development costs of new technologies, will increase profits for the company and its owners. At root, therefore, it will have no choice: As much as possible of its costs, such as educating employees, protecting against possible accidents or criminality, or sick pay, is best left to the surrounding society.

This does not show any lack of consideration or evil intent. It is the legal definition of a company, this idea about the company as a sack, which makes this course of action completely natural. Costs out, profits in. Joel Bakan, a Professor of Law at the University of British Columbia, therefore calls the current company structure an 'externalisation machine': everything that could imply costs would be best ejected from within the company's boundaries.[46] It resembles psychology's description of the way every human being has an Ego which endeavours to reject everything that it does not like about itself. It ends up 'under the carpet', in its own shadow. It is as if it is no longer there. The ego no longer sees it. It is repressed. But everything that is repressed doesn't cease to exist. It remains part of the greater Self, but now residing in the shadow.

I have discussed elsewhere the problematic nature of setting a definite limit for the human self in the brain or the skin, as traditional psychology has done.[47] I believe that our identity, our larger Self, covers our relationship to other people as well as the air, environment and the landscapes we inhabit. Correspondingly, if companies are really embedded within an industrial ecosystem,[48] then we should try to make the balance sheet reflect this. Banks cannot thrive unless their customers and the community where those customers are work and prosper too. Now seems the time to start extending the accounting for these vital relationships. The company itself has interests in the local community, in the landscape and the climate. If seen in this more systemic sense, the company cannot be truly profitable unless the surroundings also prosper

So *The Economist* is speaking from within a severely limited view when it gives the shareholders sole right of disposal over all of the company's financial surpluses – before social and environmental deficits have been settled. The profits also belong to the network of which the company is a member, not only to the shareholders.

Current bookkeeping practice provides too narrow a picture of the company's self. When relationships with the surrounding world are omitted, economic players no longer act in enlightened self-interest.

Shadow 4: Economic growth first

As with pricing, the utility model and profit-maximisation, economic growth is also a necessary and indispensable constituent of modern society. I am not against any of that, just as I would scarcely want to be against money, the soul, the sea, power, food or sex. However, we cannot afford to be ignorant of the shadow side of them in our collective behaviour.

This is not the place for a detailed review of the enormous debate about economic growth since the 1970s. This book is about the relationship between economic ideas and human emotional life. Why does the debate about growth become so emotional? Why do the boundaries become so rigid?

In his textbook, Paul Samuelson does a good job of describing the fundamental attitude to economic growth that characterises economism. He points out that in the hundred years between 1900 and 2000, the economy grew by a factor of eighteen, measured in GNP. The collective economic activity in the US thus increased by a factor of eighteen. He states that this is the most important economic fact for the entire century. Continued economic growth makes it possible for developed industrial countries to give their inhabitants more of everything: better food, larger houses, better health services, pollution control, education and pensions.

The Economist joins in with the praise of growth: "Over the past century or so . . . the western industrial democracies have experienced what can only be described as an economic miracle. Living standards and the quality of life have risen at a pace, and to a level, that would have been impossible to imagine in earlier times . . . All this has been bestowed not just on an elite, but on the broad mass of people. In the West today the poor live better lives than all but the nobility enjoyed throughout the course of modern history before capitalism."[49]

All nations continue to regard economic growth as the most central purpose of their politics, Samuelson continues. Countries that are successful in the competition for economic growth, such as the UK in the nineteenth century and the US in the twentieth century, continue to climb in the international pecking order. They also become role models for other countries that are on their way to greater wealth. "Economic growth is clearly the most important factor in the long-term success of nations," he concludes.[50] "To get rich is glorious!" Deng Xiaoping supposedly said before China joined the race.

Samuelson and Xiaoping are not alone in regarding economic growth as the best miracle cure for all of society's ills: Poverty? Just increase growth to produce more and consume more goods and services for everyone. Then take a step back and see how wealth trickles down from the rich to the poor. A rising tide lifts all boats, as the saying goes. Unemployment? Increase demand for goods and services by lowering interest rates and stimulating more investment. Then growth and employment will increase. Overpopulation? Just help economic growth to get started, and see how it contributes to reducing the birth rate as it did in the industrialised countries during the course of the twentieth century. Environmental destruction? If only people become prosperous enough, we will also be able to afford reductions in pollution and improved environmental regulation. More GNP growth leads to a reduction in local pollution – after a short-term rise. Economic growth is the foundation on which most other problems can be resolved. Correspondingly, deficient growth becomes synonymous with stagnation, human tragedy and increased conflicts about sharing a cake that no longer gets bigger.

- £ -

The concept of economic growth is among the most fundamental assumptions in economism. The economist Herman Daly, who is among the founders of the field of ecological economics, tells a story from the time when he was working at the World Bank and assigned to comment on a report concerning the relationship between economics and the environment. An early draft of the report contained the following figure:

The relationship between economics and the environment (1)

Daly thought the figure did not give the environment enough prominence, and that it would be best to draw a new figure in which there was a bigger box around the whole of this figure which could then be called the environment – in other words, the economy was framed by ecology. Then the relationship between the two would become clear.

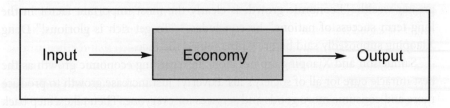

The relationship between economics and the environment (2)

The next draft then had a box around the entire figure (see above), but the outer area was not labelled Environment or Ecosystem. Daly pointed out that the larger box would have to be labelled or that the figure caption would have to explain that the economy was a subsystem of the environment. The last and final version of the report avoided having any such figure at all. It was deleted.

At a seminar somewhat later, Herman Daly asked the chief economist at the World Bank, Lawrence Summers, why the diagram had not been included and whether he believed the growing size of the economics box in relation to the size of the environment box was an important question. The chief economist's answer came quickly and firmly: "No, that is not the correct way of looking at it." [51]

There are some deep-set assumptions that collide with one another here. They have deep-seated differences that make them see the world in very different ways.

Chief Economist Summers was thinking – together with thousands of other brilliant minds – in line with the neoclassic understanding of economic growth. There are four drive-wheels or factors of production behind that growth: capital, resources, labour and technology. None of these have any clear limitations; it therefore seems certain that growth can just continue. If any one factor goes lacking, another type of resource, labour force, capital or new technology can be used to substitute for this scarcity so that growth can continue. Anything that is getting scarce will result in higher prices, and therefore attracts increased effort and ingenuity into providing it. When one price goes up it becomes profitable to invest, ensuring that sooner rather than later, the lack is overcome. The higher the oil price becomes, for example, the more investment there will be in developing new fields or in using oil more efficiently or in finding completely different forms of energy. Growth therefore 'never' needs to stop. Adaptation and ingenuity will always win in the long run.

Herman Daly, along with thousands of other growth-sceptics, believes this assumption about everlasting economic growth obviously has a dangerous shadow to it. The thing that ends up being forgotten is that the scale of the biosphere, containing the planet's ecosystems, is not infinite. So, we must ask whether collective economic growth, at one time or another, results in what might be called *uneconomic growth?* That would be a parallel to what might take place in individual companies, when they produce so much that further production becomes unprofitable. Uneconomic growth takes place when further increases in collective production results in costs to resources and well-being that are higher than the utility of what they add. The same thing happens when cells in the body start to divide more and more quickly, out of control. In medicine, this is called cancer. The downside of growth becomes greater than its upside. This first becomes widely evident when the growth boom overshoots and goes into bust and collapse in the future.

Centuries ago, when the human economy was small in relation to the environment and natural resources, the economy could grow as much as it wanted. However, when collective economic activity appropriates most of the Earth's surface, and most of the photosynthetic production of plants and marine resources, the economy ends up in a new situation. The Earth is affected by a 'cancer'. When more and more fish stocks, copper or oil are consumed by growth, it becomes increasingly difficult to find more. The emissions start to change the sea's ecosystems, the level of CO_2 in the atmosphere increases, wilderness disappears and pollution disrupts the food chains, and all at an increasing rate.

Uneconomic growth occurs when increases in production come at the expense of resources and well-being that is worth more than the items made. Certainly, many goods are produced, but at the same time so are more and more 'bads': more pollution, stress, overcrowding, income differences, water shortages, flooding, drought, hurricanes. Viewed as a whole, then, we are becoming poorer and not richer, even if the level of economic activity is frantic. Manufactured capital cannot substitute fully for natural capital. It is no use building more fishing boats when the seas are emptied of fish. Society does not become richer by clearing up after pollution and oil spills. For that reason, new indicators for natural capital are required. If all economic activity, regardless of what kind, are added into the GNP, the downturn will become evident only once the resources are so empty that the ecosystems break down. Indeed, GNP rises as long as new cars, ships and oilfields are built, but it is highly doubtful whether this growth is beneficial or sustainable, concludes Herman Daly.[52]

- $-

Here are two different perceptions of reality that are on a collision course. One is based on the idea of a optimal balanced growth of the economy. This growth is thought to be able to continue for as long as we can see into the future, thanks to the finely balanced interplay between the production factors and the market. It is important only to adjust the factors by which that growth is achieved. The second perception of reality sees physical and biological boundaries to growth which cannot be exceeded without a consequent collapse.[53] Two mythical perspectives: One puts the balanced rationality first, the other sees the whole planet system as first priority. Apollo versus Gaia. So far, economism has stood shoulder to shoulder beside the archer-god. The renegade 'eco-economists' have had to create their own research environments and publish in other journals in order to be heard.

The assumption that economic growth is necessary and indispensable looks as if it has just as much support as before. But more and more people have been frightened by the dark clouds massing in the sky (changes in the climate). Adherents of balanced economism believe that growth is necessary to finance and manage the challenges of climate change. Adherents of green environmentalism believe that is it exactly that very growth that is creating it. Can the mythical level of a debate be any clearer than that? What we see and how facts are interpreted are dominated by what pre-analytic vision resides, before discourse starts, deep in the human psyche.

Some conclusions: from monotheism to polytheism

The principal current in economic theory during the twentieth century was inspired and formulated by that part of the human psyche that the Greeks identified with Apollo. Equilibrium prices, mathematical precision and rational actors dominate. These are ideas that have morphed from being science to rigid ideological practice among a great many senior managers and decision-makers.

The hope is that the nuancing that is now taking place (at breakneck speed) in new economic research and theory also finds its way out into instruction and practice. But economism defends itself, even against the economics researchers. Prominent economists from John Maynard Keynes to Joseph Stiglitz have complained that researchers are heard only when they bring out messages which suit the prevailing ideology of the decision-makers.[54]

- $ -

The shadow of the Apollonian has grown in parallel with the breakthrough of economism. To sum up: first, prices make us narrow things down so we see and count only a small part of the overall picture. Anything that is sold on the markets for an overall price is made visible in the economic macro-figures. Anything that is not priced is left to oblivion.

Second, all consumers are perceived as rational utility maximsiers, without any questions being asked during their consumption. Buying and consuming – of whatever – are portrayed as good things in themselves. All prices are correct if purchasers are willing to pay, regardless of whether or not the purchase satisfies the requirements of the purchaser.

Third, the principle of enlightened self-interest is formulated very narrowly. Adam Smith's observation of the invisible hand's impact is undoubtedly correct and important. Markets contribute to the growth of wealth by means of mutual benefits of trade. But there is also an implicit assumption that every company is an isolated unit with a stock of property, as defined in the balance sheet. This casts a shadow over the entire network of mutual relationships. Only financial exchanges with customers, suppliers and shareholders are documented, while the rest of the relationships – such as with the local community, with the environment and climate – remain unaccounted for and therefore invisible.

- £ -

Put bluntly: if economism is followed through to its logical end, we end up 1) with tunnel vision where only prices count, 2) commending any consumption whatever, 3) constraining companies to one single purpose, and 4) regarding all economic growth as good, as long as its factors are optimally balanced.

In addition, if, like Apollo on the mountain top, we analyse society only through highly abstract economic figures, it is easy to forget the discernible fact that the economy is a wholly-owned subsidiary of something much larger, namely the planet or Gaia herself. A change in mythical perspective may bring out the fact that both society and economic activity are only possible thanks to a continuous flow of day-to-day services from the planet's ecosystems. If the mother company's capital fails, the subsidiary goes down too and ends up in the hands of the bankruptcy administrators. There, the residue is divided and sold to the highest bidder – with no extra-planetary purchasers having registered to date. When the demand for the fragments of human economy is zero, their value is also zero. That is unfortunate for the creditors.

And who are the creditors? They are the sea, the air, trees, bacteria, the finned beings, the feathered ones, and all others of our fellow creatures on this blue planet. We humans are borrowing their surplus and consuming their capital. Our economic system becomes a company that is run on behalf of its creditors and is threatening to pull them down into bankruptcy with it. Along with us, and presumably somewhat before us, all of the major mammals are being destroyed. We do not seem to be able to cope with what the dinosaurs managed: millions of years at the top of the food chain. With excessive overconfidence in our own reason and narrowly selected economic indicators, we are building our house, *oikos,* on sandy ground. Although maybe they were not as quick-witted, the dinosaurs were probably more far-sighted in practice. Who knows what kind of invisible hand they were led by?

I believe the problem does not lie with the Apollonian perspective in itself. We need Apollonian clarity to handle the anxiety, greed and other strong emotions that arise connected with large sums of money. It would be naive to exclude Apollo's perception of reality and to replace him, in an equally one-sided way, with a Dionysus or Gaia. Money is a strong, archetypical theme, firmly anchored in the both the rational and the emotional, and people can as easily lose themselves in attacking money as they can in running after it.

Wisdom includes the understanding that all knowledge is incomplete, and that all forms of rationality, regardless of how sharp and thoroughly prepared they are, have their own inherent limitations. Wisdom is also the ability to imagine things from a plurality of ideas without allowing oneself to be possessed by one or the other, while also retaining the capacity to act. "No matter how beautiful and perfect man may believe his reason to be, he can always be certain that it is only one of the possible mental functions and covers only that one side of the phenomenal world which corresponds to it." [55]

I therefore believe that we need an economic theory that pays attention to and adheres to several gods (or dimensions of value) at the same time. That would mean a transition from monotheistic to polytheistic reasoning in economic theory and practice. The word monotheism means only one god – one measure of value only. The Greek *Poly-theos* means having several gods and being able to change between these fundamentally different ways of understanding reality. Each of them personifies a distinct dimension of value. To me, the words 'multidimensional' and 'pluralistic' can mean more or less the same thing, but I prefer polytheistic.

This might imply that we will have to go from just one money to plural moneys. The idea is similar to having different kinds of 'coins', as was the case in the early days of economics, in which each was coined in the image of one of the gods. Today, in practice, this would mean different sorts of money for different types of capital. A modern variation of this is described in the next chapter.

Polytheistic money: coins showing Demeter, Goddess of fertility and corn, on the left and Poseidon, God of ocean and the marine world, on the right.

So, in line with Bruno Frey's recommendation to have several models of homo economicus, economics becomes a truly polytheistic phenomenon. Apollo's singular, clear light can be complemented by other types of light, such as Gaia and Demeter's green-coloured, Poseidon's marine blue or Hades' dark light, to reflect the many gods that live in a full-value economy. Economism does violence not just to poor people and the natural world, but also against the other gods, such as Gaia/Demeter (climate/environmental crises), Poseidon (ocean acidification), Hades (burden of debt), Chaos (currency anarchy) and Hera (social fragmentation). The other gods no longer want to be kept outside. Therefore, economism may need to expand some of its core concepts and to include a plurality of forms of capital. They are forcing their way in.

Chapter 12

A scenario for new forms of capital

Is profound economic change possible?

"What is needed is not ever more refined analysis of a faulty vision, but a new vision." – Herman Daly[1]

The energy industry constantly faces opposition from environmentalists: Should the Arctic Ocean be opened up to oil exploration? Should drilling be permitted in North Alaska's nature reserves? Should the oil companies assume the costs of upgrading environmental protection and safety equipment in oilfields with diminishing production? Should large wind farms be constructed on otherwise untouched sections of coastline? What kind of biofuels should be encouraged? What about wave energy? But coastal landscapes, agriculture and arctic ecosystems are not the responsibility of energy companies.

Logging companies receive widespread critisism for their felling methods. It was recently documented, for instance, that the Norwegian logging company Viken Skog was not respecting forest hotspots with capercaillie and rare biotopes. It typically responded that old-growth forest, grouses and beard moss lichen are not its responsibility.

Fashion, toy and garment companies buy branded goods from Asia or Eastern Europe, and force suppliers to reduce costs as far as possible in order to increase their market share at home. This is simple economic logic. The workers' conditions and the social costs to the society in which the goods are actually produced are not their responsibility.

While industry has been racing along during a long period of high prosperity, contributions to cultural work, voluntary organisations, political organisations and community projects have been slowing down. They struggle to acquire funds and members. Sociologists have demonstrated how the civil or third sector became fragmented during the last decade before the millennium. Why are there cutbacks in public and private contributions to these causes? Why do employers not set aside more time for voluntary work by their employees?[2]

All the above kinds of concerns are done away with using the same argument: *They are not profitable.* Viewed in this way, there is one common yardstick that cuts through the value conflicts outlined above – money.

-$-

Good intentions about the environment and fine words about ethics are of little help. Prices remain the most powerful source of information in a market economy. The question will be whether we can do something with the money systems that directly motivates individuals and companies both to think and to act differently? That is what I believe, and in this chapter I am putting forward a future scenario, for a more pluralistic economy. The scenario could appropriately be called *polycapitalism*.

The starting point lies in dealing with the shadows of the four guiding principles of economism that were described and discussed in the previous chapter. First, we need to include more dimensions of value than those that are measured in traditional prices. Second, we need to do this in a way which influences the choices made by individuals and stimulates a more inclusive sense of self-interest. Third, we need to provide companies with a broader set of linked objectives than the single one (of maximising profitability) that has been the sole purpose to date. Fourth, we need to embed economic growth within social and ecological limits.

We ought to be able to achieve this without drowning in centrally controlled and inert regulations such as subsidies, a variety of taxation schemes and regulations for correcting market failures in the conventional economy. But how?

The idea is to *introduce new kinds of money in addition to the one we are using today, and allow these to circulate in parallel but related markets.* (In Chapters 3 and 9, on money and credit, we saw that the manner in which money is created is not fixed once and for all.)

Normal money (pounds, dollars, euros) acts as a powerful *incentive system.* An incentive is a form of motivation that stimulates or encourages people to act in a specific way. Money is far from everything, but – as we've seen – it is pretty close. It is the strongest motivation system within a modern society: worldwide, people defy fatigue, family ties and long journeys to be able to earn money. We work and endeavour to increase the amount we make, even when our quality of life does not continue to increase. People will do more or less anything for money: give away a kidney, give birth to other people's children, break up deadly waste without safety equipment. People go to work, synchronise their diaries and align themselves towards common objectives, as long as they are paid money to do so. The market system delivers the goods to anyone who can pay. Money makes this enormous system go round. And people act accordingly, for good or ill.

Today, national currencies have a virtual monopoly, both as means of exchange and as an incentive system. This monopoly suppresses other dimensions of value, such as nature and society. The idea is to introduce complementary currencies that will function as parallel incentive systems alongside money, but with a distinct purpose. Since money is attention (Chapter 3), a new type of money could contribute to increasing attention about natural capital, globally and locally. We also need local incentive systems that will increase trust and community collaboration, and thereby strengthen social capital. So we are thus introducing complementary types of money to create new markets for *natural capital* and *social capital*. These would work in parallel with the normal market system that delivers goods and services.

A scenario of polycapitalism

This involves linking money more closely to other dimensions of value so that soul and money no longer need to be enemies – not even to be out of step with each other. We can be 'doing well by doing good' as they say. The scenario therefore describes an additional monetary system for social forms of capital, and another for natural forms of capital. In total, then, we would get three different monetary systems that envelop one another in the following way:

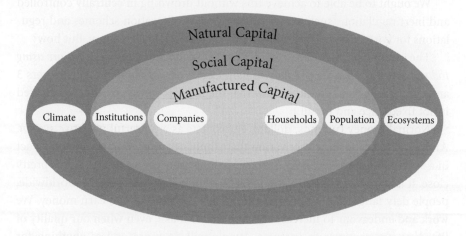

Today, when many people feel that the economy is soulless, it is mainly because it is based on a single type of thinking and a singleminded purpose, whereas the soul is always and inevitably polytheistic and pluralistic. As a psychologist, I know that the human being is highly complex, and never completely satisfied with only one form of intelligence (Piaget, Gardner), one method of learning

(Bruner), one motivation (Freud), one type of consciousness (Jung) or one pattern to work and live by (Chickzentmihaly).

I am no expert when it comes to the policy formulation and practical solutions. I am coming from a different starting point from those of economists, politicians and practitioners. My field of work is studying the way the human psyche is interwoven into a multiplicity of relationships with the world. For that reason, I would like to invite other people to join in thinking about economics in a more diverse way. I have picked out elements of the following proposals from a series of sources, but I believe the configuration as a whole is new. The proposal is presented here more as a normative possible scenario than as a detailed plan for implementation.[3] It should be perceived as an invitation to think out a new vision of the future – one that is fundamentally different, but also *plausible, relevant and maybe surprising*. A practical roadmap to implementation, is a long-term task which is not really suitable for one individual or even for a small team, but would be a collective venture if the idea caught on.[4]

We can use our best knowledge and experience available from the markets, regulations, organisational change and our own commitment. We will have to try it out. Pessimism is best suited to good times, but now it is too late to be a pessimist.

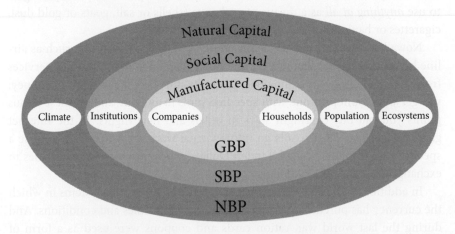

The Figure shows in a nutshell a future in which the government introduces two complementary currencies in addition to the currency we already have. These new types of money correspond to other forms of capital which can then be exchanged in new markets. Taking the UK as a starting point, we might then imagine having 'SBP' for social pounds and 'NBP' for natural pounds, in addition to GBP, the Great Britain pound. These circulate in their own specific markets, and – in general – cannot be exchanged with one another.

The anti-capitalists would prefer to control or curb the markets. Here we are taking a completely different route by letting the magic of the markets work for the common good, as Adam Smith discovered that they could, and as economists have been describing for a long time. The main difference from conventional economics is that we use different types of money to measure different forms of capital.

The three forces that drive the scenario

This scenario is made plausible by three related driving forces for change that have grown strongly over since at least the 1980s, even if they are not yet particularly evident in the mainstream: 1) introduction of new complementary currencies, 2) extended accounting for individuals and firms, and 3) expansion of what forms of capital are taken into account.

1. New types of money – complementary currencies

We start with the understanding that money is not a fixed, objective commodity, but something that is brought to life through human *imagination* and mutual trust (Chapter 3). Based on this, society or its subgroups can in principle agree to use *anything at all* as a means of exchange (shells or salt, goats or gold dust, cigarettes or bank notes).

Nowadays there are already many specialised types of currency, such as airline bonus points, for example. Airline points can only be used to buy services from the same group of companies. In reality, this becomes a form of money: you get an account printout, with specified sums in and out, and for these bonus points you can buy overnight stays in hotels and new flights. In the Internet game *Second Life*, participants go into a virtual world in which they can use a specific kind of money called 'Linden Dollars'. There are even opportunities to exchange these for normal dollars.

In addition, some chain stores have their own bonus point systems in which the currency has purchasing power subject to certain rules and conditions. And during the last world war, ration cards and coupons were used as a form of money. Even earlier, during the Great Depression of the 1930s, when it was difficult to get hold of liquid funds in official currency, there were numerous types of local money. These include the WIR (which also means 'we') in Switzerland. This economic circle still exists, and its turnover is equivalent to billions of Swiss Francs. It is a large cooperative for making reasonable loans in the WIR currency, which you can benefit from if you are a member of the circle.[5]

So, introducing other types of money is not a completely new idea. New types of money can be introduced if sufficient people agree to believe in something and to bring it into use as a means of exchange for some duration. It has been done before and will be again, as for instance in company scrips or Local Exchange Trading Systems (LETS). More later about local types of money.

Next, we take our understanding from markets and economics, that pricing is determined on the basis of the margin between supply and demand over time. Markets are decentralised and effective decision-making systems. No one can sit in a central position and control what is a correct price. Buyers and sellers must work that out in the give-and-take relationship between them, as discussed in Chapter 6 about the soul of the market. To get the pricing in new currencies to work, one will of course need both a supply side and a demand side for these currencies. Arrangements must be made for sufficient information flow between participants and, perhaps most importantly, regulations and supervision of these new markets. Only then can the markets start working to give mutual benefits to all involved parties. Further, the markets as a whole can then contribute to generating genuine wealth, i.e. balanced investment in more forms of capital than just one at the expense of the others.

2. Social and environmental accounting

In addition to currencies, new and extended accounting is required to create compliance, overview, transparency and stories about how the various types of money are flowing. All transactions must be entered into the accounts in accordance with rules adapted for the market's purposes: the measurement and growth of natural and social capital.

A lot of work has been done in these areas, but a lot of further development is still needed. We only have ten to thirty years of experience in the accounting of forms of capital such as natural and social capital.[6] In comparison, we have 500 years of experience of traditional accountancy, and even this is under constant revisioning. It is obvious that it will need a great deal of thinking, experimentation and research before well-defined standards, equalling those for current accounting practice, fall into place.

But it does not need to take 500 years. It might actually be an advantage to be able to start with a blank sheet. And there are already numerous standards to choose between, for example, Global Reporting Initiative or triple bottom line reporting.[7] Thousands of companies have already made additions to their annual reports by presenting environmental accounts (or for social or intellectual capital). Others have acquired experience with the balanced scorecard approach, in which reporting is also extended beyond the financial results, with key performance indicators for three additional categories or perspectives: 'Customer Value', 'Internal Business Processes' and 'Learning and Growth'.

The polycapitalism scenario is built on the continuation of such initiatives. So far, the results have had limited impact because environmental and social accounting has been something that most investors and analysts quickly thumb through to get to the 'hard facts' – the financial results. Environmental and social results are just icing on the cake of the financial 'bottom line'. And as other people, including Joel Bakan, author of the book *The Corporation*, have pointed out, if the manager of a company really puts social and environmental considerations *ahead of* its shareholders' interests, the board of directors would currently have a legal right and an obligation to fire that manager.[8]

These cross-pressures on the board from the stock exchange and its own shareholders *guarantee,* on the basis of current corporate governance system, that larger companies are unable to take on any costly social and environmental responsibility. CSR is possible only if it serves the company's reputation, thereby strengthening the financial results in the future. To put it bluntly: CSR is acceptable as long as it is not taken seriously (or reduces profitability even in the short term). We are therefore now seeing that the websites of major companies are full of information about their environmental and social responsibilities, while this is minimally applied in practice within its own decision-making processes. With mandatory accounting of social capital and natural capital, and with new tax rules that reward results in these areas, the internal contradictions will start to dissolve: good companies will show balances across the three types of results, and ought to gain financial tax-related benefits from that.

3. Extension to new forms of capital

In addition to new types of money and extended accounting, there is a third driving force for change in the direction I am outlining. Traditionally, the concept of capital has been limited to capital goods and financial capital. However, over recent decades, a whole spectrum of 'new' forms of capital has been proposed. This has led to a strongly growing level of interest in and research on extended concepts of capital – particularly human capital, social capital and natural capital.

'Capital goods' refers to physical objects that have been produced through work and that provide a flow of material benefits to the owner.[9] It might involve machinery, buildings, boats and so forth, which are therefore occasionally called real capital. In addition, there is financial capital such as currency and paper securities. These two cover the traditional economic meaning of the word 'capital'.

The idea behind *human capital* is that it is human competence and health that are the central wealth-creating factors in the economy. Property, land and machinery are also necessary, but without a well-educated, able-bodied population, there will be little long-term wealth-creation. Human capital is an attempt to quantify the return on investments in education, experience and health.[10]

Social capital refers to the connections and networks between people in various areas: is there reciprocity, trust and shared norms? Or is there fragmentation and mistrust? While human capital relates to characteristics within *individuals*, such as education and skills, social capital refers to the network of relationships *between* people. The quality of these relationships is crucial to a well-functioning society, and it is certainly not impossible to measure changes in such relationships over a period of time. Mistrust and weak social networks lead to increased levels of isolation, depression, violence, misuse of intoxicants and corresponding calls for security and control. This even has huge financial costs, and makes life for us more difficult and more anxious – we still know too little about just how much. But there is broad consensus that a society with a lot of reciprocity between people is also a better society, according to political scientists such as Robert Putnam and sociologists such as Pierre Bourdieu.[11] Mutual trust lubricates social interaction as well as financial development.[12]

Natural capital is a concept that has emerged in conjunction with the field of ecological economics, with the former World Bank economist Herman Daly being a central figure within it.[13] A society consuming its natural capital (trees and fertile soil, fish and clean oceans, groundwater; as well as non-renewables such as oil or copper) can achieve a high GNP growth for a period, but that is not sustainable.[14] Instead it is value destruction. Such depletion of the natural world and resources is currently viewed as value creation and entered as a positive item in GNP, because all economic activity is added to GNP. If one person pollutes and then another person cleans the pollution, both activities add to GNP, making environmental degradation frequently look good for the economy. Therefore, there is a shift away from the traditional GNP to construct indicators of national wealth that takes environmental effects into account.

Why new types of money now?

But is this approach – of adding new types of money, new accounts and new forms of capital – *realistic?* Many people think that economic models, regulations and accounting are already much too complex. Won't this cause dreadful confusion? It must be much simpler to have one type of money rather than three, and more efficient to set the pricing of all the forms of capital using the same money as unit of account? And won't they eventually be exchangeable with one another, so that in reality there is only one type of money? These are important counter-arguments, to which I will return below.

The scenario does not imply such a radical break as it might seem, because (almost) all of this is already present to some degree, concealed within the three driving forces described above. They just have to be put together inside a larger, public framework. They must be cultivated, but many of the seeds have already started growing.

What the scenario highlights about the current situation is that both markets and regulations regularly miss out essential aspects of society and nature from their view. If markets and regulation operate with only one universal type of money, their attention is shaped by this, and the other dimensions of value fall into shadow. As we saw, companies are currently legally bound to work towards creating value for their shareholders. Any managers who give priority to natural or social considerations rather than to shareholder interests, as measured in financial capital, could lose their jobs.

An example of this might be Nobel Peace Prize winner Muhammad Yunus's conflict with the telecommunications service provider Telenor, about their joint mobile phone company: Grameen Phone in Bangladesh. The Telenor management considered itself obliged, not least out of consideration for its (already very wealthy) shareholders, to breach the letter of intent about selling its stake in the company, because Grameen Phone had become so valuable. Anything it loses in ethical and social capital will not register in the financial accounts. Shareholders threatened to sue Telenor if it decided to 'give away' money to strengthen trust and community considerations in Bangladesh. Whatever they do to improve the livelihood and local communities of their workers will register only as costs. The share price is clearly seen through the lens of traditional currencies, while losses and profits in social capital remain invisible.

On the other hand, if we introduce other types of money, such as social currency and natural currency, we will be able simply to extend the self-interest of the company and its shareholders. The company can now grow along several dimensions of value at the same time. In addition, we can make it financially profitable immediately by, for example, giving tax credits to companies with good social and environmental results. So, companies that can report good social and environmental results will have a lower taxation level than companies whose social or environmental accounts are in the red.[15]

Suddenly it also becomes in the financial self-interest of the shareholders for the company to contribute to the growth of social and natural capital. The new types of money will give a wider understanding of what a company actually is. The triple bottom line sums up the contribution that the company makes to the networks by virtue of which it exists.

Markets for social capital

Social capital consists of relationships and networks between people which are maintained through continuous effort, often under the direction of not-for-profit organisations. Similar to conventional capital goods, social capital can also supply an annual 'return'. This capital generates a flow of benefits in the form of better social relationships for those that live within a defined geographical area. In that flow we find goods such as community spirit, willingness to help, trust, tolerance and security, with cumulative effects such as better health, etc.[16]

Can the mercurial dynamics of the market be used to enhance social capital? And how should social capital be measured, if this is at all possible? Where should the social currency come from? Who will issue it? There are lots of questions about a scenario with a currency for social capital. However, we are not starting from scratch. There are many experiments and rich traditions of knowledge to draw on.

A good place to start can be in the world of education. Edgar Cahn is a Washington law professor and founder of a currency he chose to call Time Dollars. He was upset at the enormous social differences between people, which were causing a lot of talent to be wasted. Children born in places with a great deal of poverty and urban violence dropped out of education. So he went to one of the most challenged schools in Chicago and offered an assistance programme. This was presented to the oldest pupils, and involved their helping younger pupils to learn. They were to act as mentors or coaches for the younger ones. Cahn started up a scheme in which the mentors were credited with Time Dollars. One hour's help was credited with one Time Dollar. Once mentors reached 100 Time Dollars, they could exchange them for a recycled PC that would belong to them.[17]

Cahn thus introduced a form of social currency based on voluntary work for other people. The results? The older pupils, who had been passive recipients of tuition until then, were suddenly given a meaningful task at school: 100 hours of making contributions to help younger pupils gave them a new feeling of importance. There was someone who needed them; they were perceived as important resources by the adults on Cahn's team. Their self-respect increased, bringing with it improvements in their own learning too. In addition, some began spontaneously to look after their mentoring pupils to ensure they were not beaten up or robbed on their way to and from school. And, perhaps most importantly, it was tangible proof of recognition when they received a PC of their own. The efforts made for other people also reinforced their own social relationships. They got to know their mentoring pupil's family and others within the mentoring group. This network led to the growth of the actual social capital, probably far in excess of the 100 Time Dollars issued. Here we see how a new type of money makes visible the hidden sources of another type of wealth. New sources of value emerge once there are ways of appreciating the efforts made.[18]

The Time Dollars, or the tokens the pupils are given as mentors, can be seen as incentives that reward particular types of action. The PC for which they could exchange their Time Dollars also has a value in ordinary money. What is the difference, we might ask, between handing out Time Dollars and handing out ordinary dollars? Could they not just as well hand out ordinary money to the mentors – for example, five dollars an hour?

The important difference lies in the *norms and institutions surrounding the use of Time Dollars*: They can only be used once one has achieved the full score – in this specific school district and for this specific purpose. They are also surrounded by another framework:[19] this type of money is connected with a specific purpose and remains within the local community, whereas ordinary money can be used anywhere and for any purpose, including soft drinks, drugs and guns. *Different types of money for different purposes.*

Many Time Dollar systems are currently in action throughout the world. And the Time Dollar system is only one of many hundreds of local initiatives used throughout the world for appreciating community services.[20] A supply of unused skills is linked to demand within the same local area. Why are there unused skills, and why is this demand not already being met with ordinary money? Well, because there are often too few paid jobs, and there is often also too little liquidity of conventional money. In addition, there is a lack of clarity around different hourly rates of pay. Time Dollars sorts this out by having 1 hour input for a common purpose = 1 Time Dollar. Since time is distributed more equally across the population than conventional money, privileging time-based participation contributes to reduced inequality. So there is an equality, trust and mutuality in the Time Dollar systems which is perceived as attractive by many people.

London has its own 'TimeBank', which has more than thirty branches in different areas of the city. Thousands of people have been involved for years. People get together for lunches, they exchange emails, and strangers help one another out. New friendships emerge around the exchanges. Every time someone receives help, it is recorded in the TimeBank accounts. People who accumulate giver-hours can get hours back themselves from other people in the network. People who want to meet other people and who have an hour left over are the people who use the system most. "There is one thing ordinary money cannot buy," says one participant, "and that is a friendly face. I always find that here."[21]

LETS, which stands for Local Exchange Trading Schemes, is a generic name for social types of currency. To date, local monetary systems such as these have been run on a voluntary basis and have therefore been vulnerable to breaks in continuity, to a critical mass that is too small, and to enthusiasts who later drop out for one reason or another. The institutions surrounding the LETS currency have not been solid enough, and this has been a significant obstacle to growth.[22] It is reasonable to ask why the introduction of new types of money should be dependent on private initiatives? Why should idealists and enthusiasts burn themselves out trying to get systems, audits, scale, trust and continuity into place? Why could not the State, whose *fundamental role* includes regulating currency and the money markets, issue several types of currency for different dimensions of value?

In the future world of the polycapitalism scenario it would be a government task to introduce and regulate *Social British Pounds*, or SBP. Ordinary GBP is issued as credit by approved banks when they lend. Similarly, local authorities can approve certain non-profit organisations as issuers of social currency. In principle, any organisation or foundation could issue SBP to its members whenever they provide programs and services that are of benefit to others and not otherwise provided by local, State or federal entities. These could be school mentors, care-givers, sports coaches, parent-child centres or other social institutions. All of these can apply for the right to issue social currency, where 1 SBP = 1 hour's documented work done for other people. Those who already receive payment in traditional currency will continue doing so. The SBP will be additional to work paid in ordinary currency, and will increase the attractiveness of and opportunities for that effort which could today be said to be underpaid and under-provided. It might be work for the kindergarten, the school band, day centres for the disabled and unemployed, visits to the elderly, circus training for twelve-year-olds, voluntary work for Amnesty International or the Red Cross, or hundreds of other opportunities that the local authorities want to prioritise.

However, not all types of social networks contribute to inclusive social capital. Some groups are inward looking and tend to reinforce exclusive membership and homogeneity. Such bonding forms of social capital may create strong in-group loyalty but also strong out-group antagonism. This is sometimes called the 'Hells Angels problem' in research into social capital. The right to issue social currency ought therefore to be reserved for organisations that increase welfare and social inclusion between people in the local society. They provide a sort of *bridging* social capital by expanding the networks, not chopping them up by strong internal *bonding*.[23]

In this future, each and every social service performed in the context of an organisation approved for issuing could receive SBP as a visible appreciation for the contribution this makes to the community. Today, such volunteers are given little or no public recognition. Nevertheless, it is exactly this type of voluntary effort which both creates and maintains local community. It has always been so. But since the financial system has now invaded the social sphere, fewer and fewer people have time for local contributions (because time is money, hence time spent with those who are unable to pay declines and social isolation grows). With a new system, such social input could gain new recognition and even enter into the public accounts.

With this system it becomes apparent that you contribute social services for the sake of something larger than yourself; that is, for the local community. The community gives back recognition in the form of a token, a little medal, a visible appreciation of the effort put in: an SBP. In that way the community *remembers* who has made the contribution, and the social currency works like a form of public remembrance.[24] This brings about a gradual increase in mutual trust within the local community. And trust in other people, both neighbours and strangers, is precisely the core of social capital.[25] Perhaps there would be a new type of competition between municipalities and counties. Which has the most inclusive social network and greatest increase in social capital – Hull or Grimsby, for example?

But it has to be possible to document the contribution, enter it into the accounts and audit it before it can be included in the social capital. With that, we find a need for some new jobs: social accountants and social auditors. They have to take responsibility for ensuring that the supply of SBP adheres to the prioritisation decided by the local community. It should not require people to drown in paperwork. Flexible Internet solutions can be utilised to automatically record the work put in. Both recipients and service providers must be able to get receipts so transactions are transparent and auditable. Another possible technical application is the use of online social networks and widespread mobile devices with cameras. In this way each transaction could be registered by way of an MMS (Multimedia Message Service by mobile phone), with images of the faces of people contributing. This would give every unit of social currency an image: a face.

This would constitute the supply side of the new type of money. We have now seen how SBP can come into circulation. What then of the demand side? What underpins and maintains the value of the SBP? What would there be to prevent inflation, in the worst case a deluge, of SBPs, making them all worthless?

-£-

The demand can arise on three levels: private, organisational and public.

Private – people use SBPs to buy services for private purposes. The following services are popular in the existing LETS systems: babysitting, pet-sitting, meals, hairdressing, advice, exercise, yoga, tuition, entertainment, help with computing, games, car maintenance, joinery services, gardening, painting, driving, running errands, book lending, dance, etc. In this way, SBPs come into private circulation and contribute to reinforcing social networks and therefore social capital.

Organisational demand arises because companies in this scenario will get reduced taxation if they can prove a positive social result in their books, as out-lined above. Companies can acquire SBPs either by having employees spend some of their time doing community work or by accepting some part of the pay-ment for their sales, typically local services, in SBPs from customers. At the end of the year, surplus SBPs in the accounts would mean that at least one out of the three bottom lines have been satisfied.

What effect would it have on companies if they had to ensure income in SBPs in order to lower taxes? Suppose a company wishes to improve its SBP results before the end of the year. It knows that there are potential customers out there with SBP purchasing power. The company can then develop strategies to increase its social results. Ingenuity and the magic of the market will ensure that services are delivered to someone who needs it in an area where this particular company has the competence (and spare capacity) to supply it. Perhaps an IT company might help a children's school with computer equipment and receive payment in SBPs. A solicitor's office provides legal advice for a not-for-profit foundation and makes part of its invoice payable in SBPs. Employees take a few days away from work to carry out some voluntary work for something they are enthusiastic about.

Public demand can take several forms. It might be worth thinking through how far the payroll tax should (or could) be paid in SBPs. The payroll tax makes it financially more expensive to employ people and therefore contributes to unemployment. Changing a tax that makes it more expensive to employ people over to an arrangement which stimulates service to the local community might seem to be a win-win situation.

Another idea is to request payment of advertising fees in the social currency, SBP. The public spaces in our towns and urban areas are often treated as a free resource, but advertising often suppresses cultural, artistic or natural expression in such public spaces. This approach would mean regarding this space, in which we all meet and move about, as a focal point for social capital. Companies that want to have access to the public space for their products would therefore be asked to pay a fee in social currency before the advertisement could be put on display and claim our collective attention.

Since social capital is something that has to be constantly renewed, it is ques-tionable whether it should be possible to accumulate SBPs over long periods of time. The degree to which social currency ought to have an expiry date is some-thing that might be considered – this is currently the case with airline bonus points. SBPs could be valid for two years from the date of issue, for example. This would stimulate circulation and prevent any accumulation of SBPs within the cycle. An exception could be if someone wants to put SBPs aside till they become pensioners. But social currency should in any case be interest-free. And, if it is intended to represent work done for the community within a specific geographical area, its validity ought also to be limited to a specific region of the country, a county or a municipality. Such issues will have to be tested and discussed before any conclusions can be drawn.

If one could find effective working arrangements and regulations so that the markets could get to work at improving social networks and social capital, this would not just be something that is 'nice to have'. It would provide an opportunity for the growth of society in a new direction altogether. And this growth would be more in line with the 'new welfare' discussed in Chapter 5. Research into social capital points consistently towards improved social integration and support from social networks, which have a relatively greater impact on health and well-being than factors such as smoking, being overweight, blood pressure and physical passivity. The impact is clearly positive also for insurance costs and economic development.[26]

According to Danish researchers, the fact that the Nordic welfare states function as well economically as they do can largely be explained by the relatively invisible but solid base of social capital. People have more trust in their fellow citizens and in the public services than do people in many other countries in the world. This social capital also makes it possible to have a more efficient business operation: fewer resources are required for bribes or for checking and monitoring whether people adhere to the rules. People are able to rely more on one another and on the State.[27]

Regardless of research findings like these, starting to account for and appreciate the time spent for the sake of local communities and social relationships outside the existing financial economy would be – in this book's perspective – important steps in the direction of greater mythical and conceptual diversity in our economy. It breaks the grip of universal money as the sole unit of account. Hera (i.e. Juno Moneta) is honoured as well, not just Apollo, as the Greeks would say. Thus, the definitions of which dimensions of values are considered real in our economic discourses would be widened.

How to invest in social capital

Sociologists have documented that school pupils' participation in activities such as music, sport, the Scouts, singing in a choir, taking part in Red Cross activities and so on is important for developing the capacity and desire to become committed to community activities later on in life. Robert Putnam points out that investment in youth activities can give returns in social capital in later years, many times over.[28]

Nevertheless, budgets and grants for areas such as these were cut back during the course of the 1980s and 1990s. There is probably a simple reason behind that: they are not profitable. In times of public and private cost-cutting, such items are easy to cut. It is much simpler to make cuts there than to resort to redundancies or cutbacks in operations. When the decision is made, the long-term costs of cutting down on investments in social capital are invisible. Reversing this trend probably depends on better documentation of the value inherent in social activities, and SBP accounting can do just that.

The software company salesforce.com, of which its Californian founder Marc Benioff is the CEO, is an example of a company that is already investing in social capital. This company business idea is to provide online webtools for applications such as sales and customer relationship management. Benioff wanted community effort to become an integral part of the operation, so foundations and non-profit organisations are allowed to use their software free of charge. In addition, one per cent of the company's shares are given away to a foundation whose board includes employees. One per cent of the profits also go straight to the foundation. Finally, Benioff has arranged for employees to use at least one per cent of their total working hours for helping the local community in which they live. He calls this the '1-1-1 solution'.

Last but not least, says Marc Benioff, the measures have had an effect on employee motivation and self-respect. They just don't work in a high-pressure software company in order to earn more money for the shareholders. They feel that they also work for other values, and that they are able to use other abilities than the one specialised skill for which they have been employed. This becomes a source of happiness and satisfaction for both employees and managers.

It is just as well that economists like Peter Drucker or Milton Friedman did not dominate that board of directors – Benioff would have lost his job because he had done the shareholders out of their claim to maximised value.

If we introduce a new market for social capital, arrangements like the ones that salesforce.com and many others have been pioneering for a number of years would become much more widespread. It implies that most companies would now want to improve their social bottom line in order to get tax reductions. What is now the exception – with companies such as Interface, Tom's of Maine, and salesforce.com in the US or Oso Hotwater in Norway – would become the rule, because the society is changing the regulatory framework of what it means to operate profitably. A company following the example of salesforce.com would be able, each year, to enter into its accounts its accrued social capital. In other words, it would receive SBPs in line with what institutions and foundations in the local community think its contributions are worth, and this would result in tax reductions.

The level of issuance of SBPs in an area would make evident what the inhabitants are doing for one another outside the close circle of family and friendships. There are many dimensions of the social landscape, both positive and negative, that could be valid purposes for issuance of SBP. Among these are education, preventative health care, cultural events open to the public, cultural heterogeneity and tolerance, commuting, family stability (and failure), reducing levels of violence and conflict, combatting drug abuse, crime prevention, civic participation, and even population control. These measures are indicators of quality of life in a community over time. They constitute the metrics of social capital. One can invest in social capital by making SBP (or maybe investing traditional currency) in projects or work that seek to improve these dimensions.[29]

To improve their community, local politicians could set up priorities among the above dimensions, which might then be used to guide and stimulate investment in and the issuing of social currency. Based on this, companies or foundations could contribute within the region. Investment in the social capital of other countries could also be assessed for approval.

The traditional model for improving social conditions is that the State collects taxes and then pays people for carrying out tasks such as the cleansing and maintenance of public places, supervising the elderly, or offering activities to young people. What is the advantage of this scenario over the traditional model? It is that we trigger the markets' capacity for innovation and combine it with the power of motivation from the new social currency. Work done for the community is accounted for and shows up in important indicators. We will gain a new system of information and incentives. Money becomes no longer just a means which, at best, can reinforce the life of the soul and emotions by paying for artistic provision, care of the elderly or the beauty of buildings. The SBP reflects human relationships more directly. In this way, *money and soul become integrated*. Social currency makes new forms of wealth visible and motivates people to form broader networks of human relationships. No longer the polarity between high moral values versus mundane profit – as in the contrast between God and Caesar – but morals and market in the same money.

Markets for natural capital

Every monetary system leads people to act in certain ways. If we have a system that reinforces the harvesting of large amounts of wild fish, truffles or oil in order to achieve higher income, then that is exactly what we will get. If we have a system that reinforces older pupils helping younger ones to learn, then – voilá! – that will also happen. It becomes less a matter of individual morals and personal choices, and more about the structures and systems that surround these choices.

If we are in agreement (for example with international authorities such as the IPCC and the Stern Report)[30] about needing to lower the emissions that have an impact on the climate, improve ecosystems and greatly reduce consumption of non-renewable resources, then we can create new monetary systems to help us do it. The complementary currencies can be used in addition to those already in existence. They make dimensions of value other than the traditional capital visible. It is probably also simpler to introduce additional new sets of money, markets and forms of capital than it is to try to patch up the existing system. Millions of people already have vested interests and enough resources to resist strongly every change.

So how do we then get started on creating markets for *natural capital*? As we saw above, capital is an asset that is capable of generating a flow of goods or services into the future.[31] An ecosystem fits this concept very well: well-functioning ecosystems bring forth an annual stream of plants and animal species which together perform ongoing 'services' such as air cleansing, water cleansing and soil stabilisation. (They don't do that for our sake, of course. Humans are just fortunate to receive it.) As with social capital, the fundamental idea is that we have to make natural capital visible in the workings of the markets, such that human decisions can take it more into account.

Why not start with an huge oak or an old pine in the forest?

How much is a tree worth?

In current economic thinking, a tree is valued on the basis of what the trunk can be sold for on the timber market at a specific time.

The tree is not valued on the basis of its inherent capacity to clean the air, nor for the aromas and biochemical signals it exchanges with other trees and creatures, nor for the soil retaining, anti-erosion powers it possesses, nor for the enrichment of the surrounding world with its leaves, nor for the shade it provides in hot countries, nor for the contribution it makes to shaping the countryside, nor for the contribution it makes to the thousands of insects that live on it and the birds which find food and shelter in it, nor for the contribution its roots make to the crumbling and aeration of stony soils, allowing the binding of CO_2 to silicon in granite to become calcium bicarbonate, which finally feeds algae in the sea and sinks to the seabed combined with carbon in the form of chalk.[32]

A tree that has stood in the same spot for one, two or perhaps three hundred years gives soul to the place and to the people who live there. The tree, an upright fellow creature in the world, patiently in its place, always the same yet a little different from one day to the next, and from winter to spring to summer to autumn. This existential contribution does not count in our hectic economic discourses.

The tree becomes silent within the framework provided by current economic pricing methods. For the rational actor, the value of the tree is calculated thus: a trunk with a volume of 0.6 cubic metres at a price of 35 GBP/m^3 equals a value of £21 before VAT. And that is that.

Why not expand this method of assessment?

Why not also start appreciating the other qualities of the tree? And why not start to evaluate the flow of the services done by the tree every day and year with a new form of money. This money would express the level of return from this unique and vital part of the natural capital. Even if this evaluation would be crude and simple, it would still be better than nothing.

As human beings, we are intelligent enough to be able to both count and account for the values of the tree in more than one way. We have sufficient feelings and understanding to be able to appreciate and measure other dimensions of value than only those that have direct utility for humans.

For example, we know that there are trees of all ages in ancient forest. Around a third of biomass consists of standing, growing trees, a third consists of standing 'dead' (fully grown) trees, and a third of lying, decaying tree trunks. All of these categories are of value to the place: to insects, fungi and birds, for microclimate-control, propagation, metabolism of nutrients, and so on. Current economics only recognises the value of some of these trees – namely the ones that are mature enough for harvesting. And they ought to be taken out as soon as they are full grown to maximise capital gains.

In addition, if we assume that long-term timber prices are on their way down, it will be worthwhile harvesting as much as possible today and putting the money into other investments which offer a higher return. If you make an annual return of up to 10 per cent on these other investments while the timber price remains stable, it is obvious what is *economically* the most rational action to take.

But if the trees are left standing, they will contribute to growth in natural capital. It takes hundreds of years for ancient forest to achieve maximum diversity. Viewed in this way, owners of forests that are allowed to stand uncut, decade after decade, are contributing to the production of increased natural capital. *Ecologically*, it would be most rational for those who choose to invest in natural capital in this way to be given a return on their investment in natural currency.

Valuation of land-based ecosystems

There are – obviously – several types of natural capital. A simple subdivision would be climate, marine, land- and coast-based ecosystems, and finally geological, non-renewable resources. In this section, I am limiting myself to land- and coast-based ecosystems.

Regardless of what happens to the climate, it is important to take care of the greatest possible amount of biological diversity. This is because it has intrinsic value, it has a value to us as people, and it contributes to climate control and to the ecosystem's general capacity to survive. Establishing the value of natural capital in one place requires biological valuations to be carried out, in the same way as we today have property values assessed. The biological valuation would need to specify the constituent parts of natural capital, and what the annual return might be. Rather than trying to express the richness of biodiversity in financial prices, as has been the trend up till now, they can be expressed in *Natural British Pounds*, or NBP. The return on the natural capital will correspond to how biodiverse it is and how productive its ecosystem services are.[33]

In the polycapitalism scenario, all economic actors will eventually be required to keep environmental accounts, as many have already begun doing today. However, in this scenario, such natural values will be entered into the accounts in terms of NBP. Values for all kinds of emissions and for the consumption of raw materials will be entered into these accounts as costs measured in NBP. The cost in NBP reflects the biological costs *directly* (i.e. to what extent ecosystem services will be needed to clear up and replenish the consumption) rather than some indirectly estimated financial costs.

Any interchange between the natural world and the economic world should be recorded as a transaction in NBP. Thus, any local pollution would enter as a cost on the polluter's NBP accounts. Likewise, any extraction of natural resources would also be a cost, and if it exceeds the annual return it would soon start showing up as depreciation of the natural capital. In this way the economy would be – eventually – firmly rooted in ecology. By making decisions based on both GBP and NBP profitability, good business sense would become much more balanced: The economy would be more directly mindful of ecology without having to wait for some slow political tax regulations to compensate for externalities.

The demand side for NBP will arise when companies and organisations want to improve their natural bottom line. In the new taxation regime, as mentioned above, financial tax relief will be granted if both social and environmental results are positive. On the other hand, there will be an increase in financial taxation in the event of corresponding deficits on the triple bottom line. The larger the surplus in SBP and NBP, the lower the tax. And vice versa: higher tax for companies running deficits in NBP.

Any owners of areas of the natural environment can sell NBP from their annual return to companies. Or they might sell 'shares' in the whole of their natural capital and therefore the rights to future annual returns. It would be the same tried-and-tested principle as applies to joint stock companies.

The owners still have the full right of disposal over the natural capital assets. The value of these will probably increase over time. In addition to their yield in NBPs they can sell tangible natural resources from the property on conventional markets for payment in GBP. This sum would go to the owner's GBP account. But if the owner extracts very large volumes of timber, game or other resources, or undertakes major interventions such as development, building roads or excavating gravel quarries, this might produce biological deterioration. Then the property's natural capital and future yearly returns in NBP will drop. New biological evaluation may be necessary to establish by exactly how much the value of the area's natural capital has diminished. Thus the owners have strong incentives to protect and enhance the biodiversity of the land.

The owner of the area is responsible, along with any co-owners, for ensuring that the natural capital is managed in the optimum way. If he or she is successful in improving biodiversity, soil and water quality, the natural capital and annual returns will increase, exactly in the way that joint stock companies' share prices and dividends usually increase when their bottom lines improve.

Suppose the property covers an old-growth forest with high biodiversity and the manager decides to construct a new forestry road to extract large volumes of timber and sell these for GBP on the raw materials market. The owner hopes to generate a positive financial result from this. But the natural capital has been weakened and the annual return of NBP may diminish. The next review of the biodiversity of the property may give the area a much lower assessment. If an owner has sold off shares in the natural capital, co-owners might demand compensation for anything extracted or better governance. If, on the other hand, the owner harvests considerably while also taking measures to strengthen biodiversity, then – according to the new assessment – value and annual return will increase once more.[34]

In this way, the value inherent in the living natural capital is made visible within the human community. Information about the quality of these areas will be conveyed and valued, and consciousness continuously raised. It is no longer just annual returns in the form of products such as timber, grain, vegetables, hunting, game animals or fish that are given a price on a goods market. Even natural capital – the ecosystems which maintain and renew the game animals, forests and shoals of fish every year – is made visible inside the economic world view. Reductions in natural capital, in the case of extraction which is too extensive or is carried out inconsiderately, will have consequences for which the owners would be made to pay.

Highly competent biologists are obviously needed for the evaluations of natural capital, in addition to well-functioning standards for carrying out assessments and making annual reports. Also needed will be independent bodies to audit the appraisals. Here, too, the system could give rise to new jobs and professions and, consequently, renewed stimulation for understanding the natural world and its ecosystems.

We thus create opportunities for income from the property's grazing land, forests, wetlands, wild bird stocks, fresh water and streams – *without* the value of the natural capital itself being reduced by over-harvesting, intensive cultivation or industrial development. The owners can also increase their income or ability to invest by actively managing natural capital items such as biodiversity and water quality on the property. Exploitation of more than can be justified biologically will rapidly be reflected in a depreciation in the market value of the property. The owners will thereby have an self-interest in maintaining and possibly also improving the natural capital. And co-owners will apply pressure – exactly in the way that active shareholders do in joint stock companies today.

In this scenario, enthusiastic landowners (of wetlands, of forests, of gardens and grazing lands) will be doing their best to take care of biodiversity because it now even gets profitable. Old dead spruces will be left to stand in peace; wild herbs, mushrooms and weeds will be cared for. Keen reindeer owners in the north of Norway will take care of both wolverines and reindeer, if the 'wolverine assessment' in their areas produces a considerable supplement to their annual income. This is not at all improbable: in a European context the wolverine is a very rare species, something that could provide an opportunity for a high NBP return even to companies that are strong in capital, which want or need to be co-owners in this type of natural capital, not least for the sake of their level of taxation.

We can think of agriculture in a similar way. The quality of the ecosystem is dependent on the use of resources, soil structure, plant quality, the well-being of domesticated animals, cultivated countryside and so on. The farms of the future could perhaps sell NBPs from water purification in wetlands, biodiversity in cultivated pasture and fresh water, CO_2 absorption by the forest and green power from wind turbines, in addition to meat and eggs.[35] Standards of appraisal in combination with new markets would set the value of this type of sale in NBP units.

As has been said, the proposal for a specific currency for natural capital is not completely new. For example, we can view carbon quotas as a form of money related to natural capital: the EU calls emissions permits a form of currency because they can be bought and sold on a specific market. In the trading system for emissions quotas, the EU has stated that an emissions permit is equivalent to one tonne of CO_2.[36] So every emissions permit is a form of security document, and can be understood as a new type of currency.

Carbon quotas as money – 'climate change currency'

The surface of our planet, Gaia, is currently managing to remove around 13 billion tonnes of CO_2 from the atmosphere a year. Of this, the sea absorbs approximately 7 billion tonnes and the soil 6 billion. Emissions of CO_2 for which people are responsible are more than double that, however – approximately 33 billion tonnes in 2007.[37] The difference of around 20 billion tonnes a year remains in the atmosphere, and is causing rising temperatures and climate disruption. These CO_2 emissions damage the natural capital constituted by the climate. The atmosphere provides us with a flow of services such as clean fresh water, suitable temperatures and protection against harmful radiation. In addition, clean air allows us to see the beauty around us, to say nothing of the fact that the air, every second, ensures we can all live and breathe. These are not exactly minor details – talk about invisible capital, or undervalued stock! It is not surprising that early peoples respected the heavens as sacred.

Let's say that we share the combined annual emissions that Gaia is able to remove equally between all of the people on Earth.[38] Every person could then emit 2 tonnes of CO_2 a year in 2008 (13 billion tonnes divided by 6.5 billion people). This 'right to pollute' is limited and therefore potentially valuable. We can translate this into a type of currency. And we could call it the climate change currency, quota currency or carbon currency – we can write this as CCC anyway.

If we say that one CCC is equivalent to one kg of CO_2, then 2 tonnes of emissions are equivalent to 2,000 CCCs. Every person in UK, the EU or on the planet could then be given 2,000 CCCs every 1st January, deposited into a specific account. Every CCC entitles a person to emit 1 kg of CO_2 from fossil sources. This constitutes the supply of currency.

As the year passes, every individual or every company that uses gas, oil or coal has to pay 1 CCC for every kg of CO_2 emissions caused by the person/company concerned. When paid, the CCCs go back to the State, and the amount of natural currency in the individual's account diminishes. This is the demand side. The UK has a lot of industry, and we like warm houses, we like flying and driving our cars. The CCC will quite quickly be in short supply, and the value of each of them could then soar. By the spring, the UK would already (collectively) have used up all of the individual balances of 2,000 CCC.[39] Then we would have to buy more CCCs from other countries (perhaps Ireland?), using normal money. That would make it smart to have a car that consumes less petrol, and perhaps to fly less. Trains, buses, bicycles and video-conferencing would also keep lots of CCC in the account. Industries that are good at cleaning up their emissions would manage with smaller purchases of CCC.

It might be profitable, not least for poor countries, to sell to others who want to emit more and are able to pay with currencies such as pounds, euros or US dollars. If emissions quotas are implemented globally according to that sort of pattern, they could contribute to poor countries becoming richer while collective emissions diminish. The poor would have something to sell on the CCC market. It is clear that the system would work less effectively if not everyone was involved. But even with just one group of countries, or a group of cities, this type of system could work by setting a cap.

The EU does not currently issue emissions permits to individuals. They are given free of charge to major industrial and power companies, and (perversely) the most to those that already emit the largest volumes of CO_2. The point of this is to get the greatest number to participate. However, gradually fewer and fewer free quotas will be issued, until the annual number issued comes down to the target emissions set for the EU in the Kyoto agreement. Politically, it would be a good message to promise everyone a personal climate quota in the form of personal amounts of climate currency deposited in an account every year. If industry is dissatisfied with not being given any of this kind of quota for free, it would be better to give proportional tax relief for a transitional period.

If people could agree on this type of system on a global basis, it might be conceivable first to provide personal quotas or 'natural currency' equivalent to 33 billion tonnes; in other words, approximately 5 tonnes per person. Year by year, this will be reduced until the total comes down to 13 billion tonnes or approximately 2 tonnes per person or even lower – until we are again at a sustainable emissions level.

It *might* be that this is too little too late, and that the atmosphere no longer provides us with all of its annual services such as controlling the temperature and an appropriate climate. The volume of CO_2 that has accumulated during the period when emissions were too high is already ominously large. It will take a long time for CO_2 concentrations to diminish again, even if emissions are cut rapidly. Air and sea have become 'fed up' with us. That makes some of us into pessimists, and some into prophets of doom. Maybe Gaia will take revenge on our thoughtlessness.[40]

No one knows the consequences for sure. It is surely still best to try to do something that will be useful to a lot of people in the short term and to everyone in the long term, instead of not doing anything at all. It is perfectly possible that people will become eager devotees of CO_2 reduction and of quota trading if the emissions quotas are shared out – not to industries, as is the case today, but straight to individuals. So individuals can use them personally or sell them to companies that need them. Money is also a form of language and shapes our attention (see Chapter 3). Starting to use several types of money would contribute to changing how we think about the world. Exploring new paths towards change with the mercurial markets might even prove quite fun – and there is a lot to be said for that.

How to invest in natural capital

Investing in natural capital is different from investing in traditionally manufactured capital, since natural capital is by definition not man-made. Nevertheless, the term 'investment' is appropriate. In economics, investment implies waiting or refraining from current consumption in order to have greater returns in the future. The same applies to natural capital: you are abstaining from immediate consumption so that the ecosystem can be left alone and allowed to regenerate.

In classic economics, the ideology of laissez-faire meant that the authorities would have to keep their fingers out of the pie if the market was to function with no intervention. Now, laissez-faire can be given a new, more profound meaning: the best way of investing in renewable forms of natural capital might be to keep your fingers out of the pie so that the ecosystems are left in peace to control themselves. In other words, you invest by reducing annual extraction and other interference to a level that is on the positive side of sustainability. Then, natural capital will be strengthened for the next year by its own devices.

Careful supportive intervention or biologically intelligent management can also help natural capital on its way, particularly in the case of agricultural land, cultivated countryside such as pastures, or areas with threatened stocks of important species.

It is a different matter with a geological natural capital, such as fossil sources of energy or metals. These are non-renewable resources which – as the name indicates – can only deplete and not increase. New deposits may be discovered, and new technology may increase the degree of extraction, but gradually the actual reserves can only be emptied.

The ecological economist Herman Daly nevertheless makes the point that even these resources can be used in a sustainable manner. He proposes that, when extracting these, an equivalent investment should be made in improving efficiencies, or in sustainably replacing those resources with renewables. The general rule would be to deplete non-renewables at a rate equal to the development of renewable substitutes. Thus, extractive projects must be paired in some way with a project that develops the renewable substitute. For example, consumption of oil reserves can be done in a sustainable way if the extracting company reinvests in new eco-technology such as windmills or in the disposal of CO_2 at the same level as extraction is proceeding. In this way the overall level of capital is maintained or increased.[41]

What will then be the relationship between the two forms of natural capital we have discussed – ecosystem services and carbon emissions, NBP and CCC? They are different, in at least three ways. 1) CCC is global, whereas NBP is more national or regional. 2) The object of CCC is not growth, but to move towards zero in net emissions; for its part, NBP can grow, based on the fact that there is no absolute ceiling to indigenous biodiversity within an area. Evolution itself seems to be moving towards larger and larger biodiversity. 3) CCC and NBP probably ought to be kept in separate accounts during the course of the year, while in the annual reports it might be appropriate to bring the two together into a figure that would highlight the company's total effect on natural capital.

Recapturing externalities

I have outlined new forms of capital and the new type of currencies that go with them, the idea being that they can address some important shortcomings in the current monetary system. It is these shadows of economic growth – negative social impacts and the destruction of the natural world – which, to many people, makes traditional financial corporations soulless, immoral, inconsiderate or profit-mad – and the associated economics as cold and arrogant.

Markets have proven remarkably successful in achieving their purposes of efficient allocation and growth in wealth. Instead of closing down the markets, banning them or protesting against them, this scenario involves setting up new markets and moneys with an altogether other purpose. The social pounds can contribute to larger wealth of social networks. The natural pounds can contribute to growth in biodiversity. We are thus moving *with* and not *against* the market. At the same time, we are moving from *the market* to *markets*. This opens up something broader than traditional growth, where all other values are subsumed under one type of money. We expand the markets to handle more than one dimension of value.

The scenario means getting to grips with the major market failure that economists long have been calling *externalities*. Externalities are quite simply side-effects of the production process or a transaction that have consequences for external third parties. That is, it is not only the producer and customer that have stakes in the production, but also others who have nothing to with the activity. The most common example is a factory that produces items for sale in distant markets, but which at the same time pollutes the local surrounding community. The costs of a diminished environment are not borne by the producer nor by the customers, but fall upon neighbours and the ecosystem surrounding the factory.

Anything that has until now been an externality – outside the market place and outside the accounts – can now be included, but in different markets: the factory that pollutes the natural world and the local environment will have to enter the emissions according to a biological assessment into its environmental accounts as a cost, and perhaps also as health effects in its social accounts. This could produce negative social and natural results, with red figures in the triple bottom line. Therefore the company will either have to pay increased taxes or ensure it has compensating earnings of equivalent value in the social and natural currencies. Through new monetary systems and expanded accounting of what we have until now been calling externalities, these externalities will be included in the visible market systems. They are placed in different accounts, but are brought into the markets, and into the forms of capital where they belong.

Opposition

Allow me to give a brief outline of three types of opposition. 1) 'Green taxes are efficient'. 2) 'It's simpler to have one type of money'. 3) 'Monetary imperialism'.

1. 'Green taxes are efficient'
The first objection can be formulated as follows: The proposal is similar to well-tried-and-tested cap-and-trade or cap-and-tax systems that are based on conventional currencies. If we want to reduce CO_2 emissions, reduce the pressure of fishing, felling or grazing, this could be arranged simply with straightforward green taxes like a cap-and-tax system. And if we do not know exactly the right price, cap-and-trade will work better. The market then sets the price in normal money. Furthermore, if the new currencies SBP and NBP can be exchanged for GBP and with one another, it will come to the same thing. People will find means of exchanging so that, in reality, it will become only one currency. It will be like exchanging UK pounds for US dollars or euros. Thus, in reality, this intricate tax relief arrangement will just be a complex, indirect tax. Nothing new.

This objection is based on a conventional understanding of money as nothing but an efficient means of exchange. *But this perspective overlooks the psychological, social, legal and institutional frames around money.* First, as we have seen in Chapters 3 and 8, money also constitutes a language and a form of attention that informs our consciousness. Whatever you pay attention to becomes real. In addition to being a means of exchange, money directs our attention and leads to certain types of action. If everything is measured on the basis of one and the same value metric, other dimensions will become invisible or suppressed.

A lot of work is today carried out in order to find the financial values of ecosystem services based on principles such as people's willingness to pay. Similarly, research is done to determine what the social contributions of culture and sports or improved health and safety is worth in pounds. However, it is profoundly difficult to work out GBP values for non-market services and goods.[42] The social and natural dimensions of value don't fit very well within the existing pricing principles.

NBP and SBP are very different types of currency, based on direct measures of other forms of capital. The normal currency (e.g. GBP) is mainly a currency based on indebtedness made up of bank money which, in principle, can be inflated to an infinite number of billions. NBP, on the other hand, is 'commodity money', linked to specific biological and natural assets. SBP is also commodity money, linked directly to time used on social and community activities, since 1 SBP = 1 hour. GBP is a participant in a global monetary system, while NBP would be national and SBP preferably local or regional. That means that regulatory frameworks must see to it that they cannot be freely exchanged for one another. For example, companies operating within an area or a country would have to acquire SBP from the same area that they operate in. With such an arrangement, local, regional and national currencies will *complement* the global ones (such as GBP and CCC). They could also counteract the booms and busts of the business cycles.

The argument against the objection will thus become: new types of money create new attention and new relationships. They will promote other patterns of behaviour based on making other dimensions of value visible in decision making. In addition, these types of money go beyond the function of being a pure means of exchange because they are surrounded by norms, institutions and regulations for accounting and exchange (outlined above) which do not apply to normal money. Green taxes are indeed efficient. I am all in favour of them. But they are not necessarily the most responsive or effective policies to bring about the profound changes needed.

2. 'It's simpler to have one type of money'
This is another type of objection, which can go like this: it is difficult enough to understand and relate to the complex, pulsing market – but what if we were to have three fundamentally different ones embedded in each other! People, politicians and economists already find it hard to understand the exact connections

between GNP, interest rates, unemployment and inflation. What would things be like if we tripled the complexity? In conventional economics, it is assumed that money gives neutral price signals in the market, so it is regarded as most efficient for all goods and services to be measured in one and the same currency. The effect is that competition is stiffer, and resources are utilised better. Several currencies will make it more difficult to compare prices, and might therefore weaken trade. This is the main argument for the euro and against the various member countries each having their own currency. The euro integrates the European market and makes trade within the area more efficient.[43]

In a similar vein, one could argue that a single world currency would make markets most efficient on a global basis. Why don't all countries use the dollar or a new world currency? Well, because many nations want to retain both their national identity and a capacity for controlling their own affairs. An important contribution to this is a country's own currency, which primarily circulates within the country's borders. That way, there is an information and exchange system binding the citizens together, and which the central authorities can have an influence on. National currencies therefore have *a national purpose*: strengthening trade and economic development within the currency's circulation area.

In other words: the fact that so many different national currencies exist tells us that the currency markets have a purpose *beyond* optimal efficiency. It is the same for social and natural capital: they have a purpose beyond what is economically most efficient, a purpose that is intended to promote other important value metrics in addition to traditional cost efficiency.

A differentiation is often made between *effectiveness* and *efficiency*. Efficiency means achieving as much as possible with the minimum possible effort. Being effective, however, means being able to achieve what you want with your efforts. Viewed in this way, social and natural currency may have somewhat lower financial efficiency, but nevertheless they can be very effective means to achieving what we really want: a society and a natural world of increasing quality.

There is a need for a few select social indicators that make it possible to keep up with the development of natural and social dimensions of value. But to date, indicators for social conditions and for the environment have been given little political attention because they do not have any direct impact on most people's lives. If we introduce exchangeable social currency and natural currency, these values could be made more evident all the way from micro to macro level. The same three series of figures will recur, from one's personal account statement to the national accounts, from municipality to parliament. It should stimulate a mutual exchange and attention which cannot be generated by other indicators as long as economic decisions are made on the basis of calculations made in a single type of money.

3. 'Monetary imperialism'

There are two variants of this objection. The first might sound like this: Regardless of what we call them, all valuations on the basis of markets and money reduce real life to figures. These new currencies would further extend the dominance of money – no thanks! We don't want money to colonise even more of our lives nor of the planet.

The second variant: Many actions are carried out without any desire for payment. Someone trains other people's children in football, someone else teaches them to play chess. Many people put in extra hours for the choir, the Red Cross or welfare association. It gives people pride and good feelings. Others spend days cleaning up beaches and streams, fighting antisocial practices by multinationals, or put out food for birds and roe deer in the winter. They do this because they want to, and because it feels meaningful. They do it out of what is called *intrinsic motivation*. Psychological research shows that children like to sit for long periods painting the same picture, but quickly stop sitting for long if they start being paid for their pictures.

Might we destroy this intrinsic motivation, if new money (NBP or SBP) is used to pay for efforts made for the natural world and the community? People might begin to *demand* such money before they would do anything at all, or they would quite simply lose interest when it becomes a 'yet another job'. That intrinsic motivation would then be crowded out by extrinsic motivation.[44] Could this become a problem for the new types of money? Would we get an expansion of imperialism, instead of an expansion of visibility and valuations?

I believe this depends on the psychological framing of the new types of money. There is no space for a long discussion of this here, but it is clear that if money makes the action purely instrumental and the work is no longer contributed for the sake of others but for the sake of (the new) money, it might have a negative effect on intrinsic motivation. However, local social currency (SBP) arises when I spend my time *for someone else and for a social purpose*. This is a very different frame from the ones around conventional money. SBP cannot be used in the shop, or to buy petrol with. I stand in front of another person and give him or her my attention. Or I need help from this other person. The SBP money that can be issued based on my work belongs first of all to the local community. It brings to light the multi-faceted network of give-and-take relationships. As long as the complementary currency is understood to be a appreciation of the efforts made to build a stronger community, it seems probable that with the presence of SBP money such efforts will increase. Experiences with Time Dollars and TimeBanks seem to confirm that participants don't view this as simply 'just money'. The symbolic meanings are different from money, which is seen in a more instrumental view. The efforts are made initially for the sake of other people, not for myself. And the SBP money is primarily recognition of the efforts made.

Nevertheless, it is important to take the objection about monetary imperialism seriously when the details of the arrangements for additional currencies are being considered.[45]

Some conclusions about polycapitalism

The idea of a triple bottom line is far from new.[46] Nor is it anything new to introduce complementary currencies.[47] *What is new is the scenario in its entirety, where 1) accounting for new types of money is based on 2) new forms of capital valued in separate markets, in combination with 3) tax arrangements which reward positive social and environmental results.* It is a vision of the future that can be tried out on a large or small scale, and, if successful, can become widely adopted in due course.

One central feature in the scenario is that the various types of money are issued in its own way and applied according to its purpose. We would need CCC for paying for petrol or flights. We could use NBPs to buy food and clothing. We could use SBPs for exchanging helpful services with one another, and companies might use SBPs for advertising and for payroll tax. Everyone with NBP and SBP surplus at the end of the year get their tax reduced. And vice versa. The main effect would be that individual attitudes and actions are more closely linked and aligned to the forms of capital and dimensions of values that are fundamentally important to society and to global sustainability. Up until now these other sources of wealth have been invisible from the economic point of view.

There are of course many 'good reasons' why this will never work.

Is it impossible to implement? Technically, to have several accounts on a bank card or a mobile phone is a piece of cake. Just as today we can have several accounts (e.g. a bank loan, savings account, credit card), in the future we could have several types of money available when making payment: one for each value dimension. It is the institutional reforms that will take time to implement.

Is this too radical a change? Today, we already have accounting for various social forms of capital. TimeBanks have been mentioned. Another example is from Norway, where there is a system where points for care work (*omsorgspoeng*) are awarded to people who are carers for young children, or for the elderly or infirm – these provide pension entitlements. Is it really such a large step from such social points to social currency? If it is possible to assign a value to timber, fish and meat, is it not possible to assign a value to the ecosystem surrounding forests, fish and cattle? With new sensor systems, Internet technologies and visualisation software, it will be easier in the future to get an overview of detailed information on developments for a lot of different variables at the same time. We no longer live exclusively in the age of bank notes and paper receipts.

Too optimistic on the use of markets? There will definitely be plenty of objections that can be directed at this proposal. Some of these have been discussed in brief above, but a great deal of thorough discussion and testing will be needed before bringing this into practice on a significant scale. Neither must we forget what the Hermes myth tells us: where markets go, trickery will always follow. Bias, the twisting of information and deft tricks will be present wherever Hermes goes. It will be best to bring along some Apollo-research and Zeus-authorities to make the scoundrel toe the line while he gets the markets to practise their magic.

Will it be too costly? Lots of researchers believe that strengthening social capital will promote financial growth as well.[48] Similarly, the destruction of natural capital will increase economic costs – the forms of capital are interrelated. As we saw in Chapter 5, a growth in wealth, measured in GNP per capita, produces limited growth in happiness. The development of natural and social capital, however, looks as if it is interrelated with higher quality of life and happiness.[49] I believe it will prove to be the case that, for human happiness, there is more to be gained from growth in natural and social capital than from further growth in material wealth.

Is it politically viable? Can a proposal like this gain broad political acceptance? If so, popular messages will be needed. I believe the message would be something such as this: 'We want to reward those that are contributing to the common good and nature with tax cuts. We want to raise taxes for those that exploit the commons and natural resources. We want to increase people's quality of life by introducing new types of money to promote growth in new forms of wealth.' I am no politician, but it is my naïve belief that this message would be broadly acceptable to the public.

Is it a plan or a vision? The scenario is at a stage at which it should preferably not be bogged down by too much detailed discussion. The fundamental question that this scenario raises is whether we can imagine our economic system being different in future. The twenty-first century is not going to be any simpler than the twentieth. Human imagination, creativity and interactions are the fundamental forms of capital we really need to start employing. At the same time, the immense human potential for inertia, fundamentalism and tyranny are always lying in ambush. They could so easily get the net upper hand, again . . . and again. These shadows would have to be more than balanced by all the social capital we manage to mobilise by developing citizens committed to their community and the planet. This is absolutely not one of the purposes of traditional money. The main ideas in this chapter are far from a set plan. What is needed at the current point is a vision of how we can get money to start working for us, rather than we working for money.

In Chapter 6, about markets, we discussed how every trade can also be seen as a gift, in a give-and-take framework. With new types of money, we expand these interactions from the narrow financial markets to wider webs of interactions. Then, both our neighbours in local communities and our wider circle of neighbours, the creatures in the natural world will be invited to participate in the extended exchange circles that I've here called the 'polytheistic economy'.

	GBP	SBP	NBP	CCC
Issued by	Banks	Third sector	Biological assessment	State/UN
Validity	Unlimited	2-3 years	1 year	1 year
Interest	Yes	No	No	No
Can pay for	Everything	Services/ advertisements	Resources	Fossil fuel emissions
Convertible	Globally	Locally	Nationally	Globally
VAT	Yes	No	No	No
Tax	Yes	Leads to deductions	Leads to deductions	Leads to deductions

Summary of proposed types of money in circulation in a country in the year 2030

Chapter 13

Conclusion
Ways forward?

"The economist, like everyone else, must concern himself with the ultimate aims of man." – Alfred Marshall

We prize the material benefits that current economic systems are able to provide. At the same time, those of us who live in wealthy parts of the world are no more satisfied than we were thirty to fifty years ago. Economic activity preys greatly upon the world's natural capital, social capital and mental health – to the advantage of a relative few, and without quality of life improving significantly even for those few.[1] Money grows, but the soul stagnates. Money seems to be pulling in one direction (effectiveness, competition, profitability, wealth) while the things of the soul pull in another (relationships, cooperation, diversity, meaning).

We therefore need – based on the terminology used in this book – to integrate money and soul. One approach to bringing together polarities is to build bridges over the chasm. But maybe money and soul were never really opposites. Rather than building bridges, this book has attempted to (re)discover the spiritual and emotional aspects contained in money and *within* economic concepts.

The economic mindset has had enormous success and influence since Adam Smith first formulated the essence of the market ideas of industrial society. These ideas easily harness powerful human needs and feelings. We are – beyond doubt – easily inspired by money and by economic growth. Nevertheless, it is as if these leave behind a feeling of loss and chronic dissatisfaction[2] – and a climate which, according to researchers, looks as if it is going to turn against humanity perhaps more rapidly than previously assumed.[3]

After the Second World War, Winston Churchill stated that democracy is the worst social system – except for everything else that has been tried. The same thing might be said of market-based capitalism. We could obviously hope for less exploitation, more ethically justifiable behaviour by corporations, along with improved government regulation within today's economic system. But moral appeals and sweet talk about corporate responsibility are of little help when economic incentives are pulling in the opposite direction. Regardless of fine words about corporate values and visions, these quickly just become instrumental means by which to serve the singular end of economic profit.

- $ -

The previous chapters have investigated how different economic ideas have their symbolic roots in a variety of deep stories. If economic thinking appears one-sided and dogmatic to non-economists, this has more to do with economism as an ideology than with economics as a discipline. Many economists are taken up with confirming that there is a strong consensus within the profession, but at the same time they know about the rapidly moving research frontier's lack of coherence and the great internal diversity of theories.[4]

A deeper understanding of the history of ideas surrounding money and economic mindsets removes the misconception that the nature of money is neutral, objective and unambiguous. Psychologically speaking, money has never been neutral, nor will it ever be. Money unavoidably brings us into a variety of relationships with other people, and into strong emotional and symbolic fields. I have tried to make this pluralism clear by seeing through the central ideas of economics into the world of language and mythology. In the idea of market we rediscovered the smooth workings of Hermes, in the idea of scarcity miserly Chronos, in the bonds of debt we found traces of Ananke, in depression dark Hades, in the cool heads of science caught glimpses of Apollo, in benevolent ideas of welfare the fatherly face of Zeus. I have drawn lines from the economy's modern *logos* to European culture's roots in *mythos*. We can hardly integrate soul and money without relating to deeper human emotions – what I (following C.G. Jung) have called the 'archetypal' level.

On a more pragmatic level, what remains is to point out and reinforce the interweaving of soul and money that is already taking place in the markets of today. At the end, I would also like to make note of four areas in which soul and money are already being integrated in new ways: in new ideas about product and service design, in the workplace, in rediscovering meaning and purpose, and finally in the experimentation being done on pluralising forms of capital.

Soul and money meet in good design

If the soul is the unique form of every individual thing, as Aristotle said, we can see this reflected in an increase in attention to product and service design. Work on product design becomes at the same time work on the soul. The products must differ from mass-produced articles, and from one another. They must be unique in a meaningful way. According to Aristotle's way of thinking, the product's soul comes to expression in its material form. The greatly increased interest in artisan products, unique luxury articles, slow food (see the grassroots movement slowfood.com), 'niche' food, organic food and locally produced food illustrates this trend. Many people no longer want standardised, anonymous, fast food. They want to know a bit more about the history, origins and characteristic nature of every single food item. We want to know the story of the olive tree grove, or where an animal grew up, where it grazed or was caught, and the names of the people involved.

Nevertheless, the majority of commerce still takes place in markets that overflow with cheap, standardised goods: they can come from anywhere (not even labelled 'Made in China' any more), they look the same everywhere in the world, and they fall to bits easily. 'We are making Norway cheaper' was the marketing jingle of the Norwegian retail chain Rimi. But was there not also something of Norway that thereby also became cheapened? The Danish interior design company Bodum has a slogan that puts this point better: 'Give up Bad Design for Good.' 'For good' also means 'for ever', of course – that is, we must do away with design that neither serves the Earth, the people who produce it, nor the people who consume it. Good design allows the product to serve its purpose throughout its useful life – in production, in use and after use.

In a narrow capitalist spirit, large sections of Western culture show a persistent disdain for aesthetics, in which anything artistic or aesthetic is subordinate to utility and the profitable. The Puritan tradition (which Max Weber pointed out lies underneath modern capitalism) has always resisted beauty as a form of waste and luxury. Based on this, the traditional perception has been that products and services must primarily be efficient and profitable. They can be pretty or chic only if that leads to higher prices or increases sales.

If, on the other hand, we start from the understanding that the aesthetic is already embodied in the product as its unique form, we are working on the basis of a consciousness that is inspired more by the Renaissance, in which beauty is a necessary and primary function. Anything we do must be beautifully done. Beauty is not an add-on. Aesthetics and beauty are terms used not just to indicate the pretty and the charming, but apply rather to all kinds of genuine expression that arouse the senses, which cut right across expectations and habits, and open people's eyes and ears. Good design makes us *more sensitive*, and the product's distinctive expression pleases us (or alarms us). Good design invites continued dialogue with the product, in contrast to a purchase which immediately leaves us feeling empty, leading us to throw it away or forget what we have bought and reach out for something else, something new.

The growth in the value of experiences and artistic designs – some speak of an *experience economy*[5] and yet others of *aesthetic capital* – is another vital area. Art is exploding out of its traditional studios, and artists are being brought in to industry and commercial services.[6] The need for creative services and professions is undergoing dramatic growth. Production processes in many industries are moving in the direction of a constantly growing spectrum of products and services. Savings gained from technological efficiencies can be reinvested in the capacity for making a larger diversity of services and goods with higher quality. In that way, every product can become virtually unique and – we hope – more durable. Both customers and the goods themselves seem to call out: 'Save us from the horrors of uniformity! We just cannot stand any more anonymous, short-lived products. Give us back our own voice and our own distinctiveness!'

The economic system has traditionally emphasised the functionality and price of products. This is in line with classical economics, in which *utility* is the basic concept. Aesthetics belongs mainly to marketing, artistic and luxury products, but doesn't have any intrinsic value. In economic theory beauty has been treated as a type of market – the art market – and everywhere else just an instrumental means subordinate to utility or market valuation.

For the soul, however, the aesthetic is an existential necessity. The soul cannot exist except in its perceivable forms, its phenomenal world. Hence the primacy of the aesthetic to soul. In the twenty-first century it will become increasingly futile to introduce products to markets without attending to their aesthetic qualities. Where would the iPod have been, for example, if it had not been for its aesthetics? The product has to be spirited away from the dogma of 'efficient production' into an aesthetic framework. Current prevailing production models may serve consumption well, but not the consumer as a whole person. Investing in quality of design and service rather than trying to crush the competition or beat last year's quarterly report is choosing beauty rather than conflict. It is choosing to serve the best in the customer, instead of exploiting the customer. It gives meaning to the employee, product, recipient, surroundings and – probably – to shareholders. I hope we will get to see more of these kinds of aesthetic business strategies in the twenty-first century.

Renewal of meaning and purpose

Don Williams, director of the Dallas-based property company Trammell Crow, said in an interview: "For me, today, work is a platform for social involvement . . . My passion today is focused on the comprehensive renewal of our lowest income neighborhoods in Dallas . . . It is unjust in America for so many of our people to not receive a good education, not to have access to a decent job, and not to have access to a decent home. That is an injustice. By the way, if you don't have an educated workforce coming up, if we have a society that is eroded over-whelmingly with drugs and crime, that's not good for business."

An organisation or company can be understood to be more than just an instrument for its shareholders. A company both can and ought to have a pur-pose beyond itself, maintains management guru Charles Handy. Without a vision of something more than itself and its own growth, there will be something lacking. If we are being honest with ourselves, it is only a greater purpose that can justify our existence. Fundamentally, business is a question of values, he says.[7] The American philosopher Jacob Needleman maintains that greed is inevitable in the absence of an inner aim, a living sense of purpose.[8]

The questions of meaning and a larger purpose in life always lead to soul and its emotions. If money provides something to live *on*, it is the soul that provides something to live *for*. Your soul relates to something that is wider and greater than yourself. This something provides a richer context for your own life. This is where our source of dignity lies – in being of service to greater values, to some-thing that goes beyond our personal sphere. We discover this dignity by partici-pating in a larger story and by making clear our own relationship with this story. Without being held by larger story or myth it is difficult, perhaps impossible, to experience life and work over time as meaningful.[9]

Workplaces where people work just for the money will be seen by increasing numbers of people as degrading and stressful. When we provide space for human development by inviting reflections on emotions, purpose and meaning at work, we are involved in the interweaving of soul and money. But, as Charles Handy points out, the tall words and visions too often end up on glossy posters and Powerpoint presentations. Simultaneously the organisation continues in practice to be treated as an instrument for providing the owners with a return on their investment. Then, paradoxically, even deepest values and human develop-ment become instrumental, and purpose and vision become nothing but tools for a greater financial return.

Care of the soul at work

In conventional microeconomics work is seen as a dis-utility, as a sacrifice that we have to carry out to in order to earn an income. Work is a commodity, a fac-tor, that we sell for money to pay for 'goods' on the consumer market.

Jeremy Bentham, the nineteenth-century British philosopher and founder of utilitarianism, wrote: "The desire for labour for the sake of labour – of labour considered in the character of an end, without any view to anything else – is a sort of desire that seems scarcely to have a place in the human breast . . . Love of labour is a contradiction in terms."[10] More recent economic theory is much more nuanced, but remnants of this perception still survive.

If it is happiness and human development we want and not yet more material wealth, then meaningful workplaces are crucial. In Chapter 5, on welfare, it became clear that work processes are in themselves a source of self-respect and happiness. Work lets people develop abilities that cannot be developed in the role of a consumer.[11] One survey estimated that 'mastering a job' increased the level of happiness by *six times* that of a comparable pay rise.[12] It is well documented that jobs with room for learning and creativity can contribute to a person's 1) cognitive complexity, 2) self-respect and 3) feeling of personal control. These are three core factors in human development.[13] At the same time they counteract stress, helplessness and other-directed self-evaluation – three familiar detriments to happiness and well-being.[14]

What does it mean to care for the soul at work? There are perhaps as many answers as there are workplaces, but one simple method would be to take some hints of direction from the four signposts leading to soul that were described in Chapter 4: form, in, down and between.

Form is connected with the sensuous and the aesthetic. Aesthetic experiences engage the whole person: body and emotions, eyes and nose, head and heart. If we make the proper arrangements for the use of art, artistic methods and games, wonderment and new ideas can be awakened. In 2006, Google was chosen as the world's most attractive company to work for, not least because it allows employees to play in shared creativity labs, and values employees bringing their own 'eccentric' interests with them to work. Even more important than gadgets, toys or creativity is the sensitivity to observe what is already there and how our bodies react to these forms that surround us and speak to us at work.

Attention to the design and procedures of the workplace, even when this applies to small details, can produce huge results. Starting the day with a poem, having a short dance break or playing the drums at lunchtime may sound 'corny' today. A fitness room seems more serious, although it is not long since that was something completely new. However, during the course of the next ten to twenty years, the enormous effect of rituals, imagination, stories and consciousness-altering music will perhaps become just as common in newly established companies and organisations as a cigarette break or Friday cakes were twenty years ago. Maybe here we have one more explanation for why more money does not increase happiness: our ability to be happy depends on the opportunity we have to open up our sense organs. However, all social classes have exactly the same access to these. And more money has very little to do with increased *sensitivity*.

In is connected with insight. The soul is deepened when given opportunity to reflect on events and experiences. Team feedback and time for reflection makes this possible. Research into teamwork shows that disconcertingly little time is set aside for learning from experience or for giving one another feedback. For a long time the organisational psychologist Chris Argyris has been pointing out how often people avoid learning from experience by covering things up, instead of reflecting together, openly, about what is happening.[15] It must be possible to give vent to feelings within a secure, open framework. Openness is a precondition of more in-depth learning, 'double learning'. The opportunity to give and receive feedback and to reflect on it within a secure framework is often a rare commodity in busy organisations. But it does not cost much, and produces better insight and clarifies differences between others and me. A person's self-respect, which is of great importance to happiness and satisfaction with life, is dependent perhaps most of all upon insight into how other people perceive him or her.

Between is obvious: People are social beings, through and through, and relationships with others are what consistently contribute most to quality of life. Colleagues at work have a special role to play. The satisfaction that we humans feel in relation to other people has many faces: greeting, caring, looking after, responding, helping, repairing, preparing food, learning, teaching, inspiring, guiding and surprising each other. Caring for relationships with other people at work is also another task of the soul. Working without friendship and closeness to other people quickly feels empty. Where there is no room for sharing emotions with one another, collaboration and affiliation will be weakened.

Down is perhaps more challenging. If we invite soul and emotions in to join us in our work, the shadow side will also emerge. Confusion, despair, troubles, loss and disappointments are never far away when we open things up to let the soul participate. But this is necessary if the deepening of the soul is to happen. Such feelings often put the brakes on our busyness, and thereby invite us to take a more in-depth look at what is going on. Is there anything pressing underneath this troubling feeling? Something that the ego is shutting off? In addition to providing opportunity for a change of direction, such feelings are possibly an early warning that greater difficulties could be on their way. Maybe it is not such a daft idea to give the soul's apparently less rational sides a chance – give them some air before a major explosion happens. We prefer 'up', but people are also 'down'. If we put a tight lid on the underworld, the pressure from below will only increase.

In summary: when we share with others the feeling of satisfaction of a job that has been beautifully completed, we might say that the soul and the work have come together. It is no more difficult, nor any simpler, than that.

Soul and money meet in polycapitalism

This fourth point is the bedrock upon which the previous items rest. Without expansion from capital to a variety of forms of capitals we will probably not get far with the above. We will slide back into monotheism, where there is only One True God: the annual financial results.

One of the core ideas in classical economics since it was formulated in 1752 by the Scotsman David Hume, has been that money is a *neutral* means of exchange. This implies that money is just a lubricant which makes trade more efficient than it would be in a system of barter. Apart from that, money does not affect commercial activities or the real economy. This conception of the neutrality of money maintains that changes in the money supply will have an effect only on relative prices, and no real effects in the long term. However, economists in the tradition of John M. Keynes, such as Joseph Schumpeter, have pointed out that this is to overlook a number of effects in the economy, not least institutional ones. The method by which money is introduced actually changes the structure of the economy.[16]

But not just economic structure is at stake with money. Money also influences our attention, relationships and dreams, as outlined in Chapter 3. We have discovered deep emotions at work in money and – since money talks so loudly – it has become the world's most common language. All this means that money is defining our relationship with both society and nature. In order to make the necessary changes in society and in ourselves we might consider introducing new kinds of money.

Then the structure of industry and society will gradually change in line with this new language and the new institutions that accompany the new forms of money. Then there will no longer be just one money with one dominant purpose, but three equivalent purposes. If we try to maintain society's social and natural capitals by first gathering financial fees and taxes, and then transferring these instrumentally into social and natural purposes, these other forms of capital will probably remain secondary and will therefore continue to suffer injury. On the other hand, if we introduce new forms of capital with new types of money, we will get *new business areas with opportunities for expanded earnings*, while at the same time companies will be working for broader and more meaningful purposes. Earning money in three different, though related, ways can, at the same time, even be fun, hip or cool because our work gets more into line with broader visions and purposes. If earning traditional money can be fun, it must be three times as much fun earning three types of money!

My scenario for this century is that historians in 2100 will be writing about the barbarity of the era of economism during the first part of this century – when those who did not comply with financial profitability as the only sovereign and inviolable purpose in all situations were pushed aside; when governments hardly ever managed to internalise externalities in any productive way; when economists in the International Monetary Fund could force countries such as Indonesia and Thailand to prioritise their financial sectors ahead of other pressing needs; when executives were pilloried in the media if they weren't effective enough in cutting costs to maximise shareholder value at all times.

It was like the inquisition of the Middle Ages, writes our historian from 2100, except that they didn't burn people at the stake. Anyone who did not live by the one true doctrine that characterised the economics of that time was eased out of his or her position. In the decades before and after 2000, companies were busily externalising as many costs as they could because they thought that if only the costs were removed from their financial accounts they would also be removed from this world. 'Busily occupied with cutting back and transferring costs to the local community and the natural world, they were sawing off the branch they themselves were sitting on. Now in 2100 we are still having to pay the unpaid costs from that period', might be how the verdict on our times would sound.

- £ -

However, profound change is possible if we change the frameworks that determine how we interact with money. Edgar Cahn, the entrepreneur who created Time Dollars, formulates this as follows: "The real price we pay for money is *the hold that money has on our sense of what is possible,* the prison it builds for our imagination." But if money possibilises the imagination, as we discovered in Chapter 3, it can also work the other way around: imagination can make new money possible. For that to happen, we have to think in a completely new way – to dare to think of truly radical innovation within finance and money.

- $ -

People need to feel at home in the world. It is high time for economics too to come home. Home to that Great House as the word *oikos* itself indicates: the shared household where we – all two-, four- and six-legged beings, all the amazing kinds of creatures, as well as the deep stories and values – live and breathe.

Notes

Introduction

1. A view recently espoused forcefully, for instance in Thomas Friedman (2006) *The World is Flat*.

Chapter 1. Money everywhere

1. *One Ring to rule them all, One Ring to find them, One Ring to bring them all and in the darkness bind them*. It is tempting to read this as a description of the nature and impact of money. As we shall see (Chapter 9) money has much in common with the dark art of alchemy, for which Faust was willing to exchange his soul in his agreement with Mephistopheles. Economist Mark Blyth (2007) of Johns Hopkins University also brings up this parallel between modern neoclassicist economic theory and Tolkien's world in a critical article that he wrote: 'One Ring to Bind Them All: American Power and Neoliberal Capitalism'.

2. James Hillman (1994) *Kinds of Power*, p.6.

3. Over the past decade there has been a turnaround in economic theory, away from the conventional presentation of *homo economicus*, based on a broad cross-discipline research front in which economics meets psychology, sociology and anthropology. When psychologist Daniel Kahneman was awarded the Nobel Prize for Economics in 2002, jointly with economist Vernon Smith, this was the tip of an iceberg moving in the direction of a much more nuanced, empirically based understanding of the people involved when economic choices are made. See Kahneman, Daniel and Testy, Amos (eds) (2000) *Choice, Values, and Frames*. A summary of emotions and economics is contained in Mabel Berezin (2005) 'Emotions and the Economy', Ch. 6 in Smeiser and Swedberg (2005) *The Handbook of Economic Sociology*.

4. Glyn Davies (2002) A *History of Money: From Ancient Times to the Present Day*, p.5.

5. The perception of the neutrality of money can be traced via classical social economics in John Stuart Mill (1852) *Principles of Political Economy*, by way of Adam Smith (1776) and back to David Hume (1752) *Political Discourses*. Hume and Mill maintained that the amount of money in itself is unimportant. If the amount of money becomes bigger than the real values within an economy, this situation that will not last long, as there will be inflation and the purchasing power of money will fall. Most people may have a tendency to believe that the nominal value of money corresponds to the real value. This was called 'the illusion of money' by John Maynard Keynes, and in 1929 Irving Fisher wrote a book on the topic, *The Money Illusion*. More recent experimental research has given the debate renewed interest: see Shafir, E., Diamond, P.A. & Tversky, A. (1997) 'On Money Illusion', *Quarterly Journal of Economics*, 112 (May), 341–74, and for a theoretical summary, see John Smithin (2000) *What is Money*.

6. Erik Dammann (1989) *Pengene eller Livet*, and Joe Dominguez and Vicki Robin (1999) *Your Money or Your Life*.

7. Tang (1992–1997) quoted in Furnham and Argyle (2000) *The Psychology of Money*, p.42.

8. Rubinstein (1981) quoted in Furnham and Argyle (2000) *The Psychology of Money*, p.45.

9. Obviously there are exceptions. There is an outline description of these in Furnham and Argyle (2000) *The Psychology of Money*. On the whole, economic psychology has been a marginal activity in the field, but has nevertheless undergone strong growth and has been fronted by the magazine *The Journal of Economic Psychology*, which started publication in 1981.

10. William Desmonde (1962) *Magic, Myth, and Money: The Origin of Money in Religious Ritual*, p.114 f.

11. A good summary was provided by John Galbraith (1975) *Money: Whence it Came, Where it Went*.

12. I have permitted myself to paraphrase Habermas slightly: In his terminology, he says: "colonization of the lifeworld by the system". Jürgen Habermas (1981) *Theorie des Kommunikativen Handels*, Band I und II. [*The Theory of Communicative Action*. Vols I and II].

13. Jacob Needleman (1993) *Money and the Meaning of Life*, p.3.

14. In Norway, NOU 2005:5 *Clear signals in a complex world*, led by Knut Alfsen, has proposed a set of 16 of this type of indicator.

15. NOU 2005:5, *Clear signals in a complex world*, for the Norwegian Ministry of Finance, p.27.

16. Ralph Waldo Emerson (1838) 'Lecture on War', *Emerson's Complete Works*, Vol.11. Quoted in Meadows, Randers & Meadows (2004) *Limits to Growth*.

17. John M. Keynes (1936) *The General Theory of Employment, Interest and Money*, NY: Prometheus Books, 1997, pp.383–4.

18. Carl G. Jung (1954) *The Archetypes and The Collective Unconscious*, in *Collected Works Vol. 9*, Part 1.

19. Cf. Gregory Bateson (1971) *Steps to an Ecology of Mind*; James Hillman and Michael Ventura, *We've had 100 years of Psychotherapy*; Per E. Stoknes (1996) *Sjelens Landskap*, Ch. 7.

20. Why am I using Greek myths and not others such as Norse, Sami or Native American myths? One reason is that there are many more surviving documentary and artistic relics from the Mediterranean area than there are from Scandinavia. There is an unbroken tradition of philosophy and culture stretching from Ancient Greece to the West (from Greek poetry and philosophy to early Christendom, St Augustine, St Thomas, the Renaissance, the Enlightenment, the Romantics), whereas we know the old Nordic customs and gods mainly through the texts of Christian monks, usually writing several hundred years after these formed part of a living religion. Any contemporary writings from the old Nordic period are mainly descriptions written by foreigners. And although the short and terse Eddic poetry that remains from the scalds and runes has a compact power, it nevertheless does not have the variation, nuance and thorough philosophical processing of the great Greek and Judaic narrative literature. However, the most important reason why I have given much more space to the Greek myths than the Nordic ones is that Western culture – in science, world view and human understanding – is far closer to the common European heritage than it is to the inheritance from our Nordic or Celtic ancestors. In our culture, the invisible mythical structures that guide thought and action have Greek and Roman names. However, it is not difficult to find parallels in other cultures: in Egypt, with the Inuit, in Polynesia, in West Africa, in the Aztec or Mayan cultures, among the Sami or Native Americans, etc. Often with distinctive names, stories and characteristic features but, amazingly, frequently with

similar faces. However, for a culture that is mainly Eurocentric, the Greek and Roman patterns are the most relevant and distinctive and thus the most powerful. With the term 'powerful' I mean influential, authoritative, controlling and tyrannical. Europeans cannot, with the aid of multiculturalism, escape from the context that has its basis in Ancient Greece and Rome. We cannot cut our linguistic and imaginal roots or change our basic modes of thought, but we can expand and reimagine them carefully and cautiously, tell better and more beautiful versions of them and in that way continue our dialogue with them. Cf. James Hillman (1995) *Kinds of Power,* pp.243–50.

21. In the introduction to Maurice Merleau-Ponty (1962) *Phenomenology of Perception,* entitled 'What is phenomenology', he describes phenomenology on the basis of four characteristics. Primarily, it is a descriptive science, which returns to the concrete phenomena as they appear to us, immediately and pre-consciously. Next, it is the phenomenological reduction that involves a loosening of habitual ties and the reawakening of a sense of wonder when faced with the phenomenon. Thirdly, he names the search for essences, or those characteristics that are necessary to the phenomenon itself. Finally, it is consideration of broad intentionality – or the directness of consciousness in the world – which produces both the perceiver and the perceived.

22. We get psychologism if, for example, via biological psychology, we reduce competitive behaviour to an outcome of a fight-or-flight response, when we understand wealth only as a means for distributing genes as much as possible, or entrepreneurship as an outcome of adaptability to ecological niches. On the basis of psychology's cognitive tradition, it is possible instead to interpret competitiveness as an outcome of social learning, wealth as an attempt at strengthening self-image, and entrepreneurship on the basis of flow or creative thought processes. Psychoanalysis would perhaps have given an interpretation of competitive behaviour as going back to the Oedipus complex, wealth to anal-fixation and entrepreneurship to sublimated libido. In contrast to psychologisms I am proposing to psychologise – which means moving through the literal to the metaphorical. It implies moving the concept away from its literal meaning in the specific subject area whence it came, to trace and speculate on what this concepts tells us about the psyche; about the soul. What images and associations come with the concept? How has that created meaning for us, in the past and now? "Psychologizing does not mean making psychology of events, but making psyche of events – soul-making", James Hillman (1976) *Re-visioning Psychology,* p.133.

23. James Hillman (1976) *Re-Visioning Psychology;* (1990) *A Blue Fire,* ed. Thomas More; (1995) *Kinds of Power;* (1996) *The Soul's Code;* (2004) *A Terrible Love of War.*

Chapter 2. The camel and the eye of a needle

1. Max Weber (1920) *The Protestant Ethic and the Spirit of Capitalism.*

2. There are obviously many other ways of interpreting these stories, more 'pleasant' ways also. For example, the gnostic traditions read the same stories in completely different ways. Others take the eye of the needle to be a low and narrow gate in the city walls of Jerusalem. Here, however, I am in search of the reading that has been (most) common in the history of the Church – with many, strong warnings against the corrupting effect of money.

3. Richard H. Tawney (1922) *Religion and the Rise of Capitalism,* London: Pelican Books, 1975, p.49.

4. Ibid., p.48.

5. Ibid., p.44.

6. Ibid., p.52.

7. Ibid., p.50.

8. Robert Heilbroner (2000) *The Worldly Philosophers,* p.23.

9. Richard Tawney (1922) *Religion and the Rise of Capitalism,* p.30.

10. Cf. 'Materialismetrenden' in Ch. 2 of Anders Barstad and Ottar Hellevik (2004) *På vei mot det gode samfunn?* SSB [Statistics Norway].

11. Karl Marx already saw clearly that capitalism was a substitute for theology. And according to Max Weber's *The Protestant Ethic and the Spirit of Capitalism,* the economy's religious background and function has become a background theme for analysis in some types of specialist environments, although seldom in economic ones.

12. "There can be economics in anything," says economist Diane Coyle (2002) in *Sex, Drugs and the Economy:* "In marriage, sport, crime, drugs trafficking, education, movies and even, yes, sex. Economics is one route towards understanding any aspect of human nature. And one of the most illuminating because of its analytical rigor." p.21.

13. James Hillman (1995) *Kinds of Power,* p.3.

14. The classic texts highlighting the growth of capitalism from religious ideas are Max Weber (1920) *The Protestant Ethic* and Richard Tawney (1922) *Religion and the Rise of Capitalism.*

Chapter 3. So, what is money?

1. M. Neary and G. Taylor (1998) *Money and the Human Condition* and G. Ingham (1996) 'Money is a Social Relation' in *Review of Social Economy,* 54:4, 243–75

2. Glyn Davies (2002) Director of the Bank of Wales and Professor of Economics at the University of Wales, writes: "Economists, and especially monetarists, tend to overestimate the purely economic, narrow and technical functions of money and have placed insufficient emphasis on its wider social, institutional and psychological aspects," *History of Money – From Ancient Times to the Present Day.*

3. Georg Simmel (1900) *The Philosophy of Money* is a classic reference text within the philosophy of money.

4. James Buchan (1996) *Frozen Desire,* p.283.

5. For an introduction to the effect of the alphabet on mind and body, see Chs 4 & 5 in David Abram (2005) *Spell of the Sensuous.*

6. Good outlines of the way technological inventions change society and economics is given by David Landes (2003) in *The Unbound Prometheus,* and by Joel Mokyr (1990) in *The Lever of Riches.*

7. When I choose the word 'imagination' and not 'fantasy', it is because most people would link the word 'fantasy' with a personal internal capacity to create mental pictures. Imagination is broader than that; it does not just relate to an internal capacity, but to our shared lifeworld – the open shared field of senses in which we all take part and in which the images aroused by money play themselves out. The 'credit crisis' of 2008, for instance is not a fantasy, nor physical, but imaginally real. See also James Hillman (1982) 'A Contribution to Soul and Money', in *Soul and Money,* p.36.

8. James Hillman (1982) 'A Contribution to Soul and Money', in *Soul and Money,* p.40.

9. William Sherden (1997) *The Fortune Sellers.*

10. Marshal McLuhan (1964) *Understanding Media,* describes money as a kind of

medium on a par with language, alphabet, roads, cars and radio: these are all extensions of humanity and define us.

11. "Average volumes are expected to exceed $3 trillion by 2007 with more than 44% of transactional volume coming from electronic trading." Quotation from the report 'Foreign Exchange' (Oct. 2006) by International Financial Services, London. Turnover was estimated by them as being US$2,700 billion per day in April 2006. At present, the current report from the Bank of International Settlements (BIS 2005) indicates US$1,900 billion/day for April 2004, *Triennial Central Bank Survey of Foreign Exchange and Derivatives Market Activity*, p.5. Foreign exchange trading has increased more than tenfold from less than US$200 billion/day in 1986. In 2006, global trade in goods and services was approximately US$14,500 billion according to the WTO annual report, which is 'only' around US$40 billion/day.

12. As it did in Malaysia in 1999, and in a series of countries since. There is internal disagreement among economists as to whether extensive global currency speculation is destructive or constructive for long-term economic development. Milton Friedman and Joseph Stiglitz would represent opposite sides here.

13. George Soros, 2003, *The Alchemy of Finance*, calls this 'human reflexivity': the fact that all of those involved are reflexive people, and not 'passive' atoms as in science, makes it impossible in principle to create any universal constants concerning financial markets. People will not obey any 'natural laws' because they are fundamentally free to change behaviour.

14. See http://www.indiodesign.com/boggs/jsgboggs.htm, downloaded 20 Feb. 2007.

15. Keith Hart (2000) *Money in an Unequal World*, p.235.

16. Many people have emphasised this point, for example Arne Jon Isachsen and Høidal (2004) *Globale Penger.*

17. Keith Hart (2000) *Money in an Unequal World*, p.237.

18. Marshall McLuhan (1964) *Understanding Media*, p.186.

19. From Jackson (1995) *The Oxford Book of Money*, as quoted in Furnham and Argyle (1998) *The Psychology of Money*, p.26.

20. Works such as Kahneman and Tversky (1979) 'Prospect Theory, An analysis of decisions under risk' and Kahneman (2003) 'Psychological Perspective on Economics' form the type of tradition which highlights the way money affects ways of thinking, and links between economic choices and attention.

21. This point is based on people working on institutional economics such as Victor Nee (2005) 'The New Institutionalisms in Economics and Sociology', Ch. 3 in Smeiser and Swedberg, eds. (2005) *The Handbook of Economic Sociology*. Economist John Smithin (2002) makes money as a 'social relationship' into a principal point in his book *What is Money?*

22. James Buchan (1996) *Frozen Desire: The philosophy of money*. James Hillman (1982) 'A Contribution' and (1994) *Kinds of Power*, are important references from psychological research.

Chapter 4. Why money and *soul*?

1. The Catholic seller of indulgences, Tetzel, coined that slogan, and also occasioned Martin Luther's dispute with his 95 theses against the Catholic Church in 1517.

2. Robert Heilbroner (2000) *The Worldly Philosophers*.

3. The words have a *pragmatic* relationship with the objects, not an ostensible one, i.e. indicative or representative. Cf. Ludwig Wittgenstein (1957) *Philosophical Investigations*.

4. Carsten Jensen (1992) *Sjelen sitter i øyet*.

5. Emmanuel Levinas (2004) *Den annens humanisme*.

6. This is a main tenet of Martin Heidegger's principle work from 1927, *Sein und Zeit* [*Being and Time*]. There is no room here for a more in-depth philosophical review.

7. Freely based on Gaston Bachelard (1958) *The Poetics of Space*.

8. Martin Buber (1923) *I and Thou*.

9. In our culture, 'internal' is often confused with subjective, or inside-the-subject, which then becomes inside-the-brain. The soul-concept, as used here, relates neither to the subjective nor the objective. Such concepts belong within the dualistic tradition from Descartes. 'Internal' and 'external' are used here not for spatial indications relative to the location of the subject, but to describing qualities in the case of lived experiences. Our life-world is neither internal nor external in a literal sense. As Maurice Merleau-Ponty (1962) writes: "Truth does not 'inhabit' only the 'inner man', or more accurately, there is no inner man, man is in the world, and only in the world does he know himself."

10. James Hillman (1976) *Re-Visioning Psychology*, p.122.

11. William Bloom (1995) *Money, Heart and Mind*, p.164.

12. Per Espen Stoknes (2008), 'The Remembering of the Air', in *POIESIS: A Journal of the Arts & Communication*, Vol X, 2008, 74–86

13. Gregory Bateson (1968) *Steps to an Ecology of Mind*, or Fritjof Capra (1996) *The Web of Life, A New Scientific Understanding of Living Systems*.

14. See David Abram (2005) *The Spell of the Sensuous* for an exposition of the life-world, p.40. Phenomenologists Edmund Husserl, Martin Heidegger and Maurice Merleau-Ponty worked out a whole philosophy of human existence around the concept of lifeworld.

15. James F. Moore (1996) *The Death of Competition: Leadership and Strategy in the Age of Business Ecosystems*.

16. There are exceptions, such as the ethics council for Norway's Petroleum Fund (the Government Pension Fund – Global), a public institution that came into being only after lengthy tussles and contra-arguments from many quarters, not least from Norway's Ministry of Finance.

Chapter 5. New welfare: Does money make the soul happy?

1. The fact that welfare should also apply to animals, plants, countryside and special locations in nature, is a thought that we have hardly begun to take on board. So far, the idea of welfare has been anthropocentric – in other words, more or less exclusively for humans.

2. Here, I am following Siri Næss (2001) 'Livskvalitet som psykisk velvære' ['Quality of life as mental well-being'] in *Tidsskrift for den Norske Lægeforening* [*The Journal of the Norwegian Medical Association*], 121, 1940–4.

3. Rafael di Tella and Robert MacCulloch (2006) 'Some Uses of Happiness Data in Economics', *Journal of Economic Perspectives*, 20:1, 25–46.

4. Other English words for quality of life are: subjective well-being, happiness and satisfaction. There is a huge overlap between their inherent meanings. Siri Næss (2001) gives a good summary of Norwegian terms in 'Quality of life as mental well-being', *The Journal of the Norwegian Medical Association*, 121, 1940–4.

5. The journal is available at www.kluweronline.com/issn/1389-4978. In addition, articles about happiness are often published in publications such as the *Journal of Economic Psychology, Journal of Economic Perspectives* and *American Economic Review*. A summary of the field is provided by Huppert et al. (2005) *The Science of Well-Being*.

6. Examples of questions taken from MMI Norsk Monitor, Oslo (1985–2005). The international World Values Survey uses eleven questions: one on overall satisfaction with life, five about positive and five about negative affects.

7. For a methodical discussion, see for example Robert Lane (1991) *The Market Experience,* part VII, or Daniel Kahneman (ed.) (1999) *Well-Being.*

8. See, for example, Davidsson (2000) quoted on p.17 in Richard Layard (2004) *Happiness.*

9. Steptoe, A, Wardle J. and Marmot, M. (2005) 'Positive Affect and Health-Related Neuroendocrine, Cardiovascular and Inflammatory Processes', *Proceedings of the National Academy of Sciences,* 3 May, 201:18, 6508–12.

10. Daniel Kahneman and Krueger, Alan (2006) 'Developments in the Measurement of Subjective Well-Being', *Journal of Economic Perspectives,* 20:1, 3–24.

11. David G. Blanchflower and Oswald, Andrew J. (2004) 'Well-being Over Time in Britain and the *USA', Journal of Public Economics,* 88, 1359–86.

12. Richard Layard (2004) *Happiness,* Ch. 3.

13. The first classic economics article that highlighted this paradox is probably Richard Easterlin, (1974) 'Does Economic Growth Improve the Human Lot? Some Empirical Evidence' in P. David and M. Reder (eds) (1974) *Nations and Households in Economic Growth: Essays in Honor of Moses Abramovitz,* pp.98–125.

14. Richard Layard (2004) *Happiness,* p.38.

15. UNDP (2001–2005) *Human Development Report.*

16. Ottar Hellevik (1999) 'Why do we not get any happier?' Statistics Norway: Samfunnspeilet 1999–2004 .

17. Richard A. Easterlin (1973) 'Does money buy happiness?' *The Public Interest,* 30 (Winter) 1–10.

18. Richard A. Easterlin (2004) 'The Economics of Happiness', *Daedalus* 133:2 (on happiness) 26–33.

19. Here are four of these, which Lane (1991) *The Market Experience* summarises p.529 ff:
1) In general, studies show that people take satisfaction from *everyday sources other than income.* The responses to the question 'What gives you most satisfaction or happiness on a daily basis?' can be given as follows (several answers possible): a) family 72%, b) TV 48%, c) friends 47%, d) music 31%, e) books, magazines, newspapers 28%, f) house/home 24%, then meals, sport, clothes.
2) *Work* has inherent qualities for creating a feeling of self-respect that contributes more to well-being than salary level does. The happiness from doing work is linked more to quality and feedback than to income.
3) *Sex and marriage* are overwhelmingly more important in quality-of-life studies than economic contributions to well-being. One woman states, "Money has never been a problem for me . . . I would change lives with anyone who has a decent sex life", p.530.
4) *Worries.* People in the wealthiest classes do not have a lower frequency or intensity of perceived worries. However, studies have also shown that there is a difference between poor and wealthy as regards *what* they worry about. Even if money cannot always buy more happiness, *economic security* can reduce the volume of *financial* worries. Lane (1991), Ch. 26.

In a more recent study by Mariano Rojas (2007), 'Heterogeneity in the relationship between income and happiness', the author summarises five theories that have been put forward to explain the income-happiness paradox: 1) The relative explanation (comparison), 2) The absolute explanation (money in excess of basic necessities provides little gain), 3) Adaptation (habituation), 4) Aspiration (sliding scale of ambition); and he puts forward his own 5) Conceptual Referent theory (there are several different culturally based definitions of happiness that people refer to when they are to determine their level of happiness).

20. In his book *Mythologies*, Roland Barthes (1957) makes a series of close readings of how certain selected practices, often unintended, gain a status of 'natural'. Unreflected on, they are upgraded to having the status of truths in the culture. We obtain increasing numbers of such myths about what for us in the modern world are natural economics, e.g. that we need the freedom of choice that the market provides with 60 different types of shampoo. Bruce Springsteen takes a dubious stance on this type of media myth about diversity when he sings "500 channels and nothing on".

21. See Richard Layard (2004) *Happiness*, p.49, or van Praag, kap 21 in Kahneman (ed.) (1999) *Well-Being*.

22. Robert Lane (1991) *The Market Experience*, p.545, Kahneman (ed.) (1999) *Well-Being*, Kahneman and Krueger (2006) 'Developments in the Measurement of Subjective Well-Being', *Journal of Economic Perspectives*, 20:1, 3–24

23. Lewis Carroll (1871), *Through the Looking Glass*, Ch. 2.

24. Tibor Scitovskyi (1976) *The Joyless Economy*.

25. "People generally underestimate the extent of hedonic adaptation to new states . . . Failures of hedonic prediction are even common in the short term," from Daniel Kahneman (2003) *A Psychological Perspective on Economics*, p.165.

26. Richard Layard (2004) *Happiness*, p.48.

27. Robert Lane (1991) *The Market Experience*, p.223.

28. "Whenever a friend succeeds, a little something in me dies," quoted in *The Sunday Times Magazine*, London (16 Sept 1973); "Envy is the central fact of American life," in Gore Vidal (1981) *The Paris Review Interviews: Writers at Work*, 5th series; and "It is not enough to succeed. Others must fail," quoted by Gerard Irvine, 'Antipanegyric for Tom Driberg' (8 Dec. 1976).

29. Thorstein Veblen (1901) *The Theory of the Leisure Class*, p.156, quoted in Heilbroner (2000) *The Worldly Philosophers*, p.229.

30. Richard Layard (2004) *Happiness*, p.151.

31. Stutzer, A. (2003) 'The role of income aspirations in individual happiness', *Journal of Economic Behavior and Organization*, 54, 89–109, quoted in Richard Layard (2004) *Happiness*, p.49/252, see http://cep.lse.ac.uk/layard/annex.pdf.

32. Blanchflower and Oswald (2004), in Layard (2004) *Happiness*.

33. John Maynard Keynes (1931) 'Economic possibilities for our Grandchildren' in *Essays in Persuasion*.

34. Paul Samuelson and William Nordhaus (2001) *Economics*, 17th edn, p.754.

35. Robert Lane (1991) *The Market Experience*, p.599.

36. Ibid., Ch. 17.

37. See Helliwell, J. (2003) 'How's life? Combining Individual and National Variables to Explain Subjective Well-Being', *Economic Modelling*, 20:2 (Mar. 2003), 331–60, which analyses

World Values Survey data; or Di Tella et al. (2003), 'The Macroeconomics of Happiness', *The Review of Economics and Statistics*, 85:4 (November 2003), 793–809, which analyses Eurobarometer and the US General Social Survey.

38. See 'Fremtidsbilder 2030' ['Images of the Future 2030'], a report from BI Norwegian School of Management to the annual conference of the NHO (the Confederation of Norwegian Enterprise) in 2007.

39. UK Government Strategy Unit (Dec 2002): *Life Satisfaction: The State of Knowledge and Implications for Government*. Accessible at: http://www.cabinetoffice.gov.uk/media/cabinetoffice/strategy/assets/paper.pdf

40. "David Cameron, the latest leader of Britain's once rather materialistic Conservative Party, has espoused the notion of 'general well-being' (GWB) as an alternative to the more traditional GDP." *The Economist*, leader article, 19 Dec. 2006.

41. The Norwegian eco-philosopher Sigmund Kvaløy Sætereng's concept of MFA (meaningful work), is one of many examples of parallel ideas.

42. Robert E Lane (1991) *The Market Experience*, Part V.

43. Richard Sennett (2003) *Respect*, and Richard Layard (2004) *Happiness*, pp.156–60.

44. A central concept in Richard Florida (2003) *The Rise of the Creative Class*.

45. Richard Layard (2004) *Happiness*, p.158. Bruno Frey (1997) *Not Just for The Money*.

46. Baard Kuvaas (2006) 'Work performance, affective commitment, and work motivation: The roles of pay administration and pay level'. *Journal of Organizational Behavior*, 27, 365–85.

47. Robert Lane (1991) *The Market Experience*, p.232.

48. Richard Layard (2004) *Happiness*, p.133. See also Joseph Stiglitz (2006) 'Good Numbers Gone Bad – Why relying on GDP accounting can lead to poor decision making'. *Fortune*, 2 Oct., p.24.

49. More recent economic research, particularly within behavioural economics, is already in rapid movement away from narrower economic self-interest. According to Prof. Alexander Cappelen at NHH (the Norwegian School of Economics and Business Administration), "the most important trend within the economics profession today is to include other forms of motivation." *Dagens Næringsliv*, p.47, (17 Feb. 2007).

50. Rafael di Tella and Robert MacCulloch (2006) 'Some Uses of Happiness Data in Economics', *Journal of Economic Perspectives*, 20:1, 25–46.

51. NOU 2005:5 *Simple signals in a complex world*.

52. Robert Lane (1991) *The Market Experience*, p.600.

Chapter 6. Markets: Who owns the invisible hand?

1. Henri Pirenne, *Economic and Social History of Medieval Europe*, quoted in Robert Heilbroner (1995) *The Worldly Philosophers*, p.21.

2. Robert Heilbroner (1995) *The Worldly Philosophers*, p.26.

3. John McMillan (2002) *Reinventing the Bazaar: a natural history of markets*, p.6.

4. "By matching sellers and buyers (supply and demand) in each market, a market economy simultaneously solves the three problems of what, how and for whom", Samuelson and Nordhaus (2001) *Economics*, pp.27–9.

5. Adam Smith (1776) *Wealth of Nations* Book II, ii, p.86, in Heilbroner (1997) *The Essential Smith*.

6. Adam Smith (1776) *Wealth of Nations* Book I, ii, pp.25–6, in Heilbroner (1997) *The Essential Smith*.

7. Right in the final phase of writing this book, I came across a more recent German article in which the invisible hand of Hermes/Mercury is linked explicitly to Adam Smith's works: Peter Bendixen (2004) 'Die Konstruktion des ökonomischen Blicks', Institut für Wirtschaftsethik Universität St. Gallen, see http://www.jsse.org/2004-2/oekonomischer_blick_bendixen.htm, downloaded 22 Feb. 2007.

8. On 27 September 1911, the wholesaler Conrad Langaard presented a statue of Mercury in bronze. It was positioned in front of the main façade where it remains today. http://www.oslobors.no/ob/historie_borsbygningen, downloaded 2 Feb. 2007.

9. Norman Brown (1947) *Hermes the Thief*.

10. The Homeric hymn to Hermes, lines 30–5, translated into English by Charles Boer (1970) *The Homeric Hymns*.

11. I wrote a few pages about Hermes in a previous book, *Sjelens Landskap* [*Landscapes of Soul*], published in 1996. This chapter – and for that matter the entire book – is an expansion on a train of thought begun in Ch. 4 of *Sjelens Landskap*.

12. The Homeric hymn to Hermes, lines 513–20.

13. The Homeric hymn to Hermes, lines 574–80.

14. Adam Smith (1776) *Wealth of Nations* Book IV, ii, p.456, in Heilbroner (1997) *The Essential Smith*.

15. Adam Smith (1776) *Wealth of Nations* Book II, ii, p.86, in Heilbroner (1997).

16. Adam Smith (1776) *Wealth of Nations* Book I, Ch. II, in Heilbroner (1997).

17. Manuel Castells (2000) *The Rise of the Network Society, The Information Age: Economy, Society and Culture*, Vol. I.

18. Keith Hart (2001) *Money in an Unequal World*, p.203.

19. Joseph Schumpeter (1942) *The Process of Creative Destruction*.

20. William H. Desmonde (1962) *Magic, Myth, and Money: The Origin of Money in Religious Ritual*. "The bull was a widespread unit of value in the early history of the Graeco-Roman culture. Representations of ox heads in a palace inventory from Cnossus indicate that the ox unit was probably used in Crete in Minoan times. In Homer values are invariably expressed in terms of oxen. The arms of Diomedes are declared equivalent to nine oxen; those of Glaucos to 100. Female slaves skilled in crafts sold for four oxen, and the three-legged pot was worth twelve." Page 109 f. Glyn Davies (2002) *History of Money - From Ancient Times to the Present Day*. "Cattle used as money were of course counted by head . . . The religious usage of cattle (for sacrifice) probably preceded their adoption for more general monetary purposes . . . They were movable, an immense advantage, forming man's earliest working capital and the linguistic origin of our . . . terms capital and chattels," pp.42–3.

21. Ibid., p.118.

22. Rafael Lopez-Pedraza (1989) *Hermes and His Children*, p.59 f., and James Hillman (1974) *Re-Visioning Psychology*, Part IV.

23. The Homeric hymn to Hermes, lines 574–84, translated by Charles Boer (1970).

24. John McMillan (2002) *Reinventing the Bazaar: A Natural History of Markets*, p.6.

25. From Charles L. S. Montesquieu (1748, trans. 1973): *The Spirit of Laws*, quoted in Andrew Samuels (1993) *The Political Psyche*, p.99.

26. As Ginette Paris (1990) indicates about Hermes in the book *Pagan Grace; Dionysos, Hermes and the Goddess Memory in Daily Life.*

27. "What is needed is an effort to distinguish between the properties of markets, of buying and selling as a form of human activity, and those of capitalism increasingly organized by states and bureaucracy." p.205 in Keith Hart (2000) *Money in an Unequal World*, Ch. 5: 'The Market from an Humanist Point of View'.

28. Samuelson and Nordhaus (2001) *Economics*, p.161: "The invisible-hand theory assumes that buyers and sellers have complete information about the goods and services they buy and sell. Firms are assumed to know about all the production functions for operating in their industry. Consumers are presumed to know about the quality and prices of goods."

29. Thomas Carlyle (1849) *Occasional Discourse on the Negro Question*: "Not a 'gay science', I should say, like some we have heard of; no, a dreary, desolate and, indeed, quite abject and distressing one; what we might call, by way of eminence, the dismal science." Regardless of how correct or otherwise Carlyle was in his assertions, the designation itself has become firmly implanted.

30. Kjell A. Nordstrøm and Jonas Ridderstråle (1999) *Funky Business.*

31. Torunn Ystaas (2001) 'Tapte Talenter' ['Lost Talents'], pp.30–1, in *Flux – Livsfilosofisk magasin [Flux – Life philosophy magazine]* no. 24, Spring 2001.

32. This is the hole that 'branding' is now trying to fill. In modern marketing, the mantra is that the product has to tell a story and appeal to the consumer's emotions and sense of identity. I believe this tries to satisfy a legitimate need, but it raises questions about how the brand-idea tries to create a general story around the *product in relation to other products.* The individual product's journey from the land and producer to the shelves and the store gets lost. The product has been given an *image,* yes, but seldom a transparent, unique story that buyers can trace back to actual people, to the producer, the creator of the concept, or the vendor. The product has gained 'wings', but not 'roots' in firm ground, in places, animals, plants and time.

33. Marcel Mauss, (1925, 1990) *The Gift: The Form and Reason for Exchange in Archaic Societies.*

34. Keith Hart (2000) *Money in an Unequal World*, pp.193–5.

35. Ginette Paris (1990) *Pagan Grace*, p.94.

36. Walter Wriston, former CEO of Citibank, is a good representative of this view. He despised politicians and bureaucrats "whose business in life it is to regulate, and who still do not understand that the world has become one huge international market place". And "The hand of government touches every aspect of human productivity. It is not only wasteful, but serves to destroy incentive and to discourage ingenuity. Their desire to control the international financial markets as they control so many national financial markets is, however, a vain wish." Quoted in Armand van Dormael (1997) *The Power of Money*, p.147.

37. See, for example, Ch. 9: 'Is Well-Being a Market Externality?' in Robert Lane (2000) *The Loss of Happiness in Market Democracies.*

38. A good classic example of the domination of this competition metaphor is found in Lester Thurow's (1985) *The Zero-Sum Solution: Building a World-Class American Economy.*

39. A broad tradition of research within economics has made the ideals of perfect markets problematic. In 2001, George A. Akerlof, Michael Spence and Joseph E. Stiglitz were awarded the Nobel Prize for their analyses of markets with asymmetric information.

40. Robert Lane (2000) *The Loss of Happiness in Market Democracies*, p.8, Chs 9 & 10.

41. Paul Samuelson and William Nordhaus (2001) *Economics*, p.27.

Chapter 7. Riches, milk and honey: Is it a sin to be rich?

1. Paul Samuelson and William Nordhaus (2001) *Economics*, p.228.

2. Morning edition of Aftenposten (17 Apr. 1998), p.56.

3. Furnham and Argyle (1998) *The Psychology of Money*, p.262.

4. Ibid.

5. Tad Crawford (1994) *The Secret Life of Money*, pp.104–7.

6. Samuelson and Nordhaus (2001) *Economics*, p.96.

7. Therefore some of the world's largest and most solid economic companies, such as General Electric in 2005 under CEO Jeffrey Immelt, began to position themselves for the new water market that is going to emerge once marginal utility means that the price of fresh water will rise in future.

8. Statistics for global gold production can be found at http://www.goldsheetlinks.com/production2.htm. Downloaded on 22 July 2007. 80% of all gold known throughout history has been produced since 1900.

9. Lynne Twist (2003) writes wholeheartedly on just this topic – *scarcity* – in her book *The Soul of Money*. The two previous paragraphs are inspired by two of hers, pp.43–4.

10. Samuelson and Nordhaus (2001) *Economics*, p.4.

11. In an interview with *Forbes* Magazine, financial consultant Russ Alan Prince states that surveys at his consultancy company indicate that wealthy people are particularly afraid of 1) being tricked by unscrupulous financial advisors, 2) being the subject of some other financial swindle, 3) having their identity stolen, 4) being unreasonably prosecuted, and 5) being the victim of violence, either to themselves or their family. *Forbes*, 23 May 2007.

12. Robert Graves (1955) *The Greek Myths* Vol. I, pp.46–7.

13. James Hillman (1987) 'Senex and Puer', in *Puer Papers*.

14. In the book *A Christmas Carol*, the Ghost of Christmas Present shows Scrooge what material surplus and riches there would be in the present if only he could release the grip of want and regain the considerateness he possessed within. Dickens' Scrooge finally changes from being someone who was in the habit of biting his nephew's and subordinate's heads off because he felt that he did not possess enough, to becoming a benefactor who is happy with present circumstances. The chronological compulsion of linear time loosens its hold, and in that way he escapes from the grip of Chronos.

15. Daniel Kahneman (2003) 'Psychological Perspective on Economics', *The American Economic Review, 93:2, 162–8.*

16. In thanks for this, Zeus later placed her in the firmament, and her image can be seen today in the constellation of Capricorn.

17. Lynne Twist here, in *The Soul of Money* (2003), p.58, refers to R. Buckminster Fuller's concepts.

18. Samuelson and Nordhaus (2001) *Economics*, p.4.

19. Interview with Gates and Buffet by Daniel Roth, in *Fortune* 152:8, Europe edition, 98–104.

20. A broad, close archetypical relationship is documented between senex, the old man, and his restoration through consuming milk. See James Hillman (1987) *Puer Papers*, p.38 f. The illustration is by Peter Paul Rubens (1625) *Cimon and Pero (Caritas Romana)*.

21. Carl G. Jung (1959) *Collected Works*, Vol 9a, §215.

Chapter 8. Accounts and bookkeeping: What story does money tell?

1. The story has been borrowed from Abraham Briloff (1972) *Unaccountable Accounting.*

2. Phenomenologist Martin Heidegger, for example, talks about "language as the house of being", and in a famous quote says: "Die Sprache spricht, nicht der Mensch" ["Language speaks, not the [hu]man]". Ludwig Wittgenstein and Jacques Derrida are key names from other such traditions which emphasise the pragmatic and constructive nature of the language.

3. This is called the pragmatic understanding of language. In philosophy, this turn of phrase is associated with the later works of philosopher Ludwig Wittgenstein (*Philosophical Investigations*, 1953). His perceptions of the active life-shaping function of language games can also be applied to bookkeeping and accounts, which have strict formal and informal rules for their 'games'.

4. Fred Kofman (1995) 'Double-loop Accounting' in Peter Senge et al. (1995) *The Fifth Discipline Fieldbook*, p.286.

5. Miriam Beard (1938) *A History of the Business Man*, quoted in Robert Heilbroner (2000) *The Wordly Philosophers*, p.22.

6. Max Weber (1920) From 'Prefatory Remarks' to *Collected Essays in the Sociology of Religion*, reproduced in Max Weber (2002) *The Protestant Ethic and the Spirit of Capitalism*, pp.153–6.

7. Luca Pacioli (1494) *Particularis de Computis et Scripturis* [*Of Reckonings and Writings*]. Quotation from Brown and Johnston (1963) *Paciolo on Accounting*, p.118, quoted in James Buchan (1998) *Frozen Desire*, p.76.

8. These are abbreviations relating to various methods for calculating the profitability of projects or business areas: ROI = Return On Investment. EBITDA = Earnings Before Interest, Taxes, Depreciation and Amortisation. ROCE = Return on Capital Employed. The choice of method and principles for calculations can be crucial to decisions about implementation or closure.

9. Erik Reinert (1996) *Det Tekno-økonomiske Paradigmeskiftet*, Norsk Investorforum, no. 3/1996.

10. From UK Cooperative Banks, quoted in John Elkington (2001) *The Chrysalis Economy*.

11. Compare this discussion to Thomas Moore (1994) *Care of the Soul*. Here, his proposals include us building a quite concrete personal space for peace of mind and contemplation, writing, art or music, to which we can withdraw at set times; in other words, a tangible space for the soul.

12. The foregoing is inspired by William Bloom (1995) *Money, Heart and Mind*, p.189.

13. Brendan Burchell (2003) 'Financial Phobia: A Report for Egg'.

14. William Bloom (1995) *Money, Heart and Mind*, p.164.

15. William Bloom (1995) *Money, Heart and Mind*, pp.198–9.

16. Marianne Gullestad has carried out research into what she calls "peace and quiet as a cultural category". We can imagine Hestia as peace and quiet personified. See Gullestad (1989) *Kultur og hverdagsliv*, Ch. 7.

17. Nanna L. Hauge (1989) *Antikkens Guder og Helter*, p.38.

18. Ginette Paris (1991) *Pagan Meditations*, p.168.

19. Robert Graves (1955) *The Greek Myths I*, p.74.

20. Finn Øystein Bergh (2004) *Økonomiskolen*, p.266.

21. See Haresh Sapra (2006) 'Accounting Reform: The Costs and Benefits of Marking-to-Market', *Capital Ideas*, The University of Chicago Graduate School of Business: http://www.chicagogsb.edu/capideas/jul06/2.aspx. Downloaded 11 June 2007.

Chapter 9. Money as credit: Faust's dark secret

1. Credit – "ORIGIN mid 16th cent. (originally in the senses [belief] [credibility]): from French *crédit*, probably via Italian *credito* from Latin *creditum*, neuter past participle of *credere* 'believe, trust'." *New Oxford American Dictionary*, 2nd edn.

2. *New Oxford American Dictionary*: 'bank'; Dee Hock (2004) 'Money – A Brief History', available from http://uniteddiversity.com/wp-content/uploads/2008/01/ moneyabriefhistorydeehock.pdf

3. Richard Kerschagl (1973): "Typical too . . . is the story of the Duke of Orleans who, as soon as he had engaged John Law, the inventor of the European bank note, dismissed all his court alchemists, adding that he had now discovered a better and surer method of making money." From *Die Jagd nach dem künstlichen Gold: Der Weg der Alchemie*, p.64. Quoted in Hans C. Binswanger (1994) *Money and Magic, A Critique of the Modern Economy in the Light of Goethe's Faust*, p.31.

4. A masterly portrayal of the story of the rise and fall of John Law is given in Ch. 6 of James Buchan (1998) *Frozen Desire*.

5. The example has been borrowed from Fred Harrison (2005) *Boom & Bust*, p.122.

6. The dramatic conclusion of the Bretton Woods system has been described in many places. In my opinion, it is well covered in Armand Van Dormael (1997) *The Power of Money*, Ch. 8.

7. This is the story of countries such as Argentina, see the description in Arne Jon Isachsen (2004) *Globale Penger*, p.29.

8. James Buchan (1998) *Frozen Desire*, Ch. 5.

9. Samuelson and Nordhaus (2001) *Economics* Ch. 2; Finn Øystein Bergh (2004) *Økonomiskolen*, p.249.

10. Samuelson and Nordhaus (2001), p.719.

11. Historically, the increase in the money supply vitalised the real economy with an increased supply for credit, creating strong growth. Money had been in short supply, hindering trade and demand. Today, further increases in the supply of money do not mean automatic growth in the real economy. The links between different types of money supply aggregates and activity in the real economy, the 'transaction mechanisms', are complex, unstable over a period of time and theoretically unclear. Cf. section 5.2–5.3 in Norges Bank (2000) *Vurdering av den norske pengemengdestatistikken* by Bernhardsen et al.

12. Armand van Dormael (1997) in his book *The Power of Money* traces the development of credit and upheavals in politics and industry from the 16th century to the collapse of the Bretton Woods agreement.

13. The public authorities are no longer guarantors for money: they print only approximately 4% (i.e. the entire stock of cash) of the money that society needs. Banks and credit institutions issue the remainder in the form of credit. The central bank is only the indirect guarantor of private customers' bank deposits up to a specific sum, because they are the banks' bank ('lender of last resort') in the event of a banking crisis arising.

14. No attempt has been made by any conspiratorial element to hide this 'secret'. It is

described in all of the more recent, thorough textbooks on economics and banking systems, under the technical term of 'fractional-reserve banking'.

15. In Norway, the required capital for credit risk is 8%, initially, in compliance with the last regulation issued by the Norwegian Ministry of Finance, which came into force on 1 Jan. 2007, based on the EU-based Basel II Regulation.

16. Credit-card industry profits have risen from $27.4 billion in 2003 to $40.7 billion in 2007, according to R. K. Hammer. Source: www.time.com, 21 Feb. 2008.

17. OECD 2005 finds signs indicative of 'low levels of financial literacy': "1) United States – 50% of adults and 66% of high school students fail basic economics test, 2) United Kingdom – fewer than 40% of respondents confident about making financial decisions, 3) Japan – only 1% of consumer education professionals believe that consumers have an adequate level of financial knowledge, 4) Australia – 37% of those with investments did not understand that investments can fluctuate in value." Even fewer can give a correct answer when asked where money comes from, and what are the differences between 'commodity money', 'flat money' and 'bank money'.

18. James Buchan (1998) *Frozen Desire*, p.123.

19. Mihaly Csikszentmihalyi (1990) *Flow: The Psychology of Optimal Experience*.

20. Meadows, Randers & Meadows (2004) *Limits to Growth – The 30-Year Update*, see foreword.

Chapter 10. Debt and interest: The prison of the soul

1. From http://www.lapresrupture.qc.ca/suicide.html. Downloaded on 22 Jan. 2006.

2. Brown, S., Taylor, K. and Price S.W. (2005) 'Debt and distress: Evaluating the psychological cost of credit', *Journal of Economic Psychology*, 26, 642–63. They conclude: "For an otherwise average individual a 10% increase in the level of individual outstanding credit would need a 7% increase in monthly income, or an 18% increase in annual savings, to offset the negative impact on their psychological well-being."

3. Yang, Livia Markoczy and Min Qi (2007) 'Unrealistic optimism in consumer credit card adoption', *Journal of Economic Psychology* 28, 170–85.

4. During the course of 2007 it became clear that failures in the 'subprime' credit market in the US had the potential to weaken the entire macro-economy; meaning that difficulties among the poor in making payments would have a major impact on society. A remarkable examination of the social and psychological consequences of the high-cost credit industry in the US is contained in the book by Christopher L. Peterson (2004) *Taming the Sharks – Toward a Cure for the High-Cost Credit Market*.

5. IMF (2001) *Manual on Monetary and Financial Statistics*, p.69.

6. The monetary base (often called the basic money supply or 'M0') also includes the banks' reserves in the central bank which are not interest-bearing.

7. Statistics Norway describes the Norwegian money supply: "The money supply (M2) was NOK 1,306 billion at the end of May 2007, of which the majority (approx. 90 per cent) comprised bank deposits. In comparison, banknotes and coins constituted only 3–4 per cent of the money supply. The remainder of the money supply comprised mainly shares in the money market fund (around 6 per cent), while bank-certificates comprised less than 1 per cent." The Norwegian situation is typical of most European countries. Source: http://www.ssb.no/m2/ downloaded 20 July 2007.

8. More precise than the term 'bank' would be 'the money-issuing sector' (which does not include types of credit institutions), and more precise than the term 'households' would be 'money-holding sector'. Norges Bank and Statistics Norway subdivide the money-holding sector into four parts: other financial ventures, municipalities, non-financial ventures and households, of which the latter is the largest part as at 2007. Source: Statistics Norway money supply statistics. Available from http://www.ssb.no/m2/.

9. Luther (c. 1520) quoted in Richard Tawney (1921) *Religion and the Rise of Capitalism*, p.91.

10. The Koran Sura 2, verse 275.

11. William Bloom (1995) *Money, Heart and Mind*, p.142.

12. Margrit Kennedy (1995) *Geld ohne Zinsen und Inflation: Ein Tauschmittel das jedem dient* [*Interest and Inflation Free Money: An Exchange Medium that Works for Everybody*].

13. Richard Tawney (1921) *Religion and the Rise of Capitalism*, London Pelican Books (1975) p.91.

14. Johan Galtung, (1996) *Peace by Peaceful Means: Peace and Conflict, Development and Civilization*.

15. *New Oxford American Dictionary*, 2nd edn: *Gage* is defined as 1) an object that is deposited as security against an obligation, 2) a pledge, usually with a glove thrown as a symbol of a desire to fight to the death, and 3) an instrument for measuring the diameter of a pipe, chain or wire. 'Gage' is thus an obligation on a person's life. 'Mortgage' emphasises this.

16. Michael Rowbotham (1998) *Grip of Death – a study of modern money, debt slavery and destructive economics*, p.31.

17. From the website about Ananke at 'the Greek Mythology Link', a website created and maintained by Carlos Parada. Downloaded from http://www.maicar.com/GML/Ananke.html on 7 Aug. 2007.

18. There are different mythical versions of the parentage of the Moirae. Some sources maintain that it is Zeus and Themis, others Chaos and yet others Ananke. This might indicate that people can always make a virtue out of necessity.

19. Aeschylos' *Prometheus Bound*, strophe 45, translated by Edmund D. A. Morshead (1908).

20. Glyn Davies (2002) *History of Money*, pp.48–9.

21. *Arrian's Discourses of Epictetus*, Fragment 8.

22. Aeschylos' *Prometheus Bound*, strophe 104, translated by Edmund D. A. Morshead (1908).

23. The story is taken from Tad Crawford (1994) *The Secret Life of Money.*

24. Philip Mayerson (1971) 'The House of Hades: Gods of the Underworld' in *Classical Mythology in Literature, Art and Music*, pp.227–47.

25. James Hillman (1979) *The Dream and the Underworld.*

26. In its 'Tilstanden i finansmarkedet 2006' [Status of the Financial Market 2006], the Financial Supervisory Authority of Norway describes the calculations for the "total debt burden for households, which constituted 160% of total income in 2004, increasing to 200% by the end of 2008", p.33. And ". . . towards the end of 2009 debt will exceed 230% of disposable income", p.28. Unsecured consumer debt (credit card and other consumer borrowing) has been growing by more than 15% per year in recent years, p.34. When this was written in 2007 the banks were stretching the limits of lending. The old rule of 2.5 times income was being stretched to 5 and 6 times, particularly for people with higher incomes, as analysed in

the journal *Dagens Næringsliv* (26 May 2007, p.110). Much of this is based on the economic conditions. But the long-term trend of increasing levels of debt in proportion to income is nevertheless clear in all Western countries; see for example the following table for the US since 1949:

USA householders	1949	1967	1973	1979	1989	1995	1999
Debt/income	32%	67%	65%	72%	85%	92%	103%

Source: Economic Policy Institute, quoted in Peterson (2004) *Taming the Sharks*.

27. Lars Gulbrandsen (2007) *Gjeld til å bære? Norske husholdningers gjeld og lånelyst sommeren 2006*, NOVA Report 11/07 and Frøydis Strøm, Harald Lunde and Eiliv Mørk (2006) "Inntektene øker, men gjelden øker mer" [Incomes are increasing, but debt is increasing more], *Samfunnsspeilet*, SSB, 11 Dec. 2006.

28. See Chs 2 & 10 in Robert Lane (2000) *The Loss of Happiness in Market Democracies*.

29. Tolkien's journal, 13 July 1956, p.12. Quoted in Stephen Goodson, 2002, 'The Mythos of J.R.R. Tolkien', *Spearhead* magazine, see http://www.spearhead.com/0208-sg.html, downloaded 23 Feb. 2006.

30. Tolkien's journal, 3–10 Aug., p.48. Quoted in Goodson, ibid.

31. A more recent, thorough and technical discussion of the structural effects on the economy of bank money is contained, for example, in Giancarlo Bertocco (2007) 'The Characteristics of a Monetary Economy: A Keynes-Schumpeter Approach', *Cambridge Journal of Economics*, 31:1, 101–22.

32. This is not the place to go into a detailed, technical discussion of proposals such as these. A detailed proposal for possible monetary reform of this type has been described recently in Joseph Huber and James Robertson (2000) *Creating New Money*. They build further on the famous economist Irving Fisher's (1935) *100% Money*, which questions, among other things, the beneficial effects on the economic conditions of 'fractional reserve banking' and proposes a transition away from debt-based money. Other people have proposed similar systems, but this is a debate that has still not been given a thorough treatment in the light of the challenges of the 21st century. Huber and Robertson's book can be downloaded here: http://www.neweconomics.org/gen/uploads/CreatingNewMoney.pdf. A completely different type of monetary system to limit consumption of resources in the economy is described by Richard Douthwaite (2006) *The Ecology of Money*.

Chapter 11. Powerful economic myths: About economic ideology in practice

1. Gassco's report to the Norwegian Ministry of Petroleum and Energy in June 2006 concludes by stating that all of the CO2 value chains they have studied have a negative present value. They do not, therefore, recommend CO2 separation.

2. "The most exciting idea in economics since 1776" writes Erik Grønn (1999) in *Forelesninger i offentlig økonomi*, p.30.

3. Efficiency vs. equality – the big trade-off. Samuelson & Nordhaus (2001) *Economics*: "The conflict between equality and efficiency is our biggest socio-economic trade-off, and it plagues us in dozens of dimensions of social policy. We can't have our cake of market efficiency and share it equally." Also Arthur Okun (1975) quoted in Samuelson & Nordhaus, p.385.

4. John Davis (2006) 'The Turn in economics: neoclassical dominance to mainstream pluralism?', *Journal of Institutional Economics*, 2:1, 1–20. David Colander, Richard P. F. Holt, and

Barkley J. Rosser, Jr. (2004) 'The Changing Face of Mainstream Economics', *Review of Political Economy*, 16:4, 485–99.

5. Mark Schneider (2006) 'Great Minds in Economics: Paul Samuelson', in *Yale Economic Review, Summer 2006*. See also Mark Skousen (1997) 'The Perseverance of Paul Samuelson's Text Book' and Agnar Sandmo (2006) *Samfunnsøkonomi – en idéhistorie*, p.335.

6. Samuelson & Nordhaus (2001) *Economics*, p.7. They quote Alfred Marshall: "It will be my most cherished ambition . . . to increase the numbers, whom Cambridge University sends out into the world with cool heads but warm hearts, willing to give some . . . of their best powers to grappling with the social suffering around them . . .", p.16.

7. By some called Hume's guillotine because it cuts off the two completely, and refers them to widely different spheres. Such a dichotomy is deeply problematic from the point of view of the philosophy of science, which points out that any way of framing research questions and selecting so-called neutral facts is already normative.

8. Samuelson and Nordhaus (2001) *Economics*, p.5.

9. Mark Schneider (2006) 'Great Minds in Economics: Paul Samuelson', in *Yale Economic Review, Summer 2006*.

10. Herbert Simon (1978) *Rational Decision-making in Business Organizations*, Nobel Lecture 8 Dec. 1978.

11. Joseph Stiglitz (2002) 'There Is No Invisible Hand' *The Guardian*, 20 Dec. 2002.

12. The 'new' ways in which research has been moving (since around 1980) are said by John Davis to be the following: "strategic interaction (game theory), the psychological characteristics of human beings (behavioral economics), experimental practices, the arguments of evolutionary psychology and non-linear complexity methods; all these constitute strategies of investigation that were largely absent in standard competitive marginalist thinking, which has been the mainstay of neoclassicism for many years". p.3 in John Davis (2006) 'The Turn in economics: neoclassical dominance to mainstream pluralism?', *Journal of Institutional Economics*, 2:1, 1–20.

13. Paul Ormerod (2006) 'Shun the rational agent to rebuild economics' in the *Financial Times*, 26 Nov. 2006, available at: http://search.ft.com/ftArticle?queryText=volterra+consulting&aje=true&ct=0&id=061106001215. Ormerod adds: "The challenge of reconstructing economic theory virtually from scratch makes it an exciting time to be an economist. It is attracting eminent researchers from other disciplines, such as mathematical sociology, computer science and statistical physics."

14. John Davis (2006) 'The Turn in economics: neoclassical dominance to mainstream pluralism?', *Journal of Institutional Economics*, 2; 1, 1-20.

15. David Colander (2000) 'The Death of Neoclassical Economics', *Journal of the History of Economic Thought*, 22:2, 127–44. The zenith of neoclassical dominance was in the 1970s, according to John Davis (2006) and came from the 'Chicago School' of economics within which Becker, Friedman, Lucas, Stigler and Hayek were key figures. They had an attitude which qualifies as economic imperialism, illustrated by the assertion that "the economic approach is a comprehensive one that is applicable to all human behavior", from Gary Becker (1976) *The Economic Approach to Human Behavior*. Quoted in John Davis, ibid.

16. Apollo shares his status as sun-god with Helios (in the same way as there are several moon-goddesses). Helios was probably an older sun-god than Apollo, who became 'promoted' to sun-god later (in both mythical and religious-historical time). We could perhaps think of Helios as being the sun itself, while Apollo is more representative of 'the bright light' and 'illumination'.

17. From the 'Hymn to Pythian Apollo', in *The Homeric Hymns,* translated into English verse by Charles Boer (1970).

18. Ovid, *Metamorphoses,* translated into English verse by A. D. Melville and E. J. Kenney (1998). Quoted from Book One.

19. Ovid, ibid., quoted from Book One.

20. Robert Graves (1955) *The Greek Myths,* I, p.79 (Ch. 21, n and o).

21. *New Oxford American Dictionary,* 2nd edn. *Oxford American Writers Thesaurus,* 1st edn, provides the following synonyms for equilibrium: "his equilibrium was never shaken, composure, calm, equanimity, sangfroid; level-headedness, coolheadedness, imperturbability, poise, presence of mind; self-possession, self-command; impassivity, placidity, tranquility, serenity; cool" – an incredibly archetypal precise description of the mythical attributes of Apollo. In the word equilibrium itself, we are approaching the essence of what it means to be Apollonian.

22. Philip Mirowski (1989) *More Heat than Light: Economics as Social Physics.*

23. Joseph Stiglitz (2002), 'There Is No Invisible Hand', *The Guardian,* 20 Dec. 2002, p.59. The last sentence from a previous article, Joseph Stiglitz (2000) 'The Insider', in *The New Republic* 17 Apr. 2000.

24. NOU 1998:11, *Kraft- og energibalansen mot 2020,* Oslo: Norwegian Ministry of Petroleum and Energy.

25. Gradually, the committee put in place a set of qualitative scenarios that could become management tools for the calculations. Immediately as these images of the future developed, it also became possible to provide more detailed 'orders' for the macro-economic calculations which were to be performed. NOU 1998:11.

26. Ronald Coase (1991) 'The Institutional Structure of Production', Nobel Lecture.

27. See for example, SSB (2006) *Statistikk 2016, Scenarier og Strategiske utfordringer,* p.9.

28. The price signals do not always emerge quickly enough to generate the 'right' reaction on the markets; delays arise in the real world, which mean that the price signals do not always convey the right information at the right time. The role of delayed price signals in relation to developments in technology and the market has been discussed by Meadows and Randers (2004) *Limits to Growth: 30 Year Update,* Ch. 6.

29. Bannock (2003) *Dictionary of Economics,* defines 'Consumer Sovereignty' thus: "In a free-market economy consumers vote with their purses for the pattern of production and consumption they want . . Although preferences are something the economist takes as given, and makes no value judgement about, they are assumed to be consistent and rational in certain ways", p.71.

30. In the Nobel Committee's reasoning for awarding the Prize to Daniel Kahneman in 2002, they state: "Economic theory relies on the assumption that economic agents may be likened to a 'homo oeconomicus'. This fictitious individual is usually governed by self-interest and makes his economic decisions by rationally evaluating the consequences of different alternatives, even in complex situations where the outcome is difficult to predict. Despite such strong assumptions, this approach has proved to be highly rewarding and has enhanced our understanding of many economic phenomena."

31. For a supplementary discussion about the devaluing of anything feminine within the Apollonian way of thinking, see for example James Hillman (1975) *Myth of Analysis,* Part 3, in particular pp.246–51.

32. This 'mental rule of thumb' is called 'availability heuristics' because elements that are more mentally available are given greater weight than they ought to be rationally or statistically. The concept of *availability heuristics* became familiar from Kahneman, D., Slovic, P. and Tversky, A. (eds) (1982) *Judgment under Uncertainty: Heuristics and biases.*

33. This grows out of the 'prospect theory' of Daniel Kahneman and Amos Tversky (1979) 'Prospect Theory, An analysis of decisions under risk'. *Econometrica*, 47, 313–27.

34. Such *relative* anchoraging to a reference point, such as that implied by the prospect theory, is in conflict with Bernoulli's analysis of benefit based on classical economics. Bernoulli presumed that personal, earlier experiences have little significance, but Kahneman and Tversky's findings are that they have. This gives rise to status quo heuristics (or anchoring and adjustment heuristics), which produces a systematic deviation from economic rational maximisation of utility. See, for example, pp.17–18 in Daniel Kahneman (ed.) (1999) *Well-Being.*

35. "Economists ignore possible circularities in the concept and rarely argue about what consumers enjoy, taking it as a matter of psychological fact." From the definition of 'utility', p.395 in Bannock et al. (2003) *Dictionary of Economics.*

36. Kahnernan (1999) *Well-Being,* Chs 1 & 21; Kahneman (2002) *A Psychological Perspective on Economics,* p.163 f.

37. Robert Lane (1991) *The Market Experience,* p.549 ff.

38. Bruno S. Frey (1997) *Not Just for the Money – An Economic Theory of Personal Motivation.*

39. 'Theory of the firm', Bannock et al. (2003) *Dictionary of Economics.*

40. Frode Geitvik reproduced in NA24 (2007) 'Selger sol for milliarder' [Selling the sun for billions], by Magnus Klever, 21 Mar. 2007. Available at: http://arkiv.na24.no/Nyhet/225191/Selger+sol+for+milliarder.html.

41. K. Basu, H. Mintzberg, R. Simons (2002) 'Memo to CEOs', in *Fast Company* 59, June 2002.

42. Both Milton Friedman and Peter Drucker believe it is immoral of executives not always to put their shareholders first: "If you find an executive who wants to take on social responsibilities (without this contributing to profitability for the shareholders), fire him. Fast." Drucker in an interview with Joel Bakan (2004) *The Corporation,* p.35. At the same time the management in many companies is so powerful, has such good networks and such great influence on the people sitting on the Board, that the principle of shareholders coming first becomes more talk than reality. Management has its own axes to grind (salaries and options) and even hoodwinks shareholders. See for example: John K. Galbraith (2004) *The Economics of Innocent Fraud.* Or Ch. 7 of Bent S. Tranøy (2006) *Markedets makt over sinnene.*

43. *The Economist* (2005) 'Profit and the public Good', pp.13–15 in 'A Survey of Corporate Social Responsibility', special section *The Economist,* 22 Jan. 2005.

44. 'Profit and the public Good', ibid., p.13.

45. Ronald Coase (1937) 'The Nature of the Firm' in *Economica* is the classic article for discussion of the producing unit's status in the economy. He maintains that standard economic theory has regarded the firm as being a 'black box'. Coase's argument is that the firm comes into existence to be able (internally) to reduce transaction costs (time for information acquisition, negotiating, entry into contracts, etc.) which would have arisen if all production had been carried out through the market. But he also assumed at that time that the firm is a limited unit that can be studied independently from its relational or systematic nature. Many years later in his Nobel Lecture (1991), he therefore called for more research into the firm's

external relationships such as entering into real contracts. Ronald Coase (1991) 'The Institutional Structure of Production', Nobel Lecture.

46. Joel Bakan (2004) *The Corporation,* Ch. 3.

47. Per E. Stoknes (1996) *Sjelens Landskap [Landscapes of Soul]*, postscript.

48. James F. Moore (1996) *The Death of Competition: Leadership and Strategy in the Age of Business Ecosystems.*

49. *The Economist* (2005) 'The world according to CSR', 20 Jan. 2005

50. Samuelson and Nordhaus (2001) *Economics*, pp.567–8.

51. Herman Daly (1996) *Beyond Growth*, p.6.

52. Herman Daly (1996) *Beyond Growth*, Part III, and Herman Daly (2005) 'Economics in a Full World', *Scientific American*, 293:3, 100–7.

53. One well-written examination of various critiques of growth, viewed from a growth-adherent's perspective, is: Daniel Ben-Ami, 'Who's afraid of economic growth?' http://www.spiked-online.com/Articles/0000000CB04D.htm, downloaded 7 Aug. 2007.

54. Stanley Alcorn and Ben Solarz (2006) 'The Autistic Economist', *Yale Economic Review*, Summer Issue.

55. Carl G. Jung (1943) The *Collected Works*, vol 7, §110.

Chapter 12. A scenario for new forms of capital: Is profound economic change possible?

1. Herman Daly (1996) *Beyond Growth*, p.48.

2. Robert Putnam (2000) *Bowling Alone*, p.407.

3. I want to describe the proposal as a 'normative scenario' to distinguish it from explorative scenarios for mapping future uncertainties. See Jay Ogilvy (2002) *Creating Better Futures*.

4. Elements of the work here develop from my extensive work on scenarios over the past ten years. Among those that are of particular relevance can be included NOU 1998:11 Kraft-og energibalansen mot 2020; SSB: Statistikk 2016; and BI 2007 Fremtidsbilder 2030.

5. See Bernard Lietaer (2001) *The Future of Money*, for more detailed descriptions. For WIR's own description: http://www.ex.ac.uk/~RDavies/arian/wir.html.

6. The classic article about economic valuation of the ecosystem services of the natural capital is Costanza, R. et al (1997) 'The value of the world's ecosystem services and natural capital.' *Nature*, 387:6230, 253–60. A later work giving review over Norwegian experiences with accounting for natural capitals is given in Alfsen and Greaker (2007), 'From Natural Resources and Environmental Accounting to Construction of Indicators for Sustainable development', *Ecological Economics*, 61:4, 600–10. As regards social capital, a key early article often mentioned is Putnam (1993) 'The Prosperous Community', which he later expanded into a book (2000), *Bowling Alone*.

7. John Elkington's work has been important to the introduction of the concept of the triple bottom line: John McMillan (2002) *The Sustainability Advantage: Seven Business Case Benefits of a Triple Bottom Line,* or John Elkington (2001) *The Chrysalis Economy*. The world's most frequently used standard for sustainability reporting (social and environmental accounting) is the Global Reporting Initiative, GRI: http://www.globalreporting.org/.

8. Joel Bakan (2004) *The Corporation*, pp.33–7.

9. Bannock et al. (2003) *Dictionary of Economics*.

10. The classic references to human capital are Gary Becker (1964) *Human Capital: A theo-*

retical and empirical analysis, with special reference to education, New York: National Bureau of Economic Research, and Jacob Mincer (1958) 'Investment in Human Capital and Personal Income Distribution', *The Journal of Political Economy.* An analysis of Norwegian human capital has been carried out by Mads Greaker et al. (2005), *Utviklingen i den norske nasjonalformuen 1985–2004.*

11. Robert Putnam (2000) *Bowling Alone,* p.21. The designation 'social capital' has many directions and definitions. Putnam points out that 'social capital' appears to have been discovered and formulated at least six times by different philosophers during the course of the 20th century. Among the most important are urbanist Jane Jacobs (1961) *The Death and Life of Great American Cities,* and the French philosopher Pierre Bourdieu (1986) 'The Forms of Capital' in John G. Richardson (ed.) *Handbook of Theory and Research for the Sociology of Education.*

12. Luigi Guiso et al. (2004) 'The Role of Social Capital in Financial Development'. *American Economic Review,* 94:3, 526–56.

13. Herman Daly (1996) *Beyond Growth* and (2005) 'Economics in a Full World'. See also Paul Hawken, Amory Lovins and Hunter Lovins (1999) *Natural Capitalism.* Jonathon Porritt (2006) *Capitalism: As If the World Matters.*

14. Some people maintain that the forms of capital can be substituted for one another, i.e. that increased manufactured capital and human capital can compensate for potential decline in natural capital. This argument is often called *weak sustainability.* The *strong sustainability* argument states that there can be no substitution of natural capital with other types of capital: No economic growth can compensate for the loss of wild deer, eagles, the wild salmon or the last choral reefs. Neither can we "become richer by cleaning up one another's pollution as more and more of the natural world is used up". Herman Daly (1996) *Beyond Growth,* p.76.

15. This can be formulated as revenue neutral, which means that the total tax level will not increase. The state will not increase the tax level, but the distribution between the taxes changes. It probably ought not to be possible to extrapolate social and environmental deficits in the way financial deficits can today.

16. Robert D. Putnam (2000) *Bowling Alone,* p.19 ff. Svendsen and Svendsen (2006) *Social Kapital.*

17. Edgar Cahn (2000) *No More Throw-away People: The Co-production Imperative.*

18. Edgar Cahn (1992) *Time Dollars,* and Edgar Cahn (2002) 'Unleashing our Hidden Wealth', *Yes! Magazine,* available online: http://www.yesmagazine.org/article.asp?ID=524. David Boyle's (1999) *Funny Money* is also an excellent introduction.

19. The framework can be viewed as both psychological and institutional. Institutional economics is part of sociology that works with economics on the way the social institutions surrounding money are understood. See Victor Nee (2005) 'The New Institutionalisms in Economics and Sociology' in Ch. 3 in Smeiser and Swedberg (2005) *The Handbook of Economic Sociology.*

20. For a summary of the Time Dollar systems, see http://www.timebanks.org/. A summary of other types of local monetary systems is contained in the database of the Complementary Currency Resource Center foundation at http://www.complementarycurrency.org/. The movement for local, complementary currency types also has its own journal: *International Journal of Community Currency Research,* see http://www.uea.ac.uk/env/ijccr/index.html.

21. Check the London TimeBank: http://london.timebank.org.uk/ or http://www.timebanks.co.uk/ for further information on the TimeBanks phenomenon.

22. Stephen DeMeulenaere (2007) 'Annual Report of the Worldwide Database of Complementary Currency Systems', *International Journal of Community Currency Research*, 11, 23–35.

23. For a discussion of 'bridging' and 'bonding' types of social capital, see Robert Putnam (2000) *Bowling Alone*.

24. Keith Hart (2000) discusses the origin of money as a form of memory in *Money in an Unequal World*, pp.15, 234 and 318.

25. Svendsen and Svendsen (2006) *Social Kapital*.

26. House et al. (1988) 'Social Relationships and Health', *Science*. Quoted in Robert D. Putnam (2000) *Bowling Alone*, p.326. In addition, see all of Section IV.

27. Svendsen and Svendsen (2006) *Social Kapital*.

28. Robert Putnam (2000) *Bowling Alone*, p.405.

29. It is possible to start out from the summary of successful cases by Sirgy, Rahtz and Lee (2006) *Community Quality-Of-Life Indicators (Social Indicators Research Series)*.

30. M .L. Parry et al. (2007) *Technical Summary. Climate Change 2007: Impacts, Adaptation and Vulnerability. Contribution of Working Group II to the Fourth Assessment Report of the Intergovernmental Panel on Climate Change.* Nicholas Stern (2007) *The Economics of Climate Change: The Stern Review.*

31. Herman Daly (1996), *Beyond Growth*, pp.80–1.

32. Stephan Harding (2006) *Animate Earth*, Ch. 5.

33. A starting point for examining the concept, valuation and status of the various types of ecosystem services can be taken in the Millennium Ecosystem Assessment (2005) *Ecosystems and Human Well-being: Biodiversity Synthesis*. For a discussion of accounting units for ecosystem services, see James Boyd and Spence Banzhaf (2007) 'What are ecosystem services? The need for standardized environmental accounting units.'

34. Development is needed particularly of models for common land and shared resources such as fish stocks, etc. However, the principle ought to be that all registered farmers/ fishermen will become co-owners within the new ownership team to ensure that they all gain a shared interest in optimising assets.

35. Wayt Gibbs (2005) 'How should we set priorities?', *Scientific American*, Sept. 2005, p.113.

36. European Commission (2004) *EU Emissions Trading. An Open Scheme Promoting Global Innovation to Combat Climate Change.*

37. Figures for carbon capture are estimated as follows: 2 GtC/year are absorbed by sea and 1.7 GtC/year are absorbed by land. This is equivalent to 7.3 $GtCO_2$/year and 6.2 $GtCO_2$/year, rounded off to 13 $GtCO_2$/year, respectively. Collective emissions generated by human activity for 2007 are estimated at 9 GtC/year = 33 $GtCO_2$/year. Instead of just CO_2 all greenhouse gases could be included in the calculations of CO_2 equivalents. That has not been done here. See the latest figures from the IPCC in Solomon, S. (2007) *Technical Summary Climate Change 2007.*

38. See Arne Jon Isachsen and Jørgen Randers in Part 1 of BI (2007) *Fremtidsbilder 2030.*

39. Emissions per capita in Norway in the year 2000 were approx. 12 tonnes CO2 equivalents per year. Private emissions (particularly for transport and heating) are less than 12 tonnes, since oil and industry are responsible for around half. Norway's Low Emissions Committee [Lavutslippsutvalget] (2006) p.41.

40. James Lovelock (2006) *The Revenge of Gaia: Why the Earth is Fighting Back – and How we Can Still Save Humanity.* For a discussion of the concept of doomsday and the myth of apocalypse within the environmental movement, see Per E. Stoknes (1996) *Landscapes of Soul,* Ch. 2, 'Apocalypse Now?'

41. Herman Daly (1996) *Beyond Growth,* pp.81–3.

42. See, among others, Daniel Kahneman et al. (1999) or Graham Loomes (2006) '(How) Can we value health, safety and the environment?' *Journal of Economic Psychology,* 27, 713–36.

43. Arne Jon Isachsen and Geir Bjønnes Høidal (2004) *Globale Penger,* p.126.

44. See Bruno Frey (1997) *Not Just for the Money* for an economic discussion of 'crowding out'. For a psychological discussion, see Sansone and Harackiewicz (eds.) (2000) *Intrinsic and Extrinsic Motivation: The Search for Optimal Motivation and Performance.*

45. Experience is needed in issues such as: What if people choose to abstain from receiving SBPs and NBPs? Would that be antisocial?

46. See Jonathan Porritt (2006) *Capitalism: As If the World Matters.* Paul Hawken, Amory Lovins and Hunter Lovins (1999) *Natural Capitalism.* John Elkington (1999) *Cannibals with Forks: Triple Bottom Line of 21st Century Business,* Adrian Henriques (2004) *The Triple Bottom Line: Does It All Add Up? – Assessing the Sustainability of Business and CSR.*

47. Richard Douthwaite (2006) *The Ecology of Money,* Bernard Lietaer (2002) *The Future of Money* and David Boyle (1999) *Funny Money.*

48. Francis Fukuyama (1995) 'Social Capital and the Global Economy', and Robert Putnam (2000) *Bowling Alone.*

49. Costanza et al. (2007) 'Quality of Life: An approach integrating opportunities, human needs, and subjective well-being'. *Ecological Economics* 61:2–3 (March), 267–76.

Chapter 13. Conclusion: Ways forward?

1. For natural capital, see Herman Daly (1996) *Beyond Growth,* Lester Brown (2003) *Plan B – Rescuing a Planet under Stress and a Civilization in Trouble,* or D. H. Meadows, J. Randers, D. L. Meadows (2004) *Limits to Growth – The 30 Year Update.* For social capital, see Robert Putnam (2000) *Bowling Alone,* David Halpern (2005) *Social Capital* or Robert Lane (2000) *The Loss of Happiness in Market Democracies.* For quality of life, see Richard Layard (2004) *Happiness.*

2. Robert Lane (2000) *The Loss of Happiness in Market Democracies.*

3. Solomon, S., et al. (2007) 'Technical Summary' IPCC; Tim Flannery (2006) *The Weather Makers: How Man Is Changing the Climate and What It Means for Life on Earth.*

4. Cf. 'The Common Ground' in Paul Krugman and Robin Wells (2006) *Macroeconomics,* pp.5–40.

5. Pine, J. and Gilmore, J. (1999) *The Experience Economy,* Harvard Business School Press, Boston.

6. Anne-Britt Gran and Donatella De Paoli (2005) *Kunst og kapital. Nye forbindelser mellom kunst, estetikk og næringsliv.*

7. Charles Handy (1996) 'The Sixth Need of Business: "Wisdom from an Oarsman"', in Bill DeFoore and John Renesch (eds.), (1996) *Rediscovering the Soul of Business,* p.232. He gains the endorsement of Mihaly Csikszentmihalyi (2003) *Good Business,* which presents renewal of meaning and introduction of flow in the work processes as the main purpose of future organisations.

8. Jacob Needleman (1991) *Money and the Meaning of Life,* p.294.

9. Lynne Twist, *The Soul of Money,* p.119. We must also be aware, of course, so we are not swallowed by the single myth in which we believe, and thus become zealots.

10. Jeremy Bentham (1746–1832) quoted in Robert Lane (2000) *Loss of Happiness,* p.73.

11. Robert Lane (1991) *The Market Experience,* p.259.

12. Andrews and Withey, 'Social Indicators of Well-Being' quoted in Lane (2000) *Loss of Happiness.*

13. Robert Lane (1991) *The Market Experience,* Part V.

14. Richard Sennett (2003) *Respect;* Richard Layard (2004) *Happiness,* pp.156–60.

15. Chris Argyris (1990) *Overcoming Organizational Defenses. Facilitating organizational learning.*

16. John Smithin (2000) *What is Money?,* and Giancarlo Bertocco (2007) 'The Characteristics of a Monetary Economy: A Keynes-Schumpeter Approach', *Cambridge Journal of Economics,* 31:1, 101–22.

Bibliography

Abram, David (2005) *Sansenes magi* [*The magic of the senses*], Oslo: Flux.

Aischylos (1985) *Promethevs i lenker* [*Prometheus in chains*], transl. by Øivind Andersen, Oslo: Gyldendal.

Alcorn, S. and Solarz, B. (2006) 'The Autistic Economist', *Yale Economic Review*, Summer Issue.

Argyris, Chris (1990) *Overcoming Organizational Defenses. Facilitating Organizational Learning*, Boston: Allyn and Bacon.

Bachelard, Gaston (1958) *The Poetics of Space*, NY: Orion Press 1964.

Bakan, Joel (2004) *The Corporation: the pathological pursuit of profit and power*, NY: Free Press.

Bank of International Settlements (BIS) (2005) *Triennial Central Bank Survey of Foreign Exchange and Derivatives Manket Activity*.

Bannock et al. (2003) *Dictionary of Economics*, London: Penguin Books.

Barstad, Anders and Hellevik, Ottar (2004) *På vei mot det gode samfunn?* [*On the way to the good society*], Oslo: SSB.

Barthes, Roland (1957) *Mytologier* [*Mythologies*], trans. by Einar Eggen, 3rd edition, Oslo: Gyldendal, 1999.

Basu, K., Mintzberg, H. Simons. R. (2002) 'Memo to CEOs', in *Fast Company* 59, June 2002.

Bateson, Gregory, 1972, *Steps to an Ecology of Mind*, New York: Ballantine Books.

Becker, Gary (1964) *Human Capital: A theoretical and empirical analysis, with special reference to education*, New York: National Bureau of Economic Research.

Bendixen, Peter (2004) 'Die Konstruktion des ökonomischen Blicks', *Journal of Social Science Education*, Institut für Wirtschaftsethik Universitat St. Gallen, http://www.jsse.org/2004-2/ oekonomischer_blick_bendixen.htm downloaded 8 Aug. 2007.

Berezin, Mabel (2005) 'Emotions and the Economy', Ch. 6 in Smeiser and Swedberg (2005) *The Handbook of Economic Sociology*, Princeton, N.J.: Princeton University Press.

Bergh, Finn Øystein (2004) *Økonomiskolen* [*The School of Economics*], Oslo: Hegnar media.

Bertocco, Giancarlo (2007) 'The Characteristics of a Monetary Economy: A Keynes-Schumpeter Approach', *Cambridge Journal of Economics*, 31:1, 101–22.

BI (2007) *Fremtidsbilder 2030* [*Images of the Future 2030*], Report to the NHO's Annual Conference 2007.

Binswanger, Hans C. (1994), *Money and Magic, A Critique of the Modem Economy in the Light of Goethe's Faust*, Chicago, Illinois: University of Chicago Press.

Blanchflower, David. G. and Oswald, Andrew J. (2004) 'Well-being Over Time in Britain and the USA', *Journal of Public Economics*, 88, 1359–86.

Bloom, William (1995) *Money, Heart and Mind*, London: Viking.

Blyth, Mark (2007) 'One Ring to Bind Them All: American Power and Neoliberal Capitalism' in Jeffrey Kopstein and Sven Steinmo (eds) *Growing Apart, America and Europe in the 21st*

Century, New York: Cambridge University Press.

Boer, Charles (1970) *The Homeric Hymns*, CT: Spring Publications.

Bourdieu, Pierre (1986) 'The Forms of Capital' in John G. Richardson (ed.) *Handbook of Theory and Research for the Sociology of Education*, New York: Greenwood Press.

Boyd, James and Banzhaf, Spence (2007) 'What are ecosystem services? The need for standardized environmental accounting units', *Ecological Economics*; 63:2/3 (Aug. 2007), 616–26.

Briloff, Abraham (1972) *Unaccountable Accounting*, New York: Harper & Row.

Brown, Lester (2003) *Plan B – Rescuing a Planet under Stress and a Civilization in Trouble*, New York: W. W. Norton.

Brown, Norman O. (1947) *Hermes the Thief*, NY: Lindisfarne Press, 1990.

Brown, S., Taylor, K. and Price, S. W. (2005) 'Debt and distress: Evaluating the psychological cost of credit', *Journal of Economic Psychology*, 26, 642–63.

Buber, Martin (1923) *Jeg og Du* [*I and thou*], trans. by Hedvig Wergeland, Oslo: Bokklubbene, 2003.

Buchan, James (1997) *Frozen Desire: The meaning of money*, New York: Farrar.

Burchell, Brendan (2003) 'Financial Phobia: A Report for Egg', University of Cambridge.

Cahn, Edgar (2000) *No More Throw-away People: The Co-production Imperative*, Washington DC: Essential Books.

Cahn, Edgar (2002) 'Unleashing our Hidden Wealth', *Yes! Magazine*, http://www.yesmagazine.org/article.asp?id=524, downloaded 5 May 2007.

Capra, Fritjof (1996) *The Web of Life, A New Scientific Understanding of Living Systems*, New York: Anchor Books, Doubleday.

Carlyle, Thomas (1849) 'Occasional Discourse on the Negro Question', *Fraser's Magazine for Town and Country*, Dec.1849, 672–3.

Castells, Manuel (2000) *The Rise of the Network Society, The Information Age: Economy, Society and Culture*, Vol. I. Cambridge, MA; 2nd edition, Oxford, UK: Blackwell.

Coase, Ronald, (1937) 'The Nature of the Firm', *Economica*, 4:16 (Nov. 1937), 386–405.

Coase, Ronald (1991) 'The Institutional Structure of Production' (Nobel Lecture), Stockholm: The Nobel Foundation.

Colander, David (2000) 'The Death of Neoclassical Economics', *Journal of the History of Economic Thought*. 22:2, 127–44.

Colander, D., Richard P. E and Rosser, B.R. (2004) 'The Changing Face of Mainstream Economics', *Review of Political Economy*, 16:4, 485–99.

Costanza, R., et al. (1997) 'The value of the world's ecosystem services and natural capital.' *Nature*, 387:6230, 253–60.

Costanza et al. (2007) 'Quality of Life: An approach integrating opportunities, human needs, and subjective well-being', *Ecological Economics* 61:2–3 (March), 267–76.

Coyle, Diane (2002) *Sex, Drugs and Economics*, New York: Texere.

Crawford, Tad (1994) *The Secret Life of Money*, New York: Allworth Press.

Csikszentmihalyi, Mihaly (1990) *Flow: The Psychology of Optimal Experience*, New York: Harper and Row.

Csikszentmihalyi, Mihaly (2003) *Good Business: Leadership, Flow and the Making of Meaning*, New York: Viking.

Daly, Herman (1996) *Beyond Growth*, Boston: Beacon Press.

Daly, Herman (2005) 'Economics in a Full World', *Scientific American*, Sept. 2005.

Dammann, Erik (1989) *Pengene eller Livet* [*Your money or your life*], Oslo: Dreyer.

Davies, Glyn (2002) *History of Money: From Ancient Times to the Present Day*, Cardiff: University of Wales Press.

Davis, John (2006) 'The turn in economics: neoclassical dominance to mainstream pluralism?', *Journal of Institutional Economics*, 2:1, 1–20.

DeFoore, Bill and Renesch, John et al. (ed.) (1996) *Rediscovering the Soul of Business*, San Francisco: New Leaders Press.

DeMeulenaere, Stephen (2007) 'Annual Report of the Worldwide Database of Complementary Currency Systems', *International Journal of Community Currency Research*, 11, 23–35.

Desmonde, William H. (1962) *Magic, Myth, and Money: The Origin of Money in Religious Ritual*, NY: Free Press of Glencoe.

Dormael, Armand Van (1997) *The Power of Money*, NY; New York University Press.

Douthwaite, Richard (1999) *The Growth Illusion: How economic growth has enriched the few, impoverished the many and endangered the planet*, Devon: Green Books.

Douthwaite, Richard (2006) *The Ecology of Money*, Devon: Schumacher Briefings.

Easterlin, Richard (1974) 'Does Economic Growth Improve the Human Lot? Some Empirical Evidence' in David and Reder, (ed.), *Nations and Households in Economic Growth: Essays in Honor of Moses Abramovitz.*, NY: Academic Press, pp.98–125.

Economist (2005) 'A Survey of Corporate Social Responsibility', topic section in *The Economist*, 22 Jan. 2005.

Elkington, John (1998) *Cannibals with Forks: Triple Bottom Line of 21st Century Business*, Gabriola Island, B.C.: New Society Publishers.

Elkington, John (2001) *The Chrysalis Economy*, Oxford: Capstone.

Elkington, John (2002) *The Sustainability Advantage: Seven Business Case Benefits of a Triple Bottom Line*, Gabriola Island, B.C.: New Society Publishers.

European Commission (2005) *EU Emissions Trading. An Open Scheme Promoting Global Innovation to Combat Climate Change*, Luxembourg: Office for Official Publications of the European Communities.

Fisher, Irving (1929) *The Money Illusion*, London: Allen & Unwin.

Fisher, Irving (1935). *100% Money*, Works Vol. 11, ed. and introduction by William J. Barber, London: Pickering & Chatto, 1997.

Flannery, Tim (2006) *The Weather Makers: How Man Is Changing the Climate and What It Means for Life on Earth*, London: Allen Lane.

Frey, Bruno S. (1997) *Not Just for the Money – An Economic Theory of Personal Motivation*, MA: Edward Elgar Publishing.

Friedman, Thomas (2006) *The World is Flat*, NY: Farrar.

Fukuyama, Francis (1995) 'Social Capital and the Global Economy: A Redrawn Map of the World,' *Foreign Affairs*, Sept./Oct. 1995.

Furnham and Argyle (1998) *The Psychology of Money*, London: Routledge.

Galbraith, John K. (1958) *The Affluent Society*, Boston: Houghton, 1998.

Galbraith, John K. (1975) *Money: Whence it Came, Where it Went*, Boston: Houghton.

Galbraith, John K. (2004) *The Economics of Innocent Fraud*, Boston: Houghton Mifflin.

Galtung, Johan (1996) *Peace by Peaceful Means: Peace and Conflict, Development and Civilization.* NY: Sage Publications.

Gran, Anne-Britt and De Paoli, Donatella (2005) *Kunst og kapital. Nye forbindelser mellom kunst, estetikk og næringsliv* [*Art and capital. New links between art, aesthetics and economic life*], Oslo: Pax.

Graves, Robert (1955) *The Greek Myths,* Harmondsworth: Penguin.

Greaker, M. Løkkevik, P. and Walle M. (2005) *Utviklingen i den norske nasjonalformuen fra 1985 til 2004: Et eksempel på bærekraftig utvikling?* [*Norway's national wealth 1985–2004. An example of sustainable development?*] SSB Reports 2005/13.

Grønn, Erik (1999) *Forelesninger i offentlig økonomi* [*Lectures in public economics*], Oslo: Cappelen akademisk.

Guiso, L., Sapienza, P. and Zingales, L., (2004) 'The Role of Social Capital in Financial Development', *American Economic Review,* 94:5 (Dec. 2004).

Gulbrandsen, Lars (2007) *Gjeld til å bære? Norske husholdningers gjeld og lånelyst sommeren 2006* [Sustainable debt? Norwegian households' debt and desire to borrow, summer 2006], NOVA Report 11/07.

Gullestad, Marianne (1989) *Kultur og hverdagsliv* [*Culture and everyday life*], Oslo: Universitetsforlaget.

Habermas, Jürgen, (1973) 'Dogmatism, Reason, and Decision: On Theory and Praxis in our Scientific Civilization,' in *Theory and Practice,* trans. by J. Viertel, Boston: Beacon Press.

Habermas, Jürgen (1981) *Theorie des Kommunikativen Handels. Band l und II* Frankfurt a.M.: Suhrkamp.

Halpern, David (2005) *Social Capital,* NY: Polity Press.

Harding, Stephan (2006) *Animate Earth,* Devon: Green Books.

Harrison, Fred (2005) *Boom & Bust: House Prices, Banking and the Depression of 2010,* NY: Shepheard-Walwyn.

Hart, Keith (2000) *Money in an Unequal World,* London: Profile Books.

Hauge, Nanna L. (1989) *Antikkens Guder og Helter* [*The gods and heroes of the ancient world*], Oslo: Cappelen.

Hawken, Paul, Lovins, Amory, and Lovins, Hunter (1999) *Natural Capitalism: The Next Industrial Revolution,* London: Earthscan.

Heilbroner, Robert (2000) *The Worldly Philosophers,* London: Penguin Books.

Hellevik, Ottar (1999) 'Hvorfor blir vi ikke lykkeligere?' ['Why are we not getting any happier?'] SSB: *Samfunnsspeilet* [*Mirror on society*] 1999–2004.

Helliwell, John E. (2003) 'How's Life? Combining Individual and National Variables to Explain Subjective Well-Being', *Economic Modelling,* 20:2 (Mar. 2003), 331–60.

Henderson, Hazel (1991) *Paradigms in Progress,* Indianapolis, Ind.: Knowledge Systems.

Henriques, Adrian and Richardson, Julie (2004) *The Triple Bottom Line: Does It All Add Up? – Assessing the Sustainability of Business and CSR.* London Sterling, VA: Earthscan.

Hillman, James (1975) *Re-Visioning Psychology;* New York: Harper & Row.

Hillman, James (1979) *The Dream and the Underworld,* New York: Harper & Row.

Hillman, James (1982) 'A Contribution to Soul and Money', in *Soul and Money,* CT: Spring Publications.

Hillman, James (1987) 'Senex and Puer', in *Puer Papers,* Dallas: Spring Publications.

Hillman, James (1990) A *Blue Fire,* ed. Thomas More; London: Routledge.

Hillman, James (1995) *Kinds of Power,* New York: Currency Doubleday.

Hillman, James (1996) *The Soul's Code,* NY: Random House.

Hillman, James (2004) *A Terrible Love of War,* New York: The Penguin Press.

Hock, Dee (2004) 'Money – A Brief History', downloaded from http://www.terratrc.org/articles-briefhistory.html on 20 Jan. 2007.

Huber, Joseph and Robertson, James (2000) *Creating New Money,* London: The New

Economics Foundation.

Hume, David (1752) *Political Discourses*, Edinburgh: A. Kincaid & A. Donaldson.

Huppert, F., Baylis, N., Keverne B. (ed.) (2005) *The Science of Well-Being*, London: Oxford University Press.

Ingham, G. (1996) 'Money is a Social Relation' in *Review of Social Economy* 54:4, 243–75.

International Monetary Fund (IMF) (2000) *Monetary and financial statistics manual*, Washington, D.C.: International Monetary Fund.

Isachsen, Arne J. and Bjønnes, Geir H. (2004) *Globale Penger* [*Global money*], Oslo: Gyldendal.

Isachsen, Arne J., Stoknes, Svein O. and Bjønnes, Geir H. (1999) 'Den store gjettekonkurransen' ['The great guessing game'], Oslo: SSB Notater.

Jacobs, Jane (1961) *The Death and Life of Great American Cities*, New York: Random House.

Jensen, Carsten (1992) *Sjelen sitter i øyet* [*The soul is in the eyes*], Oslo: Dokument.

Jung, Carl G. (1954) *The Archetypes and The Collective Unconscious*, in *Collected Works Vol. 9 Part 1*, Princeton: Bollingen.

Kahneman, Daniel and Krueger, Alan (2006) 'Developments in the Measurement of Subjective Well-Being', *Journal of Economic Perspectives*, 20:1, 3–24.

Kahneman, Daniel and Tversky, Amos (1979) 'Prospect Theory, An analysis of decisions under risk', *Econometrica*, 47, 313–27.

Kahneman, Daniel and Tversky, Amos (eds) (2000) *Choice, Values, and Frames*. NY: Cambridge University Press.

Kahneman, Daniel (2003) 'Psychological Perspective on Economics' *The American Economic Review*, 93:2, 162–8.

Kahneman, Daniel, Diener, Ed, Schwarz, Norbert (eds) (1999) *Well-Being: The Foundations of Hedonic Psychology*, NY: Russel Sage.

Kahneman, Daniel, Slovic, P. and Tversky, A. (eds) (1982) *Judgment under Uncertainty: Heuristics and biases*. NY: Cambridge University Press.

Kennedy, Margrit (1995) *Interest and Inflation-Free Money: Creating an Exchange Medium that Works for Everybody and Protects the Earth*, Philadelphia: New Society.

Keynes, John M. (1931) 'Economic possibilities for our Grandchildren' in *Essays in Persuasion*, London: Macmillan.

Keynes, John M. (1936) *The General Theory of Employment, Interest and Money*, NY: Prometheus Books, 1997.

Kredittilsynet (2007) *Tilstanden i finansmarkedet 2006* [*The financial market in Norway 2006*], Report: February 2007, Oslo: Kredittilsynet.

Krugman, Paul, and Wells, Robin (2006) *Macroeconomics*, NY: Worth Publishers.

Kuhn, Thomas S. (1970) *The Structure of Scientific Revolution*, Chicago: University of Chicago Press, 2nd edn.

Kuvaas, Baard (2006) 'Work performance, affective commitment, and work motivation: The roles of pay administration and pay level', *Journal of Organizational Behavior*, 27, 365–85.

Kydland, Finn and Prescott, Ed (1977) 'Rules rather than discretion: The inconsistency of optimal plans', *Journal of Political Economy*, 85, 473–90.

Landes, David (2003) *The Unbound Prometheus*, Cambridge: Cambridge University Press.

Lane, Robert (1991) *The Market Experience*, Cambridge: Cambridge University Press.

Lane, Robert (2000) *The Loss of Happiness in Market Democracies*, London: Yale University Press.

Layard, Richard (2004) *Happiness,* New York: Penguin Press.

Levinas, Emmanuel (2004) *Den annens humanisme [Humanism of the other],* trans. and introduction by Asbjørn Aarnes, Oslo: Aschehoug.

Lewis, Carroll (1872) *Through the Looking Glass,* London: Macmillan.

Lietaer, Bernard (2002) *The Future of Money: Creating New Wealth, Work and a Wiser World,* London: Century; new edn.

Loomes, Graham (2006) '(How) Can we value health, safety and the environment?', *Journal of Economic Psychology,* 27, 713–36.

Lopez-Pedraza, Rafael (1989) *Hermes and His Children,* Einsiedeln, Switzerland: Daimon.

Lovelock, James (2006) *The Revenge of Gaia: Why the Earth is Fighting Back – and How We Can Still Save Humanity,* London: Penguin.

Mauss, Marcel (1925) *The Gift: The Form and Reason for Exchange in Archaic Societies,* London: Routledge, 1990.

Mayerson, Philip (1971) 'The House of Hades: Gods of the Underworld' in *Classical Mythology in Literature, Art and Music,* NY: Wiley.

McLuhan, Marshall (1964) *Understanding Media: The Extensions of Man Critical Edition,* CA: Ginko Press, 2003.

McMillan, John (2002) *Reinventing the Bazaar: a natural history of markets.* NY: Norton.

Meadows, Randers & Meadows (2004) *Limits to Growth: The 30-Year Update,* VT: Chelsea Green Publishing.

Merleau-Ponty, Maurice (1962) *Phenomenology of Perception,* trans. to English by Colin Smith, London: Routledge, 1989.

Mill, John Stuart (1852) *Principles of Political Economy,* London: John W. Parker.

Millennium Ecosystem Assessment (2005) *Ecosystems and Human Well-being: Biodiversity Synthesis.* World Resources Institute, Washington, DC.

Mincer, Jacob (1958) 'Investment in Human Capital and Personal Income Distribution', *The Journal of Political Economy,* 66:4, 281–320.

Mirowski, Philip (1989) *More Heat than Light: Economics as Social Physics,* Cambridge: Cambridge University Press.

Mokyr, Joel (1990) *The Lever of Riches,* New York: Oxford University Press.

Moore, James F. (1996) *The Death of Competition: Leadership and Strategy in the Age of Business Ecosystems,* Chichester: Wiley.

Moore, Thomas (1996) Care of the Soul, New York: HarperCollins Publishers.

Næss, Siri (2001) 'Livskvalitet som psykisk velvære' ['Quality of life as mental well-being'], *The Journal of the Norwegian Medical Association,* 121, 1940–4.

Neary, M. and Taylor, G. (1998) *Money and the Human Condition,* Basingstoke: Macmillan.

Nee, Victor (2005) 'The New Institutionalisms in Economics and Sociology' Ch. 3 in Smeiser and Swedberg, ed. (2005) *Handbook of Economic Sociology,* Princeton, N.J.: Princeton University Press.

Needleman, Jacob (1993) *Money and the Meaning of Life,* New York, Doubleday.

Nordstrøm, Kjell A., and Ridderstråle, Jonas (1999) *Funky Business,* Stockholm: BookHouse Publishing.

Norges Bank (2000) *Vurdering av den norske pengemengdestatistikken. Rapport fra en arbeidsgruppe [Assessment of Norwegian money supply statistics. Working party report]* by Bernhardsen et al. External version.

NOU 1998:11, *Kraft- og energibalansen mot år 2020 [The power and energy balance towards the year 2020*], Royal Norwegian Ministry of Petroleum and Energy.

NOU 2005:5 *Enkle signaler i en kompleks verden: Forslag til et nasjonalt indikatorsett for bærekraftig utvikling* [*Simple signals in a complex world. Proposals for a national set of indicators for sustainable development*], led by Knut Alfsen, Royal Norwegian Ministry of Finance.

OECD (2005) *OECD's Financial Education Project: Improving Financial Literacy*, Barbara Smith, Ottawa, 9 June 2005.

Ogilvy, Jay (2002) *Creating Better Futures: scenario planning as a tool for a better tomorrow*, N.Y.: Oxford University Press.

Ormerod, Paul (2006) 'Shun the rational agent to rebuild economics' in *Financial Times*, 6 Nov. 2006.

Ovid (1989) *Forvandlinger – på danske vers* [*Metamorphoses – in Danish verse*], translated to Danish by Otto Steen Due, Copenhagen: Centrum.

Paris, Ginette (1990) *Pagan Grace; Dionysos, Hermes and the Goddess Memory in Daily Life*, CT: Spring Publications.

Paris, Ginette (1991) *Pagan Meditations*, Woodstock, CN: Spring Publications.

Parry, M. L. et al. (2007) *Technical Summary. Climate Change 2007: Impacts, Adaptation and Vulnerability. Contribution of Working Group II to the Fourth Assessment Report of the Intergovernmental Panel on Climate Change*, Cambridge University Press, Cambridge, UK, 23–78.

Peterson, Christopher L. (2004) *Taming the Sharks – Toward a Cure for the High-Cost Credit Market*, Ohio: Akron.

Porritt, Jonathan (2005) *Capitalism: As If the World Matters*, London: Earthscan.

Putnam, R. D. (1993) 'The Prosperous Community', *The American Prospect*, 4:13, 35–42.

Putnam, Robert (2000) *Bowling Alone*, NY: Simon & Schuster.

Reinert, Erik (1996) *Det Tekno-økonomiske Paradigmeskiftet* [*The techno-economic paradigm shift*], Norsk Investorforum, no. 3/1996.

Rojas, Mariano (2007) 'Heterogeneity in the relationship between income and happiness', *Journal of Economic Psychology*, 28, 1–14.

Rowbotham, Michael (1998) *Grip of Death: a study of modern money, debt slavery and destructive economics*, Charlbury, Oxfordshire: Jon Carpenter Publishing.

Samuels, Andrew (1993) *The Political Psyche*, London: Routledge.

Samuelson, Paul and Nordhaus, William (2001) *Economics*, 17th edn.

Sandmo, Agnar (2006) *Samfunnsøkonomi – en idéhistorie* [*Social economics – a history of ideas*], Oslo: Universitetsforlaget.

Sansone and Harackiewicz (eds) (2000) *Intrinsic and Extrinsic Motivation: The Search for Optimal Motivation and Performance*, San Diego, California: Academic Press.

Sapra, Haresh (2006) 'Accounting Reform: The Costs and Benefits of Marking-to-Market', *Capital Ideas*, The University of Chicago Graduate School of Business: http://www.chicagogsb.edU/capideas/jul06/2.aspx, downloaded 11 June 2007.

Schneider, Mark (2006) 'Great Minds in Economics: Paul Samuelson', *Yale Economic Review*, Summer 2006.

Schumpeter, Joseph (1942) *The Process of Creative Destruction*, London: Unwin.

Senge, Peter, et al. (1994) *The Fifth Discipline Fieldbook*, London: Nicholas Brealey Publishing.

Sennett, Richard (2003) *Respect*, London: Allen Lane.

Shafir, E., Diamond, P. A. and Tversky, A. (1997) 'On Money Illusion', *Quarterly Journal of Economics*, 112 (May), 341–74.

Sherden, William A. (1997) The Fortune Sellers, New York: John Wiley.

Simmel, Georg (1900) *The Philosophy of Money*, 2nd edn, trans. to English by Tom Bottomore and David Frisby, London: Routledge, 1990.

Simon, Herbert (1978) *Rational Decision-making in Business Organizations*, Nobel Lecture 8 Dec. 1978.

Sirgy, Rahtz and Lee (2004) *Community Quality-Of-Life Indicators (Social Indicators Research Series)*, Boston: Kluwer Academic Publishers.

Skousen, Mark (1997) 'The Perseverance of Paul Samuelson's Economics', *The Journal of Economic Perspectives*, 11:2 (Spring 1997), 137–52.

Smeiser and Swedberg (eds) (2005) *The Handbook of Economic Sociology*, Princeton, N.J.: Princeton University Press.

Smith, Adam (1776) *An inquiry into the nature and causes of the wealth of nations*, London: Strachan/Cadell.

Smith, Adam (1997) *The Essential Smith*, ed. Robert Heilbroner, W. W. Norton, New York.

Smithin, John, ed. (2000) *What is Money*. NY: Routledge.

Snowdon, Brian and Vane, Howard (1999) *Conversations with Leading Economists: Interpreting Modem Macroeconomics*, MA: Edward Elgar.

Solomon, S., et al (2007) 'Technical Summary', *Climate Change 2007: The Physical Science Basis. Contribution of Working Group 1 to the Fourth Assessment Report of the Intergovernmental Panel on Climate Change*, NY: Cambridge.

Soros, George (2003) *The Alchemy of Finance*, Hoboken, N.J.: Wiley.

SSB (2006) *Statistikk 2016: Scenarier og strategiske utfordringer* [*Statistics 2016: Scenarios and strategic challenges*], Report 2006/18, Oslo: SSB.

Tibor Scitovski (1976) *The Joyless Economy: The Psychology of Human Satisfaction* , US: Oxford University Press, 1992.

Steptoe, A., Wardle J. and Marmot, M. (2005) 'Positive Affect and Health-Related Neuroendocrine, Cardiovascular and Inflammatory Processes', *Proceedings of the National Academy of Sciences*, 3 May, 201:18, 508–12.

Stern, Nicholas (2007) *The Economics of Climate Change: The Stem Review*. London: Cambridge University Press.

Stiglitz, Joseph (2000) 'The Insider', *The New Republic*, 17 Apr. 2000.

Stiglitz, Joseph (2002) 'There Is No Invisible Hand', *The Guardian*, 20 Dec. 2002.

Stiglitz, Joseph (2002) Globalization and its Discontent, New York: W. W. Norton & Co.

Stoknes, Per E. (1996) *Sjelens Landskap* [*The landscape of the soul*], Oslo: Cappelen.

Stoknes, Per E. (2008), 'The Remembering of the Air', *POIESIS: A Journal of the Arts & Communication*, Vol X, 2008, 74–86

Stoknes, Per E. and Hermansen, Frede (eds) (2004) *Lær av Fremtiden: Norske organisasjoners erfaringer med scenariobasert strategi* [*Learn from the future: Experiences of Norwegian organisations in scenario-based stategy*], Oslo: Gyldendal.

Strøm, F, Lunde, H. and Mørk, E. (2006) 'Inntektene øker, men gjelden øker mer' ['Incomes are increasing, but debt is increasing even more'], *Samfunnsspeilet* [*Mirror on society*] SSB, 11 Dec. 2006.

Svendsen, Gert and Svendsen, Gunnar (2006) *Social Kapital: En introduction* [*Social capital: an introduction*], Copenhagen: Hans Reitzels Forlag.

Tawney, Richard H. (1926) *Religion and the Rise of Capitalism*, Richard Tawney, London: Pelican Books, 1975.

Di Telia, Rafael, MacCulloch, Robert J. and Oswald, Andrew J. (2003) 'The macro-economics of happiness', *Review of Economics and Statistics*, 85:4, 809–27.

Di Telia, Rafael and MacCulloch, Robert (2006) 'Some Uses of Happiness Data in Economics', *Journal of Economic Perspectives*, 20:1, 24–46

Tranøy, Bent Sofus (2006) *Markedets makt over sinnene* [*The market's power over the mind*], Oslo: Aschehoug.

Twist, Lynne (2003) *The Soul of Money*, New York: W. W. Norton & Co.

UNDP (2001–2005) *Human Development Report*.

Veblen, Thorstein (1901) *Theory of the Leisure Class*, NY: B. W. Huebsch, 1924.

Weber, Max (1920) *Den Protestantiske Etikk og Kapitalismens Ånd* [*The Protestant ethic and the spirit of capitalism*], trans. by Sverre Dahl, 2001.

Weber, Max (1920) *The Protestant Ethic and the Spirit of Capitalism*, 3rd edn, California: Blackwell Publishing, 2002.

Wittgenstein, Ludwig (1953) *Philosophical Investigations*, Oxford: Blackwell, 1957.

Wormnæss, Odd (1987) *Vitenskapsfilosofi* [*The philosophy of science*], 2nd edn, Oslo: Gyldendal.

WTO (2006) *Annual Report 2006*.

Yang, Sha, Markoczy L. and Qi, M. (2007) 'Unrealistic optimism in consumer credit card adoption', *Journal of Economic Psychology*, 28, 170–85.

Ystaas, Torunn (2001) 'Tapte Talenter' ['Lost talents'], pp.30–1, in *Flux – Livsfilosofisk magasin* [*Flux – Life philosophy magazine*] no. 24, Spring 2001, Oslo: Flux.

Index